The Indian Army
of the
Empress
1861-1903

The Indian Army

of the

Empress

1861-1903

Alan Harfield

SPELLMOUNT

TUNBRIDGE WELLS · KENT

In the Spellmount/Nutshell Military list:

The Territorial Battalions – A pictorial history
The Yeomanry Regiments – A pictorial history
Over the Rhine – The Last Days of War in Europe
History of the Cambridge University OTC
Yeoman Service
The Fighting Troops of the Austro-Hungarian Army
Intelligence Officer in the Peninsula
The Scottish Regiments – A pictorial history
The Royal Marines – A pictorial history
The Royal Tank Regiment – A pictorial history
The Irish Regiments – A pictorial history
British Sieges of the Peninsular War
Victoria's Victories
Heaven and Hell – German paratroop war diary
Rorke's Drift
Came the Dawn – Fifty years an Army Officer
Kitchener's Army – A pictorial history
On the Word of Command – A pictorial history of the
  Regimental Sergeant Major
Marlborough – as Military Commander
The Art of Warfare in the Age of Marlborough
Epilogue in Burma 1945-48
Scandinavian Misadventure
The Fall of France
The First Victory – O'Connor's Desert Triumph
Blitz Over Britain
Deceivers Ever – Memoirs of a Camouflage Officer

In the Military Machine list:

Napoleon's Military Machine
Falklands Military Machine
Wellington's Military Machine

In the Nautical list:

Sea of Memories
Evolution of Engineering in the Royal Navy Vol I 1827-1939
In Perilous Seas

In the Aviation list:

Diary of a Bomb Aimer
Operation 'Bograt' – From France to Burma – Memoirs of a Fighter Pilot
A Medal for Life – Capt Leefe Robinson VC

First published in the UK in 1990 by
Spellmount Ltd
12 Dene Way, Speldhurst
Tunbridge Wells, Kent TN3 0NX
ISBN 0-946771-03-0

© Alan Harfield 1990

British Library Cataloguing in Publication Data
Harfield, Alan
   Indian Army of the Empress – Pictorial history series)
   1.   Great Britain. Army. Indian Army history
   I. Title   II. Series
   3555.00454

Design by Words & Images, Speldhurst, Kent
Typesetting by Vitaset, Paddock Wood, Kent
Printed by The KPC Group, Ashford, Kent

Illustrations

Half title page:
Headquarters encampment of the Field Force at Fort Jamrud.

Title page:
2nd Punjab Cavalry. AMOT
A group of officers of Skinner's Horse, 1879.

Contents & Acknowledgements pages:
Sketches in the camp of the Indian troops at Malta. ILN

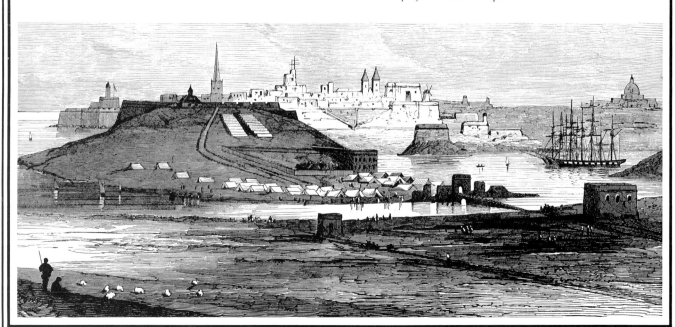

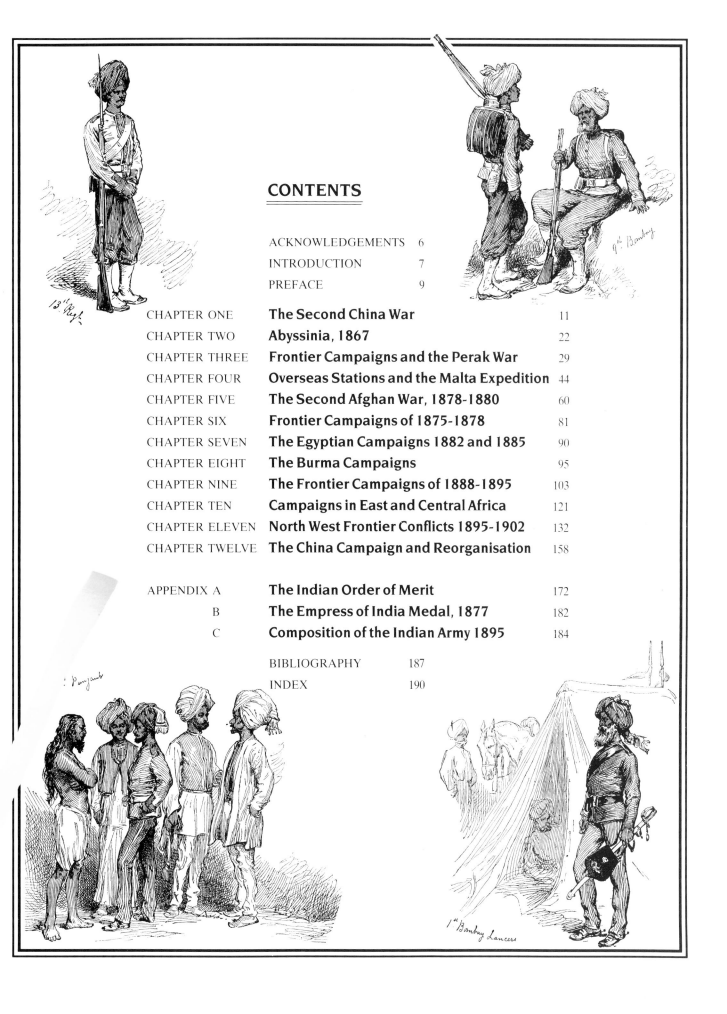

CONTENTS

ACKNOWLEDGEMENTS

GLOSSARY AND NOTES

Much of the information contained in this publication has been obtained from the National Army Museum, London, and the Army Museums Ogilby Trust at Aldershot. I am most grateful to Dr P. B. Boyden, BA PhD, for his very kind help at the National Army Museum and to Colonel P. S. Newton, MBE FMA FRSA, the former Secretary of the Army Museums Ogilby Trust, who kindly permitted me to copy many of the illustrations in the Trust collection for reproduction in this work.

As the theme of the book is the awarding of campaign medals to officers and men of the Indian Army, I extend my sincere gratitude to Major J. M. A. Tamplin, President of the Orders and Medals Research Society, for his advice and help, also for permitting me to photograph medals in his collection for use in the book.

Photographic reproduction has been by Bryan Carpenter of Town and Country Photographers, and the sketch maps and plans have been drawn by Andrew Kettlety to whom I also extend my gratitude.

Finally, I wish to acknowledge the continued help and advice that I have had from Mr W. Y. Carman, FSA FRHistS, who has also made his extensive collection of Indian Army material available to me in order that I may complete my research for this illustrated publication.

May 1990   AH

Titles of units have been given in various forms throughout the book and such names have been taken from contemporary documents such as Indian Army Lists, Government General Orders (GGOs) and reports etc. Therefore titles will appear, for example, as follows: Goorkha, Gurkha; Punjaub, Punjab; Scind, Scinde; Sikh, Seikh. The ranks given are also subject to a variety of spelling and the following table sets out the cavalry, infantry and equivalent British Army ranks.

Cavalry	Infantry	British Rank
Rissaldar Major	Subedar-Major, Subadar-Major	(Senior Indian Officer)
Rissaldar, Risaldar, Ressaidar	Subedar, Subadar	Lieutenant
Jemedar, Jemadar	Jemedar, Jemadar	2nd Lieutenant
Kot Daffadar	–	Troop Sergeant Major
–	Havildar-Major	Sergeant Major
Daffadar	Havildar	Sergeant
Lance-daffadar	Naik, Naique	Corporal
Acting lance-daffadar	Lance-Naik, Lance Naique	Lance Corporal
Sower	Sepoy	Private

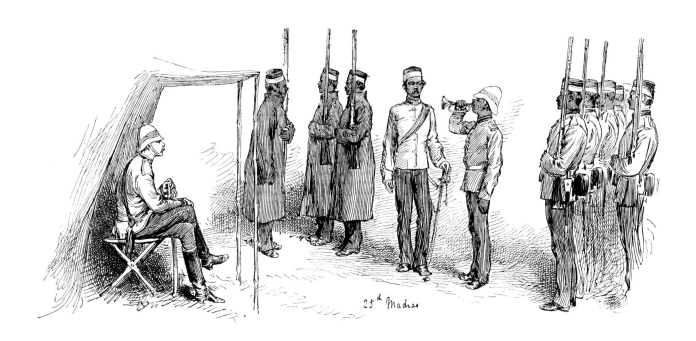

25ᵗ Madras

INTRODUCTION

by John Duncan

On the first day of November 1858 a royal proclamation was read aloud to the people of Allahabad and in other major cities throughout the whole of the sub-continent of India. It began with these words:

VICTORIA, by the Grace of God of the United Kingdom of Great Britain and Ireland, and of the Colonies and Dependencies thereof in Europe, Asia, Africa, America and Australasia, Queen, Defender of the Faith.

WHEREAS, for divers weighty reasons, we have resolved, by and with the advice and consent of the Lords Spiritual and Temporal, and Commons, in Parliament assembled, to take upon ourselves the government of the territories in India, heretofore administered in trust for us by the Honourable East India Company.

NOW, therefore, we do by these presents notify and declare that by the advice and consent aforesaid, we have taken upon ourselves the said government; and we hereby call upon all our subjects within the said territories to be faithful, and to bear true allegiance to us, our heirs and successors, and to submit themselves to the authority of those whom we may hereafter, from time, to time, see fit to appoint to administer the government of our said territories, in our name and on our behalf.

Many more such paragraphs followed. Reposing her 'special trust and confidence in the loyalty, ability and judgement of our right trusty and well-beloved cousin Charles, John, Viscount Canning' Queen Victoria goes on to appoint him 'our first Viceroy and Governor', to administer the territories and to act in her royal name and on her behalf. Assuring the 'native Princes of India' that treaties made with them by the East India Company will be scrupulously maintained, she looked 'for the like observance on their part. We desire no extension of our present territorial possessions, and, while we will permit no aggression upon our dominion or our rights to be attempted with impunity, we shall sanction no encroachment upon those of others.'

Like most declarations of its kind the proclamation is both self-assertive and grandiloquent, but it would be wrong to regard it merely as a triumphant dictat issued by an occupying power. It is said that Queen Victoria herself suggested some of the provisions. But whether the words are those of the monarch or of her ministers, the lengthy document must be taken as a clear statement of British policy towards India at the time. The fact that there are a number of recognisably liberal and enlightened ideas expressed – Victorian values at their best, perhaps – is the more remarkable, coming as they did so soon after the atrocities committed by both sides during the Indian

Mutiny and at a time when civil order had by no means been restored!

For example, 'the solace of religion' is acknowledged with gratitude, but there follows a stern warning to all those in authority that any interference with the religious belief and worship of others will incur Her Majesty's 'highest displeasure'. Similarly, the next provision insists that all citizens must be 'freely and impartially admitted to office' on the basis of education, ability and integrity, and regardless of race or creed. In the framing of legislation, due regard will be paid to the 'ancient rights, usages and customs of India'. The proclamation goes on:

WE deeply lament the evils and misery which have been brought upon India by the acts of ambitious men, who have deceived their countrymen by false reports, and led them into open rebellion. Our power has been shown by the suppression of that rebellion in the field; we desire to show our mercy by pardoning the offences of those who have been misled, but who desire to return to the path of duty.

After setting out the terms 'of grace and amnesty' extended to all offenders 'save and except those who have been, or shall be, convicted of the murder of British subjects', the proclamation ends with this resounding paragraph:

WHEN, by the blessing of Providence, internal tranquility shall be restored, it is our earnest desire to stimulate the peaceful industry of India, to promote works of public utility and improvement, and to administer the government for the benefit of all our subjects resident therein. In their prosperity will be our strength, in their contentment our security, and in their gratitude our best reward. And may the God of all power grant to us, and to those in authority under us, strength to carry out these our wishes for the good of our people.

The Queen's proclamation was immediately followed by a much shorter one from the new Viceroy – all rupees paid to public readers were certainly well-earned that day – in which he declared that henceforward 'all acts of the government of India will be done in the name of the Queen alone', and made it clear that from 'the many millions of her Majesty's native subjects' there would be exacted a loyal obedience 'to the call which, in words full of benevolence and mercy, their Sovereign has made upon their allegiance and faithfulness.'

At the highest level, these two documents gave legal substance to the great change which had already overtaken British rule in India, and which was to have a most profound effect upon the histories of both countries. The shock of the Indian Mutiny – or the Sepoy Mutiny as it is sometimes called –

and the sense of outrage felt when news of the various horrors reached the British public, brought home to them a sense of their own responsibility for the Indian Empire, and convinced the government of the day that it was no longer possible to administer the vast territories by means of an antiquated system, created and expanded on an *ad hoc* basis over many years, which interposed between the Crown and the subject peoples the whole apparatus of the Honourable East India Company, with its own Court of Directors, its own complicated management structure, conventions and arcane procedures and, above all, its own standing armies.

The Directors fought hard to maintain their unique and privileged position. They laid no fewer than three petitions before Parliament, in January, April and in June 1858, each couched in the most elegant prose and each presenting a cogent set of reasons either for preserving the *status quo*, or for changing it as little as possible. But their pleas fell on deaf ears. Of those people in Britain who held any views on the matter at all, by far the great majority believed that the time for direct rule under the British crown had come. Accordingly an Act for 'the Better Government of India' was laid before Parliament, passed with little opposition through both Houses, and received the royal assent on 2 August 1858.

Knowing that they were beaten, the Court of Directors held a 'last solemn assembly' a month later, and issued final instructions to their 'servants in the East' with these words:

Let Her Majesty appreciate the gift – let her take the vast country and the teeming millions of India under her direct control; but let her not forget the great corporation from which she has received them, nor the lessons to be learned from its success.

In the whole history of the British Empire probably no other event has been chronicled in greater depth, or in more detail, than the Indian Mutiny. However a number of salient points stand out. For example, it was not a sudden and spontaneous uprising lacking all precedent, but the climax of a lengthy period of unrest occasioned by grievances of various kinds, real and imagined, an over-stretching of resources, lack of imagination and failure of leadership on the part of East India Company officers.

It is in the shadow of these great issues and great events that the author begins his account of the exploits of those regiments who fought in the many campaigns, in India and overseas, from the time of the formation of the Queen's Indian Army until 1903, when a further major reorganisation took place. Old India hands of an earlier generation used to say that 'things were never the same after the Mutiny'. And yet, the author shows, officers and men served the Raj and the Queen Empress with devotion, loyalty and gallantry.

The first British Officer to be killed in the Sepoy Revolt – Colonel John Finnis.

PREFACE

The congregation of military officers, civilians and their wives attended the morning church service at St George's Church in the Meerut cantonment on Sunday 10 May 1857 and, following the service, returned to their bungalows or to the Mess for tiffin and a quiet afternoon. Towards sunset the residents were preparing to attend the evening service at the church, completely unaware of the unrest that existed in the Sepoy Lines which were some way from the European bungalows. The events that followed have been described in many books. However, one eye-witness report recounts the happening of that fateful Sunday evening as follows '. . . between 5 and 6 o'clock in the evening I was in my bungalow in the rear of the lines of the 11th NI, where I have resided since my arrival at the station, when, as I was dressing preparatory to going for a ride with Colonel Finnis of the 11th NI my attention was attracted to my servants and those in the neighbouring compounds . . . looking steadily into the lines of the 11th, whence a buzzing murmuring noise proceeded, such as I have often heard in case of fire, or some such alarm . . .' The witness was a Medical Officer stationed at Meerut who, following the strange conduct of his servant, went to the gate of his bungalow when he heard firing coming from the Sepoy Lines . . . he then saw a European non-commissioned officer who told him to return to his bungalow and change out of uniform. His story continued '. . . I walked into my bungalow, and was doffing my uniform, the bullets by this time flying out of the 11th lines into my compound, when the havildar-major of the 11th rushed into the room, terrified and breathless, and exclaimed "Fly Sahib, fly at once, the regiments are in open mutiny, and firing on their officers, and Colonel Finnis has just been shot in my arms . . ."'

A number of officers, hearing the unrest in the Sepoy Lines, had gone to the lines to remonstrate with their men but in the confusion the men of the 20th Regiment Bengal Native Infantry seized their arms and whilst the 11th Regiment were being addressed by their Commanding Officer, Colonel John Finnis, some men of the 20th Regiment opened fire and Colonel John Finnis fell fatally hit and thus became the first victim of the mutiny of Bengal troops. Not all native troops joined the mutiny and a high proportion of them remained on duty and loyal to the Honourable East India Company. Some saved the lives of Europeans, often at the risk of their own, but others were bent on killing, burning and what they saw as revenge for what they considered to be injustice to their comrades. Sepoys who were in jail were released and lawless elements in the city and villages joined the mutineers in a wave of arson, looting and violence. The few hours following the death of Colonel Finnis were terrifying for those who made up the European community of Meerut, but after a while the mutineers marched off to Delhi, leaving the cantonment in a state of desolation and abandoning the bodies of the murdered, with bungalows and houses ablaze.

This outbreak signalled the start of the conflict that became known as the Sepoy Mutiny and was the beginning of the end of the rule of the Honourable East India Company in India and the demise of their army. Much has been written on the events of the mutiny in which there are many accounts of great heroism of loyal sepoys, and equally in recent years accounts have been written about the atrocities committed by not only the mutineers, but also by some men serving in British regiments who had been incensed by the way that some of the European women and children had been brutally murdered.

The story of those dramatic events has no place in this account which is devoted to the officers and men of the re-formed army that was to become the Indian Army of the Empress.

The records of the regiments of the Indian Army are full of accounts in which the Indian soldier served the Empress bravely and with great distinction and the campaign medal awards abound with medal rolls of Indian Army units. A song sheet published in 1898 by Francis Day and Hunter, gives a picture of how, by the end of the century, the Indian soldier had more than redeemed himself in the eyes of the British public. The song, *How India Kept Her Word* which was sung on the London stage by Mr Leo Dryden, included a reference to the ultimate bravery award, the Victoria Cross, and contained the following lines:

> Though mutineers some of them might have been,
> They were not trusted soldiers of the Queen,
> Not everywhere burns duty's sacred lamp,
> And disaffection lurks in every camp.
> Britannia, do not blame, I beg of you,
> The loyal many for the trait'rous few;
> When once again the star of peace has beamed,
> Then India's pledge to you will be redeemed.
> They only plead for one reward,
> Repaying every loss,
> The right to wear like Britain's sons,
> The great Victoria Cross.
> > India's reply in the days gone by,
> > To other nations may have been absurd,
> > But when Britains flag unfurl'd,
> > They prov'd to all the world,
> > How the Sons of India kept their word.

The following pages recount the story of the regiments who fought in the many campaigns, both in India and overseas, during the period from the formation of the Queen's Indian Army until the turn of the century, and ends the story at the time of the reorganisation of 1903. The story follows the actions based on the campaign medals and bars that were issued to the officers and men who served in the Indian Army during the reign of Queen Victoria – the Empress of India.

HOW·INDIA·KEPT·HER·WORD.

Written by
J. P. HARRINGTON,

Composed by
GEORGE LE BRUNN,

CHORUS.
India's Reply in the days gone by,
To other nations may have been absurd,
But when Britain's flag unfurl'd, They prov'd to all the world,
How the Sons of India kept their word.

SUNG BY

LEO·DRYDEN.

Copyright.
LONDON: FRANCIS, DAY & HUNTER, 142 CHARING CROSS ROAD, (OXFORD·STREET·END)
Publishers of Smallwood's Celebrated Pianoforte Tutor. Smallwood's 55 Melodious Exercious, Etc.
NEW YORK, T. B. HARMS & Cº 18 EAST 22 Nº STREET.
Copyright MDCCCXCVIII in the United States of America, by Francis, Day & Hunter.
H. G. BANKS, Lith.
Price 4/-

CHAPTER ONE

The Second China War

Prior to the royal proclamation that was read to the population in the major cities of India on 1 November 1858, which brought the sub-continent of India under the control of the Crown, and therefore resulted in the formation of the Indian Army, the country was under the control of a private commercial company – the Honourable East India Company. The company, known as 'John Company' had, over the years that it held control of India, formed its own military force. The massive military organisation was divided into three armies, each with its own commander-in-chief, and these were under the control of the three Presidencies of Bengal, Madras and Bombay.

Units of these armies generally served in India, although there were occasions when regiments, detachments or sometimes volunteer battalions served outside India. The officers and men of the East India Company armies served to protect the Factories at Canton, provided garrisons for the far eastern outposts of Prince of Wales Island (later to be known as Penang Island), Malacca and Singapore. Volunteers from India also served with distinction in the Java campaign and later provided garrison troops for the company settlements on the west coast of Sumatra, although at one period the Sumatran settlements were an independent Presidency under the Honourable East India Company.[1]

In India, in addition to the three armies of the Honourable East India Company, there was also the 'army in India', which consisted of regular regiments of the British Army, who were generally posted for long spells of duty to serve the Raj. Such units were, in effect, rented from the Crown, and all costs were met either by the East India Company itself or by the Government of India.

There were problems within the vast armies of 'John Company' and over the years grievances grew within the army although the trouble was not obviously apparent to those in command, the senior officers generally believing that the soldiers would always be completely loyal and therefore did not heed warning signs. Grievances built up, particularly in the Bengal Army and the event that came to be known as the Indian, or Sepoy, Mutiny erupted on Sunday 10 May 1857 when regiments mutinied at Meerut. The outbreak quickly spread and although many units of the Bengal Army rebelled a number of units remained loyal, as did many of the men of the units that

Song sheet cover of 'How India Kept Her Word'.

became disaffected. Fortunately the smaller armies of Madras and Bombay presidencies remained loyal to their British Officers and to the rule of law.

The area of disaffection quickly spread from Meerut to other cantonments, such as Delhi, Cawnpore, Lucknow etc and it quickly became obvious to the Company authorities that the outbreak could not be contained without a great deal of fighting and it was perhaps significant that the training given to the officers and soldiers who mutinied stood them in good stead when faced with British regiments and other Indian units that had been brought in from the rest of India as well as from Britain, Ceylon and Singapore. The battles of the mutiny are well recorded and it is not intended to recount the story of the subsequent events following the outbreak of Meerut in this work.

Immediately prior to the outbreak the total strengths of the armies of the Honourable East India Company were given as:

Bengal Army	137,500
Madras Army	49,000
Bombay Army	48,000

In addition there were Local Forces of 40,000 and Military Police consisting of 39,000 men, making a total Indian Force of 313,500. At this time the total number of British troops serving in India was only 38,000 which proved to be inadequate to meet the contingency, thus reinforcements had to be brought in from other commands.

The Peel Commission was set up as a result of the Sepoy Mutiny and was required to consider and report on the future organisation of the 'native' army in India. It recommended that '. . . the Native Army should be composed of different nationalities and castes, and as a general rule mixed promiscuously through each regiment . . .' It did not, however, state whether it meant all nationalities and castes or only some. Bombay and Madras had a 'mixed regiment' system whereby soldiers of various races and religions served in regiments, but this system was not introduced into the Bengal Army, nor into the Punjab Frontier Force, until 1864.

The period following the outbreak of the Sepoy Mutiny and the conclusion of hostilities brought about the need for a major reorganisation of the armed forces in India and by the end of 1860 the Bengal Army had been reformed with the following infantry regiments on establishment:

Men of the 70th Bengal Native Infantry drawing rations at the
Commissariat Stores at Canton.   The Illustrated London News

Under Commander-in-Chief, Bengal	15 Regular regiments
	30 Irregular and Extra regiments
	18 Punjab regiments
Under Government of India	7 Punjab regiments
	5 Sikh and Guides regiments
	6 regiments of the Hyderabad Contingent
	3 regiments of the Nagpur Irregular Force
	7 Local Corps[2]

A total of 91 regiments. However in 1861 three of the regular regiments were disbanded together with 5 of the irregular regiments and 4 of the Punjab Regiments, thus leaving a total of 79 regiments in the Army. It had been ruled that, as a result of the lessons learned in 1857, the British Army garrison in India should not fall below 80,000. Every garrison in India was to include British troops on a ratio of 1 to 3. In practice the British Army strength was only about 65,000 and as a result of this inability to maintain an adequate presence the Indian regiments were reduced to a total strength of about 135,000. Further changes were brought about by the major reorganisation resulting from the transfer of power which included the transfer of all the former East India Company European Regiments to the British Army.[3] All Artillery were transferred from the Presidency armies to the Royal Artillery, less five mountain batteries of the Punjab Irregular Force and four batteries of the Hyderabad Contingent.

The Madras Army was little affected by the mutiny in 1857 although a few additional units were raised for local security purposes only. During 1857 the 8th Light Cavalry refused to serve in Bengal and were disbanded. During the post-mutiny reorganisation the 5th, 6th and 7th Light Cavalry were disbanded from 31 December 1860. In addition the following units, which had been raised during the Bengal Mutiny, were all disbanded during 1860:

1st, 2nd, 3rd and 4th Extra Regiments (these were regiments which had been formed to provide garrison troops in place of regular battalions who had been sent to serve 'outside' of Madras).
Madras Sappers Militia (this unit garrisoned Fort St George)
Pegu Police Battalion (formed for service in Pegu, in Burma)

The changes in the Bombay Army were also less far-reaching than the Bengal Army. Of the thirty-two infantry battalions only two actually mutinied, these being the 21st and 27th Regiments, Bombay Native Infantry. During the reorganisation of 1861 the Bombay European infantry and artillery, together with the Bengal and Madras European infantry and artillery unit, were transferred to the 'Crown' (the British Army). The units that had been formed during the mutiny were disbanded with the exception of the 3rd Sinde Horse and 30th Jacob's Rifles. The Marine Battalion was brought into the system and became the 21st Bombay Native Infantry, or Marine Battalion, and the 1st and 2nd Belooch Regiments became the 27th and 29th Regiment, Bombay Native Infantry respectively.

While the army in India was undergoing a period of reorganisation and restructuring there were overseas commitments to be considered and to the east events were taking place that were to lead to the Second China War. The policy of the Chinese during the early 1850s attempted to force the British to remain within the confines of Hong Kong. Minor actions took place at Canton during 1856 and 1857 and a decision was taken to bring in reinforcements to Hong Kong in order that an expedition could be mounted against the Chinese port of Canton. During March 1857 troops for service in China

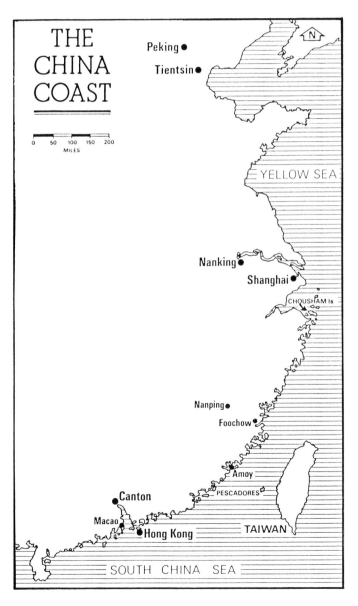

were assembled at Singapore and joining this combined British and Indian force was a major portion of the 12th Regiment, Madras Native Infantry under the command of Brevet Major M. B. Cooper.[4] The mutiny in India was to have a marked effect on the operations in China as a number of the regiments were diverted to India to help suppress the mutiny. Meanwhile, in China the campaign to secure the river route to Canton continued and on 12 December 1857 the Earl of Elgin attempted to negotiate with High Commissioner Yeh, who was in command at Canton, but Yeh ignored the British demands and a joint British and French expedition, under the command of Rear-Admiral Sir M. Seymour, moved to take Canton. The force, less the naval vessels, was made up of 'Troops from the garrison of Hong-Kong ie, 59th Regiment, Artillery, Engineers and a portion of the Madras Troops.' There were, in addition, Marines, the Naval Brigade and French troops and sailors, totalling some 5,700.[5] An attack was planned on the city of Canton, the allied force having occupied the island of Honan to the north, and the troops under the command of Major-General Sir Charles Thomas Van Straubenzee included a detachment of the 38th Regiment, Madras Native Infantry. The landings were carried out as planned and the Chinese position at Fort Lin was taken, with the Allied forces losing 130 men killed or wounded, of which 96 were British. The Chinese continued to hold out until 5 January 1858 when the Allies entered the city and 'secured the treasure and captured Yeh and the chief officials'. High Commissioner Yeh was sent to Calcutta as a political prisoner during February 1858. The Chinese government continued to delay in settling the trading treaties and the situation continued to deteriorate when the British representative, Lord Elgin, was virtually refused entry into the country. It became necessary for the Allied force to attack and capture the forts at Taku, and in the meantime the Chinese were conducting harassment tactics against the British around the Canton area. After the capture of one village, correspondence was discovered which confirmed that the Emperor of China had no intention of keeping the Tientsin Treaty of 1858 and orders had been given that the British were to be prevented from entering the Pei-ho River and trading on the Yang-tse.

By the end of 1859 the British force had been built up at Canton and, apart from the British Army element of three battalions of infantry and one of Royal Marines, a Brigade of Bengal Army troops had been added. This battalion consisted of the 47th Regiment Bengal Native Infantry (Volunteers), which arrived in June 1857; 65th Regiment Bengal Native Infantry and the 70th Regiment Bengal Native Infantry which arrived in China in February 1858. During the following year a field force was formed to proceed to Peking to enforce the treaty of 1858. The three Bengal regiments were placed under orders to return to India and were replaced in the Field Force by the 3rd and 5th Regiment, Bombay Native Infantry and, in addition, the 21st Regiment, Madras Native Infantry arrived at Hong Kong on 2 April 1860 to take over the garrison duties.[6]

On 8 March 1860 a despatch was sent by the British Minister in China to the Imperial Government at Peking asking for the ratification of the treaty of Tientsin, plus compensation and an apology for the act of the Chinese forces firing on 'Her Britannic Majesty's ships from the forts at Taku in June 1859'.

British units began to gather at Hong Kong in March 1860 under the command of Lieutenant-General Sir J. Hope Grant, KCB, and by the end of May the expeditionary force amounted to 14,000 all ranks. The force was moved to the combat area by 120 transport vessels which were escorted by a naval force of 70 ships. The 1st Division, with two brigades, had two Indian regiments serving in each of the brigades. The composition of the 1st Division was:

1st Brigade
2nd Battalion, 1st (Royal) Regiment of Foot
2nd Battalion, 31st (Huntingdonshire) Regiment of Foot
Ludhiana Sikh Regiment
2nd Brigade
1st Battalion, 2nd (Queen's) Regiment of Foot
2nd Battalion, 60th (King's Royal Rifle Corps)
15th Regiment Punjaub Infantry

The 2nd Division also consisted of mixed British and Indian brigades, the actual units being:

3rd Brigade
1st Battalion, 3rd Regiment of Foot (The Buffs)
44th (East Essex) Regiment of Foot
8th Regiment Punjaub Infantry
4th Brigade
67th (South Hampshire) Regiment of Foot
99th (Lanarkshire) Regiment of Foot
11th Regiment Punjaub Infantry
19th Regiment Punjaub Infantry

In addition, the Cavalry Brigade serving with the Expeditionary Force consisted of one British regiment plus Probyn's Horse and Fane's Horse. The actual figures given for the Indian regiments that were at the encampment at Ta-lien-wan Bay on 9 July 1860 were given as follows:

Regiments	Officers	Men	Horses
Probyn's Horse	17	446	433
Fane's Horse	15	347	327
Madras Mountain-train	7	168	39
Madras Sappers and Miners	8	245	—
8th Punjaub Infantry	15	763	—
15th Punjaub Infantry	15	943	—
19th Punjaub Regiment	19	463	—

The 70th Regiment Bengal Native Infantry at Canton (Messing arrangements). ILN

The Loodiaah (Ludhiana) Sikh Regiment, c1860.   AMOT

The total force at that time was given as 419 officers, 10,491 men and 1,731 horses.[7] It is noted that the Ludhiana Sikh Regiment, and the 11th Punjaub Infantry are not included in the foregoing return, as these two regiments, together with a battalion of British Royal Marines, remained behind to defend Shanghai against any attack that might be mounted by the Chinese units who were occupying Su-chou.

By 25 July the French had joined forces with the British at Ta-lien-wan and the whole force re-embarked with the exception of a rearguard that had been left at Odin Bay which consisted of four companies of the 99th Foot, 417 men of the 19th Regiment Punjaub Infantry, as well as artillery and '200 European and 100 Indian soldiers' who, due to illness, were still confined to the field hospital.

The expedition arrived off the Pei-ho and disembarkation was delayed due to bad weather but eventually commenced on 1 August. The landing was made one mile seaward of the South fort and the troops had to wade through water and knee-deep mud for half-a-mile before they reached dry land. The 2nd Battalion, 60th Regiment formed up on the right with the 15th Regiment Punjaub Infantry in the centre, and the 2nd (Queen's) Regiment on the left. Having established a foothold, the Allies were then delayed due to bad weather which continued until 11 August. The 2nd Division formed a line of battle, with the cavalry taking position on the right. The Tartar cavalry mounted an attack but this was repulsed by the fire of fifteen Armstrong guns. At this time Stirling's half battery, being unable to follow, were left in the rear with an escort of 30 men of Fane's Horse. An attack was made on this party by about 100 Tartars but was repulsed by the party of Fane's Horse, led by Lieutenant Ernest August Murray MacGregor, who was shot in the shoulder and severely wounded.[8]

The advance continued slowly with the Chinese defending positions with guns and jingalls,[9] also with some counter-attacks by Tartar cavalry which were armed, generally, with bows and arrows.

Sikh Cavalry and troops about to depart from Odin Bay.   ILN

A report submitted by Lieutenant-General Sir J. Hope Grant gives the details of the casualties during the actions on the 3, 12 and 14 August.

'1st Sikh Cavalry (later this unit was known as Probyn's Horse) – 2 Officers,[10] 2 Sergeants and 2 rank and file wounded. (Sowar Muttah Sing was wounded in the chest and later died.)
Fane's Horse – 1 killed (Sowar Nurzeer Khan). 1 officer, 1 Jemadar and 4 Sowars wounded.
Madras Sappers – 1 sepoy missing.'

Following the engagements the 2nd Division occupied the captured entrenchments and the 1st Division returned to their camp which was between Hsin-ho and the Pei-ho River. The whole force consolidated their positions and prepared for a renewed attack on the Chinese positions on 21 August. During this period a bridge was built over the Pei-ho River and on 21 August an allied attack was mounted with a force consisting of British units, French infantry and with 200 Madras Sappers. The Chinese forts opened fire at 5am but the return fire gradually silenced the Chinese guns and, after two hours, two of the enemy magazines exploded which demoralised the defenders. An attack was then launched on the northern fort with the 1st Battalion, 3rd Regiment (The Buffs) and the 8th Punjaub Infantry moving forward. By this time the Chinese started to show surrender flags on the southern forts, and when the infantry reached the lower north fort the defenders surrendered, leaving the way open to Tientsin.

The negotiations at Tientsin were delayed by the Chinese Commissioners playing for time in the hope that the Allied army would be stopped from advancing to Peking by the onset of winter weather conditions. The depot which had been established at Odin Bay was abandoned and the 19th Punjaub Infantry and the Royal Artillery moved to the front. The advance towards Peking resumed on 8 September with a force under the command of Brigadier Reeves which included British units and Fane's Horse. This advance force was supported on 10 September by a French formation of about 3,000 men and on 12 September the 2nd Brigade followed, supported by Probyn's Horse.

They halted at Ho-hsi-wu in order that a field force under one command could be established before making any further advance towards Peking. On 13 September 1860 the Chinese Secretary, Thomas Wade, and Harry S. Parkes set off for Tung-chou to meet with the Chinese Commissioners and an agreement was reached whereby Lord Elgin, with an escort of 1,000 men, should proceed to Tung-Chou where the convention would be signed and then Lord Elgin would proceed to Peking with his escort to ratify the old treaty.

A party led by Mr Harry S. Parkes again proceeded to Tung-chou on 18 September and on this occasion he was accompanied by 'an escort of Fane's Horse, under the command of Lieutenant W. C. Anderson' and by Mr Loch, the private secretary to Lord Elgin. The party met with the Chinese Commissioners and following this, Parkes divided his force leaving Lieutenant Anderson, fifteen of his sowars together

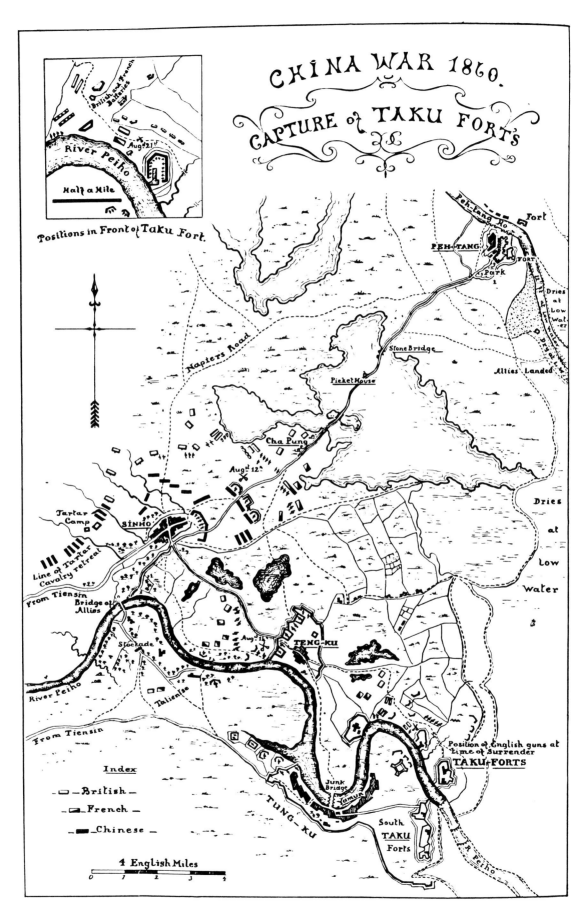

CHINA WAR 1860.
CAPTURE of TAKU FORTS

Positions in Front of Taku Fort.

Half a Mile

River Peiho

Aug.st 21.

*Landing of Sikh
Regiment horses at
Odin Bay, Talien Wan.
ILN*

The gunboat Havoc
*with Fane's Horse on
board, en route to the
Peh-tang.
ILN*

Napiers Road

Stone Bridge

Picket House

Peh-tang Ho

Fort

PEH-TANG

Park

FORT

Dries
at
Low
Water

Allies Landed

Cha Pung

Aug.st 12.

Dries

at

Low

Water

Tartar Camp

SINHO

Line of Tartar Cavalry retreat

From Tiensin

Bridge of Allies

Stockade

River Peiho

Talienfoo

From Tiensin

Aug.st 14.

TENG-KU

Position of English guns at time of Surrender

TAKU-FORTS

Junk Bridge

Tamen

TUNG-KU

South TAKU Forts

R. Peiho

Index

British

French

Chinese

4 English Miles

0 1 2 3 4

with Mr Bowlby, the correspondent of *The Times*, and Mr de Norman, an Attache to the British Minister at Shanghai, at Tung-Chou. Parkes noted that the area had been occupied by Chinese troops and, leaving Mr Loch to return to the British lines, he returned with Trooper Phipps of the King's Dragoon Guards. He, together with all of his small party, were taken prisoner by the Chinese and taken off to Peking.

It had been the intention of the Chinese to ambush the British troops and to kill as many of them as possible in the hope that this would deter the Allies from advancing to Peking. In the action that followed, another defeat was inflicted upon the enemy with the 15th Punjaub Infantry and 1st Sikh Cavalry (Probyn's Horse) taking a major role. *The London Gazette* report on the action records that 'their cavalry (Chinese) hovered in large masses on our entire left flank, so that Sir J. Michel was unable to perform the flank movement that had been intended, until the 1st Sikh Cavalry had, by a brilliant charge, discomfited the Tartar Horse'. This enabled the Allies to advance and drive the enemy back for some miles. Of the Allied force, the Indian Army casualties were:

Probyn's Horse	–	6 wounded
Fane's Horse	–	6 wounded
15th Punjaub Infantry	–	5 wounded

On the following day a party went to Tung-chou, under a flag of truce, to try to make contact with Mr Parkes and his party but the local Chinese officials denied all knowledge of the whereabouts of the British party, which included the detachment from Fane's Horse.

On 21 September another attack was made on the Chinese in the vicinity of Pa-li-chiao and once again the cavalry charged the enemy force and 'did great execution' which resulted in the Chinese retreating to a point only six miles from Peking. The action resulted in further casualties to the Allied force, including one death and nineteen wounded in the Indian units that took part in the action.[11] As the enemy withdrew to Peking it gathered a force of some 50,000 to defend the city, many of which were cavalry who were well mounted and fierce fighters, and due to this the Allied force waited until all reinforcements had arrived from Tientsin. The British were concerned with the abduction of the Parkes' party and continued to try to negotiate their release. The Chinese now regarded them as 'prisoners of war' which was not acceptable to Lord Elgin. By 3 October Prince Kung, the Chinese High Commissioner, was still playing a delaying game but when he failed to meet the Allied demands, the advance on Peking was begun on 5 October with a force of about 10,000.

The British advanced and bivouacked along the road to the An-ting Gate, close to the Tartar parade ground and the French moved forward and took possession of the gardens of the Summer Palace. On 9 October an ultimatum was given to Prince Kung demanding the surrender of Peking and Chinese Forces by 13 October. At noon on 13 October the An-ting Gate opened and the allied troops entered the city.[12]

Mr Parkes and Mr Loch, together with a Frenchman and a Sikh Sowar, were released by the Chinese. It was later that the bodies of 'Mr de Norman, Lieutenant Anderson, Mr Bowlby, one English soldier and 12 Sikhs' were sent in. Thirteen Sikh sowars were released unharmed. The account of the event made by Duffadar Jowalla Sing of 1st Troop Fane's Horse was translated by Captain Walter Fane, and a copy was sent with Lord Elgin's despatch.

Lord Elgin entered Peking on 24 October 1860 to sign the treaty and a military parade was held to impress the Chinese with a show of strength. The allied troops gradually withdrew from Peking and North China and by the end of November the majority of the British force had re-embarked. The cavalry embarked at Taku and the 1st Sikh Cavalry (Probyn's Horse) lost fifteen horses during this time due to the bad weather.

In July 1861 a decision was taken that Fane's Horse, together with some British units, would leave China in the autumn. The Commander of the British Forces submitted a report on the conduct of the Indian units which was the first of many commendations that the Indian Army was to receive over the remaining years of Queen Victoria's reign. The report reads: 'The 1st Sikh Irregular Cavalry, under Major Probyn, and Fane's Horse, under Captain Fane have performed their work most admirably. On more than one occasion these Regiments have been opposed to, and have successfully charged a vastly superior force of the enemy's cavalry.' He also recommended Major Probyn and Captain Fane for favourable notice. The report continued with commendations for the two companies of Madras Artillery under the command of Captain H. E. Hicks, and the two companies of Madras Sappers, under Captain Shaw Stewart, for the 'good and useful services in the operations which preceded and led to the fall of the Taku Forts.' The infantry units were also praised and it is well worth recording:

The 8th Punjab Infantry has been ably commanded throughout the campaign by Captain (C. H.) Brownlow. Captain Shebbeare, an excellent officer, the Commandant of the 15th Punjab Infantry, was unfortunately compelled by ill health to leave just when active operations were commencing; but the regiment has been efficiently commanded by Lieutenant (W. L.) Randall. The 11th and 19th Punjab Infantry have been employed in garrisoning the depots, &c., whilst the 3rd and 5th Bombay Native Infantry and the 21st Madras Native Infantry have formed portions of the garrisons of Hong Kong and Canton.

The report, written by Lieutenant-General J. Hope Grant, concluded:

I have much pleasure in informing your Excellency that the behaviour of the Indian Troops, both in camp and in garrison, has been everything that I could wish for.

The Indian Army had, indeed, shown that it was not only loyal but also an efficient fighting force.

There were still problems in the Shanghai area and during April and May 1862 a combined British and Indian field force operated against the Tai-pings who continued to make raids on the Settlement. The Indian Army provided two units for this operation, these being:

5th Bombay Native Infantry

British Officers	8
Native Officers	11
NCOs & men	504

22nd Punjaub Native Infantry

British Officers	10
Native Officers	12
NCOs & Men	577

During the operations on 27 and 29 April and 1 May the two units lost one officer killed and 4 wounded.

The operations around Shanghai concluded with the taking of Ka-ding which completed an area of 30 miles radius from the city which was then free of Tai-pings.

The Second China War, as the conflict became known, brought a new campaign medal which was issued to both British and Indian troops. The medal is described as follows:

Obverse – the diademed head of Queen Victoria and the legend 'Victoria Regina'.

Reverse – A collection of war trophies with an oval shield, with the Royal Arms in the centre, all positioned under a palm tree. Above is the legend 'ARMIS EXPOSCERE PACEM'. In the exergue is the word 'CHINA'.

The medal was designed by William Wyon, RA. Six bars were issued with the medal, although men in Indian Army units have only qualified for three, these being 'Canton 1857' (28 December 1857-5 January 1858); 'Taku Forts 1860' (21 August 1860) and 'Pekin 1860'.[13]

The ribbon is 32mm wide. The original issue had five equally spaced stripes, from left to right, blue, yellow, red, white and green. This ribbon was later replaced by one of crimson with yellow edges.

The China War Medal, with clasp 'Pekin 1860'.

1   Bastin, John, *The British in West Sumatra, 1685-1825*, Kuala Lumpur, 1965.
2   Mollo, B. *The Indian Army*, 1981, p91.
3   The units transferred to the British Army establishment were:

1st (Bengal European) Fusiliers	became	101st Regiment
1st Madras (European) Fusiliers		102nd Fusiliers
1st Bombay (European) Fusiliers		103rd Fusiliers
2nd (Bengal European) Fusiliers		104th Fusiliers
2nd Madras (Light Infantry) Regiment		105th Regiment
2nd Bombay (Light Infantry) Regiment		106th Regiment
3rd (Bengal Light Infantry) Regiment		107th Regiment
3rd (Madras) Regiment		108th Regiment
3rd (Bombay) Regiment		109th Regiment

4   *The Straits Times*, Singapore, Vol 13, No 836, 17 March 1857.
5   *Frontier and Overseas Expeditions from India*, Vol VI, 1911, p404.
6   Harfield, A. *British & Indian Armies on the China Coast (1785-1985)*, 1990.
7   *Frontier and Overseas Expeditions from India*, op cit, pp443-444.

8   *The London Gazette* dated 4 November 1860.
9   *Jingalls* – or Gingall. A long tapering gun 'six to fourteen feet in length, (with) a stand or tripod'.
10 Lieutenant Stuart and Ensign McCauley. The two officers listed are Lieutenant George *Stewart*, of the 17th Bengal Native Infantry and Ensign Edward *Macauley*, of the 23rd Bengal Native Infantry, both of whom were serving with the 'Seikh Irregular Cavalry' (Indian Army List, 1861).
11 Casualties were:
Fane's Horse – Lieutenant F. P. Luard, 3 Duffadar, 10 Sowars.
15th Punjaub Infantry – Lieutenant G. A. A. Baker, Subadar Kurruck Sing, 2 Sepoys, 1 Bugler.
1st Sikh Irregular Cavalry (Probyn's Horse) – Sowar Ahmud Khan (died).
12 Report dated 13 October 1860.
13 Gordon, Major Lawrence L. *British Battles and Medals*, 1962, p189.

CHAPTER TWO

Abyssinia, 1867

While some regiments of the Indian Army were engaged in action in China the larger part of the reformed Indian Army, who were now truly 'Soldiers of the Queen', were busily engaged in reorganisation and training. It was intended that with a new civil administration, which it was hoped would bring peace and stability to the country, the army would have time to complete the reorganisation and be able to act as an efficient fighting force should the need arise.

During the period 1861-67 the army, which was still grouped under the three Presidential commands, Bengal, Madras and Bombay, continued to garrison the areas and cantonments that had been defined by the East India Company prior to the mutiny. The reorganisation included a change in the allocation and promotion of officers within regiments. Prior to the mutiny the Company's army officers remained on the strength of their parent regiment and, should a regiment be engaged in action and suffer casualties among its officers or should a regiment be struck by an epidemic, the promotion prospects were greatly increased and in many cases officers were promoted to fill vacancies where senior officers died. Other officers serving in other regiments, who often had longer service in the army, were 'passed over' under this arrangement. In 1861 the system changed and the officers of each of the three Indian armies were grouped into their respective pools, these being the Bengal, Madras and Bombay Staff Corps. These pools of officers provided manpower for civil posts, military departmental posts, headquarters and staff appointments as well as normal regimental posts. At this time the British Officer establishment in each unit was reduced and the posts they held were deemed to be on the 'staff' of the regiments. Indian Officers were theoretically given the command of companies and troops. Promotion was regularised and was generally controlled by length of service and not seniority within a regiment. Under this new regulation the following table shows the time scale for promotion:

	years' service
Lieutenant to Captain	11
Captain to Major	20
Major to Lieutenant-Colonel	26
Lieutenant-Colonel to Colonel	31[1]

The 'service system' had faults, as in practice the Indian Officers were promoted from 'the ranks' and were at an age where they were not easily able to assimilate required knowledge to make them effective company or troop officers. In reality the British Officer, who should have been acting as adviser, was carrying out the duties of Company Commander, with the Indian Officer merely advising on matters relating to the soldiers' domestic affairs.

Other problems were caused by British officers who served on civil employment being able to return to regimental duties at any time. Whilst serving with the civil administration they received their promotion in due course as they completed the required amount of service. At the age of fifty-five, officers were considered to be too old for civil or political duties and were then returned to the Army for posting into senior positions in regiments. Thus an officer who had spent the majority of his career serving away from troops could be placed in command of officers and men without any experience, except that gained as a young subaltern. The system continued until the disasters of the Second Afghan War and, as a result of the failures in that campaign, the system was changed in 1882 whereby officers who returned to the Army at the age of fifty-five years received promotion, honorary in some cases, and were then retired on the appropriate pension. Those serving with troops should not serve longer than seven years in command and would be required to relinquish command when reaching the age of fifty-two years.[2]

The next overseas campaign which involved units of the Indian Army took place in 1867. Britain effected a Treaty with the Emperor of Abyssinia and in 1848 Mr Plowden was appointed Consular Agent and a treaty of commerce was ratified three years later. In 1855 Lij Kassa fought his way to the throne and became Emperor Theodore III. The Consular Agent, Mr Plowden, was murdered in 1860, and was replaced by Captain Charles Duncan Cameron.[3] He arrived in Abyssinia in 1862 and shortly afterwards he and a number of other Europeans were taken prisoner by Emperor Theodore and were tortured. A Mr Hormuzd Rassam was sent as an Envoy to the Emperor to negotiate the release of the prisoners. After nearly a year of negotiations the prisoners were released in 1866 but were rearrested the following month together with Mr Rassam, who was the British Political Agent in Aden, and the other two members of his party. These were Lieutenant William Francis Prideaux, Bombay Staff Corps, and Dr Heni Jules Blanc of the Bombay Medical Establishment.[4] In addition to this party being

Officers of the 4th Bengal Cavalry, c1865. AMOT

imprisoned, the Emperor had asked for a number of British workmen to be sent to his country and even these men were eventually imprisoned.

Following more diplomatic negotiations, which also failed, a state of war was declared in November 1867 and preparations were then made to mount an expeditionary force to secure the release of the European prisoners. In the meantime arrangements were already in hand to mount the operation. Bombay was chosen as the base for the expeditionary force and General Sir Robert Napier, KCB, GCSI was appointed Commander of the expedition. He considered that a force of 12,000 would be required, together with adequate transportation which would be a combination of mules, camels, carts and 3,000 coolies.

On 25 July 1867 the Secretary of State for India issued orders for collection of transport, and the officers to command the various operational posts were selected. All the officers and men were to be drawn from the Indian Army establishment. It was decided that troops would be sent from Bombay and that the regiments used would be relieved, where necessary, by troops from the Bengal and Madras establishments. The advance party left Bombay on 16 September 1867 to reconnoitre a landing place on the shores of the Red Sea, and on 7 October an advance Brigade sailed from Bombay. In addition one brigade was embarked at Calcutta and some minor units at Vingorla, Calicut, and Karachi. It is recorded that 205 sailing vessels and 75 steamers were employed in the ferrying of the expeditionary force.[5] During the voyage, fever and dysentery broke out on one of the troop transports and 45 out of 270 coolies died. Although it had been recommended that 3,000 should be employed, in fact only 2,000 were employed.

Due to rough weather the reconnoitring party did not reach Massowah until 1 October and, finding the harbour unsuitable, moved on to Malkatto in Annesley Bay where they arrived on 4 October. The final landing place was at Zula and the ships conveying the advance brigade arrived on 4 November, landed, and immediately a search was carried out to establish a suitable route to Kamali, a distance of about 62 miles.

The total strength of the Indian Army element of the expeditionary force was:

Cavalry
10th Regiment, Bengal Native Cavalry (Lancers)
12th Regiment, Bengal Native Cavalry
3rd Regiment, Bombay Native Cavalry
3rd Regiment, Scinde Horse
Infantry
21st (Punjab) Bengal Native Infantry
23rd Bengal Native Infantry
2nd Bombay Native Infantry (Grenadiers)

The landing place, Abyssinia, 1867.

3rd Bombay Native Infantry
5th Bombay Light Infantry
8th Bombay Native Infantry
10th Bombay Native Infantry
18th Bombay Native Infantry
25th Bombay Light Infantry
27th Bombay Native Infantry (1st Baluchis)

In addition, 1 Company Bombay Native Infantry (Marine Battalion), Bengal Coolie Corps (2,000 men) and 1,000 men of the Bombay Army Works Corps accompanied the expedition, as well as No 1 Company Native Artillery and 4 Companies Bombay Sappers and Miners and 3 Companies Madras Sappers and Miners.[6]

The 10th Regiment, Bengal Cavalry, with the Mountain Train reached Senafe on 6 December and on the following day the 3rd Light Cavalry arrived. During the last week of December a reconnaissance was made of the road leading from Senafe to Adigrat, a distance of 37 miles. Because of the terrain and the climate, this distance was divided into three marches. On 2 January 1868 Sir Robert Napier arrived at Annesley Bay and he then organised a depot at Senafe to ensure that adequate supplies would be available at that staging post. It had been intended to provide a railway link but the construction of the line proved to be difficult and by 31 January only three miles had been completed.

The Commander-in-Chief reached Adigrat on 6 February where a permanent post was established. A deputation, led by Prince Kassai arrived and met the British delegation. It was reported that the general conduct of the Abyssinians was satisfactory and, despite the climate, the health of the troops was generally good. The force advanced to Adabaga and at this stage the Commander-in-Chief ordered all officers' servants, cavalry syces and grass cutters back to base at Annesley Bay.

On 25 February Sir Rober Napier advanced to Dyab, a stream between Adabaga and Hauzen, to meet with Prince Kassai during which time the Prince promised safe custody for convoys, but even with this assurance the Commander-in-Chief took care to ensure that convoys were prepared for attack. On the following day the force commenced its advance towards Antalo and after a difficult march a halt was made at Dongolo, and this was followed by another day's march, which proved to be extremely difficult. As a result only eight miles were covered and a camp was established on the banks of the Agula.

The combined British and Indian force continued to advance over difficult terrain and the column made slow progress, with some days as little as 6½ miles being achieved. Whilst the main column advanced towards Magdala, the Sappers were establishing a telegraph line from the coast at Zula to Adigrat, a distance of 101 miles, which provided communications from the base that had been established at that location back to the landing area. During the advance the route had been prepared by the 'Advance Guard' which was commanded by the Deputy Quartermaster General, Lieutenant-Colonel Robert Phayre, Bombay Staff Corps who, with his pioneer force of 'a hundred

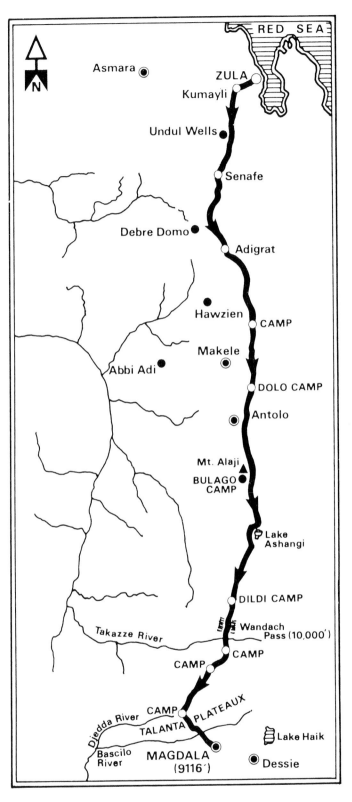

The Line of March of
Napier's Army to Magdala

and fifty sabres, two companies of native infantry, a company of Punjab Pioneers, and a company of Bombay Sappers',[7] explored the country and as well as patching up the tracks as he moved forward, he was able to produce maps of the area which were very necessary in the wild unsurveyed country. On 28 March the main force reached Santara, a point 4½ miles beyond the Takazze River. They encamped at this point for two days, having now marched 313 miles from the coast. The report of this site shows that there were vast changes in temperature, the camp being on the edge of Wadela tableland and 10,000 feet above sea level. The report reads 'Here the thermometer varied between 20° and 110° in the tents.'[8] The fortress at Magdala, which was the stronghold of Emperor Theodore III, was in the mountains and the route to the fortress was intersected by ravines, making the approach extremely difficult. From information received it was planned to follow a south-westerly direction and on 31 March the First Brigade moved to Gahso and then on the following day on to Abdikum, whilst on that day, 1 April, the Second Brigade moved to Gahso. On 1 April the strength of the combined force in Abyssinia was given as being 'nearly' 11,000 fighting men and 15,000 followers. They were spread over a wide area:

Headquarters and 1st Brigade, 1st Division	Abdikum
Headquarters 1st Division and 2nd Brigade	Gahso
Support element 1st and 2nd Brigades, 1st Division	Between Wandach and Antolo
2nd Division	Antolo, Adigrat and Senafe

The next phase of the advance was delayed whilst waiting for supplies to be brought up to the forward troops, and on 9 April the main body of the expeditionary force advanced five miles to the brink of the Bashilo valley and camped within sight of Theodore's army. The two armies met and initially Theodore mistook the Naval Brigade for transport and despatched 6,000 of his army to capture the guns and baggage. The Naval Brigade opened fire on the enemy with rockets and partially checked the advance. The 4th (King's Own) Regiment in skirmishing order, and supported by a wing of the 1st Baluchis, a detachment of Royal Engineers, and the Bombay Sappers, were able to advance to the Arogi (Arogie) plain and commenced firing on the Abyssinians who gradually fell back and were driven off the plain. However, the enemy inflicted some casualties on Sir Charles Staveley's right flank attacking from a cactus grove on Fahla hill. A Battery with an escort advanced from a defile and were in turn attacked by Theodore's men who charged down the mountain side. Although the battery opened fire, the enemy continued to advance but were checked by a detachment of 23rd Bengal Native Infantry who charged forward and met the enemy in close combat, fighting with bayonets against the Abyssinian spears. The enemy were driven off, leaving a great number of dead behind but some of the Indian troops suffered spear wounds. The action lasted from 4pm and was finished by 7pm; however, the conditions were extremely bad as heavy rain fell during the greater part of the action. Theodore's troops retreated but where possible put up stubborn defence and mounted counter-attacks.

By dawn on 11 April the 1st and 2nd Brigades took up positions on the Affijo plateau and the Arogie plain. The 1st Baluchis were moving forward in skirmishing order when a flag of truce was sent by Theodore, and Sir Robert Napier's terms were sent to the Emperor. These called for the surrender of himself, his army to surrender, and the British prisoners to be released immediately. During the temporary lull in the action Theodore assessed the situation and, deciding that his position was not as serious as he had first thought, sent an insulting letter to Sir Robert Napier. However, typical of this unstable monarch, he had yet another change of plan and sent the British captives to Sir Robert Napier's camp shortly after sunset. On 12 April Theodore sent an apology to the British for his previous letter, and on the following day Theodore planned to escape from Magdala but his troops declined to follow him and thousands of them surrendered to the combined British and Indian force.

The period of armistice having passed, Sir Robert Napier planned to resume the attack but before his plan could be put into operation news was received that Theodore was plotting to escape. The Scinde Horse held Bashilo and provided detachments to seal other routes, and a party of fifty troopers went to Fahla Hill to deal with some of Theodore's troops who wished to surrender. Sir Charles Staveley moved forward and occupied the high ground at Fahla and Selassie. The advance commenced at 8.30am and under cover of artillery guns a company of the 1st Baluchis ascended a spur on the right of Falha Hill, supported by two companies on the other spur, and by midday the hill had been secured. The 2nd Brigade then moved on to capture the other high ground at Selassie. On reaching the summit, the troops found a force of about 20,000 enemy, who then laid down their weapons and surrendered without a fight.

Having secured this high ground, the Armstrong guns and mortars were moved up to the summit by the use of elephants. In the meantime Emperor Theodore decided to continue to fight the British force and joined his own artillery at Islamgie, intending to move into his citadel at Magdala with his artillery and defend himself from his fortress. However, his plans were disrupted by the arrival of a detachment of the Bombay cavalry who, together with a detachment of the British 33rd Regiment, upset Theodore's plans and caused him to retire with only two of his guns. At this stage he was mounted on his horse and, firing off his rifle, called for a champion from the British force to come

The 27th Bombay Native Infantry (1st Baluchis), under the command of Major H. Beville.   AMOT

The capture of Magdala, 13 April 1868.

forward and meet him. After some exchange of shots Theodore and his men withdrew to the fortress. The British Commander prepared to attack the fortress which is described as follows: 'beyond the Isamgie saddle the rock of Magdala rose in a steep scarp to a height of 300 feet. A double line of defence, in each of which was a small gate, crowned the scarp; this was approached by a steep and rugged path'[9] and any attack on such a position would inevitably lead to a great number of casualties. Unfortunately the strength of the enemy garrison was not known although Theodore was occasionally seen. The British force commenced the attack by artillery and rocket fire from a distance of 1,300 yards. The attack was made by the 33rd Regiment, supported by a detachment of Royal Engineers, and 'K' Company of the Madras Sappers and Miners carrying powder bags, ladders, etc formed the storming party. Two companies of the 10th Bombay Native Infantry remained at Selassie to guard the surrendered arms and to clear the enemy off the mountain. Artillery fire commenced at 3pm but during this first bombardment the enemy kept under cover. At 4pm the order to storm the fortress was given and the attacking infantry came under fire from the enemy, who fired through loopholes, fortunately without inflicting too many casualties. By scaling over the wall by means of ladders, the attacking force was able to mount a flank attack on the defenders of the gate and succeeded in driving the enemy back up a narrow path, inflicting heavy losses. The attacking force, mainly the 33rd Regiment, gained the summit and planted the English standard whereupon the followers of Theodore surrendered. As soon as the Emperor

saw that further resistance was futile he committed suicide.

Theodore's Queen was found in her house in the fortress by soldiers and was placed in the care of Captain Speedy.[10] When consulted by Sir Robert Napier as to the disposal of the body of her husband, she requested that he be buried in the church. After an examination which established the cause of death as a self-inflicted wound, Theodore, King of Kings and Emperor of Abyssinia, was buried quietly and without military honours.

Following the dismantling of the fortress and arranging for safe conduct for those Abyssinians who wished to return to their homes, Magdala was handed over to Queen Masteeat. The British force gradually withdrew to the coast, which was 381 miles from Magdala. On 24 May Sir Robert Napier reached Senafe and held a review of troops to commemorate the birthday of Queen Victoria. Prince Kassai was present and, as he had proved friendly and helpful to the Expeditionary Force, he was given a gift of arms on the following day on the understanding that they were to be used only in the defence of his own country. The gift included 12 howitzers and mortars, 725 muskets and 350,000 rounds of ammunition, as well as other items from the commissariat stores.

The Commander-in-Chief and the last column reached Zula on 2 June and by 11 June the expeditionary force had re-embarked with the exception of the 25th Bombay Native Infantry, who remained at Zula as a guard for the stores that were still to be recovered. The casualty figures for the campaign were given as follows:

British troops –	Officers	Other ranks
Deaths	11	35
Invalided	–	333
Indian army troops		
Invalided	–	570
Followers	–	6,056 (of which 512 died)

A medal was issued to British, Indian and Naval personnel who took part in the operation. The Abyssinian War Medal was granted for the period 4 October 1867 to 19 April 1868 and is described as follows:

Obverse – A small veiled and coronated bust of Queen Victoria, surrounded by an ornate nine-pointed star, between each point of which is one of the letters of the word 'Abyssinia'.

Reverse – The name of the recipient with his regiment or ship within a laurel wreath.[11]

The size is 32.5mm diameter and the ribbon is 38mm wide. White with a broad red stripe down the centre. The medal was designed by Owen Jones and engraved by Joseph S. Wyon and Albert B. Wyon.

The following officer and men of the 23rd (Punjab) Bengal Native Infantry were 'admitted to the 3rd Class (of the Indian Order of Merit) in consideration of their conspicuous gallantry in the expedition to Abyssinia.'

> Subadar Khurruch Sing
> Sepoy Futteh Sing
> Sepoy Jowalla Sing
> Bugler Khooshall Sing

The awards were promulgated in G.G.O. No 782 of 1869.[12]

The Abyssinian War Medal.

1   Heathcote, T. A. *The Indian Army – The Garrison of British Imperial India 1822-1922*, 1974, pp136-137.
2   Heathcote, op cit, p137.
3   Charles Duncan Cameron served as an Ensign in 69th Foot from 10 May 1846, transferred to the 45th Foot on 12 June 1846, promoted to Lieutenant he retired on 17 June 1851 and was granted the Honorary Rank of Captain from 27 March 1855.
4   *Indian Army List 1867*, pp461g and 524.
5   *Frontier and Overseas Expeditions from India*, Vol VI, 1911, p69.
6   *Frontier and Overseas Expeditions from India*, op cit, p82.
7   Myatt, Frederick, *The March to Magdala*, 1970, p102.
8   *Frontier and Overseas Expeditions from India*, op cit, p71.
9   *Frontier and Overseas Expeditions from India*, op cit, p75.
10 *Speedy, Captain Tristram Charles Sawyer.* He had served in the British and Indian Armies but resigned with the intention of settling in New Zealand. Speedy visited Abyssinia en route to New Zealand and after exploring the country he joined Theodore's camp and held an independent command in Theodore's army. He then acted as Vice-Consul for a while but continued his journey to New Zealand in 1864. He farmed in New Zealand and commanded a company of Militia during the second Maori War. In view of his knowledge of Abyssinia he was invited to return to Abyssinia and arrived at Zula where he borrowed a horse and joined the expedition at Sanafe. Following the Abyssinian campaign, he moved to India where he became District Superintendent of Police at Oudh from 1869 to 1871. Early in 1872 he moved to the Straits Settlements and took up the post of Deputy Commissioner of Police. In July 1873 he gave up his police appointment to return to India to recruit soldiers for the Mantri (Chief) of Perak. He then served with the British force during the Perak Campaign of 1875-76.
11 Gordon, Major Lawrence L, *British Battles and Medals*, 1962, p200.
12 Hypher, P. P., *Deeds of Valour performed by Indian Officers and Soldiers, During the period from 1860 to 1925*, Simla, 1927, p.21.

CHAPTER THREE

Frontier Campaigns and the Perak War

During the period 1854-95 the Indian General Service Medal was issued, together with twenty-three bars (or clasps), of which two bars were awarded for actions that took place before the formation of the Indian Army, these being 'Pegu' (28 March 1852 to 30 June 1853) and 'Persia' (5 December 1856 to 8 February 1857). A third bar covered a period of almost nineteen years, spanning service with the East India Company and the Indian Army; this was the bar 'North West Frontier' which was awarded for a variety of actions during the period 3 December 1849 to 22 October 1868.

In April 1858 an expedition was despatched against Hindustani fanatics and the Khudu Khels. The force under the command of Major-General Sir Sydney John Cotton, KCB, was made up of detachments of Peshawar Light Horse, 7th and 18th Irregular Cavalry and the Guides Cavalry, the Peshawar Light Field Battery, the Peshawar Mountain Train Battery and the Hazara Mountain Train Battery, a detachment of the Bengal Sappers and Miners, and the following infantry units: Guides Infantry, 8, 12, 18 and 21 Bengal Native Infantry, together with two British Foot regiments the 81st and 98th Foot, making a total force of 4,877 men.

The force assembled on the left bank of the Kabul River, opposite Nowshera and crossed the frontier on 26 April. It operated in several columns and captured and destroyed three strongholds of the Khudu Khels and the fanatics without opposition. On 3 May they advanced towards Sitana where the main concentration of the fanatics were gathered and, after a sharp conflict, the place was taken and destroyed. The expeditionary force lost one native officer (Subadar Dalu Mal, 18th Punjab Infantry) and five men were killed. One British and one Indian Officer were wounded as were 27 Indian soldiers.[1]

At the end of the following year, December 1859, an expedition was launched against the Kabul Khel Wazirs to punish them for harbouring rebels who had killed Captain Richard Mecham of the Royal Artillery (Bengal).[2] The expedition was commanded by Brigadier-General N. B. Chamberlain CB, and consisted of Nos 1 and 2 Punjab Light Field Batteries; the Peshawar and Hazara Mountain Train Batteries; a detachment of Bengal Sappers and Miners; 2nd Punjab Cavalry; the 4th Sikh Infantry; 1st, 3rd, 4th, 6th and 24th Bengal Native Infantry; and the Guides Infantry. The whole force, amounting to about 4,000 men, moved into the Waziri country on 22 December where they met with resistance from the Waziris, which was overcome after some stubborn fighting. The enemy eventually submitted and as the aim of the expedition had mainly been achieved the Indian Army withdrew across the frontier, having had one soldier killed and 18 wounded.[3]

The next frontier campaign was against the Mahsud Waziris, who in March 1860 attacked the frontier town of Tank and were only prevented from destroying the place by the gallant defence put up by 158 men of the 5th Punjab Cavalry, led by Risaldar Saadat Khan, who were stationed at the town. A force was assembled on 16 April 1860 and this was again led by Brigadier-General N. B. Chamberlain CB, and consisted of the Guides Cavalry; 3rd Punjab Cavalry; Multani Cavalry; Nos 2 and 3 Punjab Light Field Batteries; the Punjab and Hazara Mountain Trains; and Bengal Sappers and Miners. The infantry support was provided by the Guides Infantry; 4th Sikh Infantry; 1st, 2nd, 3rd, 4th, 6th, 14th, 24th (Pioneers) Punjab Infantry; and the 25th (Gurkha) Punjab Infantry, as well as the 6th Punjab Police Battalion. It was a formidable force, as was the opposition which were the Mahsud Waziris with a strength reported to be between 4,000 and 7,000. The Indian troops were split, leaving part of the force at Palosin, under the command of Colonel Lumsden,[4] and at reveille on 23 April the enemy attacked the camp with approximately 3,000 men. Such was the intensity of the attack that there was a considerable loss on both sides, Lumsden suffering 63 killed and 166 wounded. Following this action a negotiated settlement was attempted but the Mahsuds would not accept the British terms and on 2 May General Chamberlain's force advanced and on 4 May he reached the Barari Pass where the enemy were gathered in considerable strength. Reports varied but it was generally agreed that the enemy had mustered a force of between 4,000 and 7,000 men. Two columns of attack were mounted with the left column being under the command of Lieutenant-Colonel Lumsden while the right column was under the command of Lieutenant-Colonel Green.[5] This latter column, which included the Hazara Mountain Train Battery and the 1st, 2nd and 3rd Punjab Infantry, had to advance over difficult ground and was fiercely opposed by the enemy. After the first repulse the column returned to the attack and finally the enemy line broke and, typical of the tribesmen of the North West Frontier area, they were able to withdraw back into the hilly terrain without any great difficulty. The British force lost two officers,

The Guides, a group photographed c1865.

Lieutenant Aytoun[6] serving with the 2nd Punjab Infantry, and one Indian officer; and 28 men were killed. Also 5 Indian officers and 80 men wounded. On the following day Chamberlain's force advanced and after Kaniguram they reached the Mahsud town of Makin which was stubbornly held by the enemy. This was taken on 11 May and destroyed and it was then decided that as the British force was experiencing difficulties in re-supply it would withdraw, which it did, reaching the Bannu valley on 18 May. The total casualties for the expedition was 100 killed and 261 wounded.[7] For his services on this operation Brigadier-General Chamberlain was created Knight Commander of the Order of the Bath. All members of the expedition received the Indian General Service Medal with clasp 'North West Frontier'.

Two other actions resulted in the award of the IGSM with the clasp 'North West Frontier', these being in 1864 and 1868. Prior to these two operations the Umbeyla expedition of 1863 qualified participants for the award of the medal plus the clasp 'Umbeyla', but before dealing with the latter, the events of the operations of 1864 and 1868 will be briefly covered.

During the period 5 December 1863 and 2 January 1864 a force of Mohmands and Bajouris, under Sultan Muhammed Khan, attacked the fort at Shabkadar and Lieutenant Bishop (6th Bengal Cavalry) was killed.[8] Two days after this first attack

the fort was again attacked and detachments of the 8th Bengal Native Infantry and 4th Sikh Infantry were engaged. During the following three weeks the Mohmands and Bajouris were stirred up by a number of fanatical mullas, and by 1 January 1864 a body of about 5,600 had assembled to attack the fort. A British force was assembled under the command of Brevet Colonel A. F. Macdonell, CB, consisting of three troops of the 7th Hussars; 2nd and 6th Bengal Cavalry; the 3rd Battalion Rifle Brigade; the 2nd Gurkha Regiment and a detachment of the 4th Sikh Infantry. The combined British and Indian force moved out to confront the enemy on 2 January and quickly defeated and dispersed the larger enemy force. Following this action the award of the IGSM and clasp was awarded to those troops taking part in the campaign and authorised by G.G.O. No 116 of 1864.

In the autumn of 1868 an expedition was formed to move against the Bazotee Black Mountain tribes who had gathered in some strength in the Agror Valley and had attacked the police post at Ughi. The first attempt to quell this uprising was repulsed as the force led by Lieutenant-Colonel O. E. Rothney of the 5th Goorkha Regiment was outnumbered and had to defend itself against the strong enemy party instead of actively bringing the situation under control. A number of villages under British control were burned by the tribesmen and a larger force was assembled. During the assembling of this group, three units distinguished themselves by performing long marches during the very hot month of August. The 20th Bengal Native Infantry marched 232 miles in ten days and the 31st Bengal Native Infantry covered a distance of 422 miles in twenty-nine days, while two companies of the Bengal Sappers and Miners travelled 600 miles to join the expedition in the same time. The combined British and Indian force was under the command of Brigadier A. T. Wilde, CB, and consisted of two brigades made up from the following units:

20th Hussars; Guides Cavalry; 9th Bengal Cavalry;
   16th Bengal Cavalry
D Battery, F Brigade, Royal Horse Artillery
E Battery, 19th Brigade, Royal Artillery
No 2 Battery, 24th Brigade, Royal Artillery
Peshawar and Hazara Mountain Trains
2 and 7 Companies, Bengal Sappers and Miners
1/6th, 1/19th, 38th and 77th Regiments of Foot
2nd Sikh Infantry, 2nd, 19th, 20th, 24th, 30th and 31st
   Bengal NI
23rd (Pioneers) Bengal NI
1st, 2nd, 4th and 5th Goorkha Regiments.

The operations commenced on 3 October with the combined force moving out of the Ughi Valley and the two brigades split and dealt with the enemy troops at Kilagai and Mana-ka-Dana. The 2nd Brigade took Kilagai without any opposition, whilst 1st Brigade met with some resistance at Mana-ka-Dana. On 4 October the enemy positions at that location were overrun by the 1st and 5th Goorkha Regiments. By 5 October the heights at Machai Peak were taken by the 20th Bengal NI supported by the 1st and 5th Goorkha Regiments. Over the next ten days the combined army combed the area without meeting very much opposition and the enemy negotiated for a settlement, except for the Pariari Saiads who continued to oppose the combined force. After a number of their villages had been destroyed and a fine imposed, the campaign was brought to a close with the loss of 5 men killed and 29 wounded. G.G.O No 86 of 1870 authorised the issue of the IGSM with clasp 'North West Frontier' to the officers and men who took part in the campaign.

In the years leading up to 1863 a number of Hindustani fanatics stirred up trouble in the Sittana area and, as the situation deteriorated, it became obvious that an expeditionary force would need to be sent into the area before peace could be restored. The expedition was formed under the command of Brigadier-General Sir Neville Chamberlain KCB consisting of half of C Battery, 19th Brigade, Royal Artillery, half of No 3 Punjab Light Field Battery, the Peshawar and Hazara Mountain Train Battery. The cavalry support was provided by detachments of the Guides Cavalry and the 11th (Probyn's Horse) Bengal Cavalry, with an infantry contingent made up of the 71st Regiment of Foot (Highland Light Infantry), 1st, 3rd, 5th, 20th and 32nd (Pioneers) Punjab Native Infantry and the 5th Goorkha Regiment in the 1st Brigade.

The infantry units in the 2nd Brigade consisted of the 6th, 14th and 23rd (Pioneers) Punjab Native Infantry, plus the 3rd Sikh Regiment, 4th Goorkha Regiment, as well as the 101 Bengal Fusiliers (1st Royal Munster Fusiliers). The whole force was supported by the 4th and 5th Companies of the Bengal Sappers and Miners. The advance column, under the command of Lieutenant-Colonel A. T. Wilde, entered the Umbeyla (also spelt Ambela) Pass on 20 October and met with some opposition, which was driven back. The main column followed on the next day. However, the fanatics had persuaded the Bunerwals to join the other tribes to oppose the British. A reconnoitring party met with a superior force and were driven back to the main body. The 20th Bengal Native Infantry formed the rearguard and held back the enemy with great steadiness until the party reached camp after dark. The British casualties were 3 killed, including Lieutenant W. A. B. Gillies serving with the Hazara Mountain Battery, and 23 wounded.

The enemy strength had increased considerably with the addition of the Bunerwals, causing the combined British and Indian army to change plans as to the conduct of the campaign. The decision was made to take up a defensive position and to try to entice the tribesmen to attack in order to break their strength in attempting to overrun the position. The situation remained fairly stable until 25 October when picquets on the right of the defence line were threatened by the Mahaban tribes. This threat was countered by Major C. P. Keys, who commanded that location, by attacking the tribesmen who were driven back and dislodged from a ridge and a conical hill which they had occupied in some strength. On the following day the Bunerwals launched an attack on the left flank which lasted for several hours, during which time the 20th Punjab Native Infantry again distinguished themselves by their determined stand. The position was finally relieved by a gallant charge by the 6th Punjab Infantry. During this heated confrontation three officers and 25 men were killed.[9] One British and seven Indian Officers and 84 men were wounded during this action and it was estimated that the enemy lost about 250 men killed.

On 27 October the enemy received reinforcements from Swat and other parts of the country and it was estimated that the enemy force had been built up to not less than 15,000 men. Three days later, 30 October, a determined attack was made on the British camp from the front and the right. A small but important post, known as Crag Picquet, was subjected to such a determined attack that the detachment of 1st Punjab Infantry manning the post were forced to retire. The picquet was immediately retaken by a determined bayonet attack made by the 1st Punjab Regiment, led by Major C. P. Keys, Lieutenant G. V. Fosbery of the 4th Bengal European Regiment serving with the 1st Punjab Infantry, and Lieutenant H. W. Pitcher, 4th Punjab Infantry. Lieutenants Fosbery and Pitcher were both awarded the Victoria Cross.[10] The day's fighting cost the combined force 14 killed and 41 wounded with Major Keys and Lieutenant Pitcher being among the wounded.

The supply line proved to be untenable and a new route was planned which would lead down to the plains through the villages of Khanpur and Sherdara and, to enable this route to be used, parties were sent out to cut a new road towards Ambela. The detachments covering the working parties came under attack on 6 November and, due to the stubborn resistance by some of the covering parties who had stood their ground too long, they were subsequently overwhelmed. The combined British and Indian force lost 38 men killed and 40 wounded. Among those killed were Major G. W. Harding, 2nd Sikh Regiment; Lieutenant T. B. Dougal, 79th (Cameron Highlanders) Regiment of Foot; and Ensign C. B. Murray, 71st (Highland Light Infantry) Regiment of Foot.[11]

Over the period 11 to 13 November the enemy mounted heavy and almost continual attacks on Crag Picquet and finally, during the morning of 13 November the post was attacked in great force and the defenders were forced to evacuate the position. It was during this attack that Lieutenant Davidson, who was in command, was killed. The post was retaken by a gallant counter-attack by the 1st Punjab Infantry supported by the 14th Punjab Native Infantry and a detachment from the Guides. However, the whole action brought losses to the force which amounted to 51 killed and 107 wounded. After a lull in the fighting it was determined to move camp on 18 November and the enemy saw this move as being a complete withdrawal and immediately launched an attack in large numbers. Every attempt to break the British line was repulsed but not without considerable loss on both sides. The enemy were estimated to have lost nearly 400 men during this action and the Field Force lost 43 killed and 75 wounded. Four officers were killed during this engagement, these being Lieutenant A. R. Chapman, 101 Bengal Fusiliers, and Lieutenant W. F Mosley serving with the 14th Punjab Infantry; and two British Army officers, Captain C. F. Smith and Lieutenant T. S. G. Jones.[12]

On the following day further skirmishing took place during which time Captain R. B. Aldridge was killed and on 20 November the enemy again attempted to take Crag Picquet. Although they did gain possession for a short time, this vital position was again retaken due to the storming of the post by the 5th Goorkha Regiment and the 71st Regiment of Foot. Having driven the enemy off once again, the cost to the combined force was high, with 27 killed and 110 wounded, which included Brigadier-General Sir Neville Chamberlain who was injured during the counter-attack on Crag Picquet.

Over the next three weeks little action took place but it did become necessary for Sir Neville Chamberlain to relinquish command to Major-General Garvock, due to the severity of his wounds. At this time the expedition received reinforcements which brought the total combined British and Indian Army up to approximately 9,000 and, although attempts were made to negotiate, it soon became clear that the only way to settle the dispute was by military means. While the attempts for a negotiated peace were under way the enemy strength had increased by an estimated 10,000 these being tribesmen from Dir, Bajaur and Kunar, although some of the original tribesmen left for home as there had been no quick victory and spoils to be gained. On 14 December the force under Major-General

Garvock advanced towards the village of Lalu and, dividing into two columns, stormed the enemy's position driving them down towards Ambela, destroying Lalu in the process. A number of counter-attacks were mounted by the enemy, all of which were repelled. A charge by the 1st Punjab Infantry finally scattered the enemy in the area of the camp. The last engagement of the campaign was on 16 December, when two columns moved forward into the valley. The tribesmen took up strong positions to resist any further advance but, being outflanked by the first column, they retreated without firing a shot. An attempt was made to cut them off from the pass into Kunar which resulted in a sudden and fierce attack by the enemy, led by a number of fanatics. The main thrust of this attack was met by the 23rd and 32nd Native Infantry who wavered under the onslaught but recovered, counter-attacked and killed the attacking party. The remaining enemy were gradually driven back into the mouth of the pass. The casualties for this action were 8 killed, including Lieutenant Alexander serving with the 23rd Punjab Native Infantry,[13] and four officers and 76 men wounded. On the following day the Bunerwal chiefs negotiated for peace, while the Swatis left and returned home and the Hindustani fanatics fled into the hills. A small party led by Kunar tribesmen entered Malka, the stronghold of the fanatics and destroyed the place. The Field Force, having completed its work, returned to the plains. The total cost in casualties for a small frontier campaign was high, with 15 British Officers, 4 Indian Officers, and 219 men killed; and 21 British officers, 27 Indian Officers and 622 men wounded. During the campaign, two awards of the Victoria Cross were made; these were to two British Officers, although they were serving with Indian Army units. It was to be another fifty years before an 'Indian' Officer or soldier was to be honoured with this highest award for valour.

The Indian Army units had again proved themselves efficient and steadfast during this campaign and full trust had been placed in the Indian soldier even when he was fighting men of his own country, although not of his own race. The IGSM with the clasp 'Umbeyla' was awarded to those who took part in the campaign and the award was confirmed by G.G.O. No 812 of 1869.

The Northern and North Eastern Frontier of Bengal were also problem areas and during the period December 1864 to February 1866 events occurred which led to a campaign which came to be known as the 'Bhutan War' (also spelt 'Bhootan'). A number of raids were made into the British territory from Bhutan and events came to a head when the British Mission was deliberately insulted. The government of Bhutan ignored the British complaints and an expeditionary force was organised to move into Bhutan to settle the matter. The expedition was made up in four columns which moved into the country as follows:

Right Column –
  half the Eurasian Company of Artillery, one Squadron of 5th Bengal Cavalry, one company of Bengal Sappers and Miners, and the 43rd Bengal Native Infantry.
  This column was to move to Gauhati and advance to Dewangiri.

Right Centre Column –
half the Eurasian Company of Artillery, one Squadron of the 5th Bengal Cavalry and two squadrons of the 14th Bengal Cavalry, one Company of Bengal Sappers and Miners, and a wing from the 12th and 44th Bengal Native Infantry.
The route for this column was from Goalpara to Bissen.

Left Centre Column –
half No 5 Battery, 25th Brigade Royal Artillery (mountain guns) and
half No 6 Battery, 25th Brigade Royal Artillery (mortars), one company of Bengal Sappers and Miners, a wing of the 11th Bengal Native Infantry and the 3rd Goorka Regiment.
The column was to assemble at Cooch Behar and move against Baksa and Bala.

Left Column –
half No 5 Battery, 25th Brigade RA (mountain guns), and half No 6 Battery, 25th Brigade RA (mortars), two squadrons of the 5th Bengal Cavalry, one company of Bengal Sappers and Miners, a wing each of the 11th and 18th Bengal Native Infantry and the 30th Bengal Native Infantry.
This column was tasked to move from Jalpaiguri against Dhalimkot and Chamurchi.

The left column marched on 28 November and arrived before the hill fort at Dhalimkot on 5 December and on the following day the fort was taken, following a bombardment of several hours. The casualties included the loss of three officers and seven men killed. The officers and some of the men died due to the premature exploding of a shell.[14] The column then returned to the plains and marched eastwards along the foot-hills and, after a skirmish with the enemy, the post at Chamurichi was attacked and taken, with only the loss of two men killed and three wounded. The left centre column met with a quicker success, occupying the fort of Baksa with little opposition on 6 December and, having negotiated the Bala Pass, the town of Tazagong was captured on 21 December.

The right column, under command of Lieutenant-Colonel R. Campbell, of the 43rd Native Infantry, left Gauhati on 2 December and entered the Daranga Pass on 10 December. The column advanced through the pass towards the fort of Dewangiri. The fort had, in the meantime, been taken by a party of Military Police who had attacked by another route and had succeeded in capturing the position. On 17 December the column was broken up and, whilst the main portion returned to the plains, Lieutenant-Colonel R. Campbell remained at the fort with six companies of the 43rd Bengal Native Infantry, two guns of the Eurasian Battery and a company of Sappers. Meanwhile the right centre column advanced and reached its objective by 8 January 1865 unopposed. With the objects of the expedition having been accomplished, orders were given to disband the field force. However, the enemy suddenly made a number of attacks, almost simultaneously, on Dewangiri, Bissengiri, Baksa, Tazagong in the Bala Pass and at Chamurchi.

The attack on Dewangiri took place on 29 January and after a fierce battle the enemy succeeded in surrounding the post and cutting off the water supply as well as communications to the plains. It was decided that the position would have to be evacuated, which it was before daylight on 5 February, but in the dark the column lost its way, which resulted in some of the wounded being lost as well as the guns which had to be thrown down a ravine to prevent them falling into enemy hands. In addition all the baggage of the column was lost. The column suffered a number of casualties, these being one officer and five men killed, and one officer and 32 men wounded. The attacks that were made on Bissengiri and Baksa, on 25 and 26 January respectively were held off without too much difficulty by the detachments of the 44th Bengal Native Infantry and the 3rd Goorka Regiment. The enemy made a concerted attack on Tazagong on the following day which was only repulsed with difficulty, and for several days the post was 'hard pressed' even after reinforcements had arrived. The unsuccessful attempts to dislodge the enemy resulted in casualties, including one officer, Lieutenant Millett (serving with the 11th Bengal Native Infantry) killed with two officers and 13 men wounded.

The post at Chamurchi was also attacked, but was held with difficulty until a detachment of the 30th Bengal Native Infantry arrived as reinforcements. The overall situation was such that in order to make any form of progress it was necessary to strengthen the Field Force, and a company of Sappers and Miners and five infantry units joined the force. The infantry consisted of three regiments from the Indian Army and two from the British Army stationed in India, these being the 19th, 29th and 31st Bengal Native Infantry and the 55th and 80th Regiments of Foot. The Force was then reorganised from four columns into two brigades, with Brigadier-General J. M. B. Fraser-Tyler taking command of the 'Left Brigade' and Brigadier-General H. Tombs CB VC, commanded the 'Right Brigade'. The reformed brigades quickly advanced and on 15 March 1865 the enemy was defeated at Tazagong by part of the Left Brigade and both Baksa and Chamurchi were relieved by 24 March. Following some skirmishing, the final advance to Dewangiri was made on 1 April and on the following day the final assault on the enemy was made by three companies of the 29th Bengal Native Infantry, led by Lieutenant Edwin Beddy and supported by detachments of the 12th Bengal Native Infantry and the 55th Regiment. Lieutenant Beddy was commended by Brigadier General Tombs for his leadership during the attack and described him as 'a most gallant young officer, who had already distinguished himself more than once.' The enemy made a determined defence but were eventually overrun and of the estimated 3,000 defenders, 130 were killed and when they eventually retreated from their positions they left about 120 wounded behind to be cared for by the British. The loss to the Force was, comparatively, quite small, with seven men killed and four officers and 99 men wounded.

This was practically the end of this small war. However, it was necessary to keep the Force on the frontier during the winter, during which time the troops suffered badly due to the hard winter, and having to live under 'field' conditions. Negotiations were still being held for the return of the guns that had been taken by the Bhutiahs. Part of the combined force moved into Bhutan early in February 1866 and captured an important bridge over the Mona River on 7 February but, due to lack of supplies, the force then halted and consolidated their position and on 23 February the Bhutiahs handed over the guns and the whole of the army then withdrew to Dewangiri. This was the end of the campaign and the force was disbanded and all the troops returned to their stations. The IGSM was awarded to all who were actively engaged in the operation, together with the clasp 'Bhootan', both of which were authorised by G.G.O. No 86 of 1870.

progress had been made despite the difficult terrain. The force had been continually fired upon as it advanced but no determined defence had been made by the Lushais. A number of villages were destroyed during the advance when considered necessary by the continued harassment, and during this first stage the force suffered 6 men killed and eleven wounded. On 9 January 1872 a further advance was made through Pachui and Chipiu to Kungnung. The latter place was defended and during the assault four men were killed and 11 wounded including Brigadier General Bourchier. On 1 February the advance continued through very mountainous and densely wooded country until Champhai, the principal village, was reached. Although the advance was through difficult country, very little

9th Regiment Bombay Native Infantry at Poona, 1869.　　AMOT

The next action involving the Indian Army, for which a separate clasp to the Indian General Service Medal was issued, occurred during the years 1871 and 1872. The locations of the disturbances on this occasion were on the Eastern and South Eastern frontiers of Bengal and concerned the Lushai clans who had been making raids into British territory. When the raiders abducted a planter named Winchester and his daughter, it was decided that an operation should be mounted to secure the release of the captives, also to bring the Lushais under control. Accordingly, in the autumn of 1871 two columns were formed so as to make a two-pronged attack, these being mounted from Cachar and Chittagong respectively. The Cachar Column, under the command of Brigadier-General G. Bourchier CB, consisted of half of the Peshawar Mountain Battery, a company of Sappers and Miners, and 500 men from each of the 22nd, 42nd and 44th Bengal Native Infantry. The column advanced into Lushai territory on 21 November and by 29 December good

resistance was met and, having attained its objective, the force commenced its return march on 21 February and reached base at Cachar on 10 March.

In the meantime, the Chittagong Column, under command of Brigadier-General C. H. Brownlow CB, consisting of half of the Peshawar Mountain Battery, a company of Bengal Sappers and Miners, the 27th Bengal Native Infantry and the 2nd and 4th Goorkha Regiments, left Chittagong early in December. It advanced to the village of Vanunah arriving at that location on 14 December. Continuing to press forward, a skirmish took place on 18 December which was quickly dealt with by the 2nd Goorkha Regiment. On 30 December Savunga was reached and secured without any great resistance and on 4 January 1872 a detachment of the 2nd Goorkha Regiment attacked and took the village of Chief Lal Gnura, during which time one man was

Mary Winchester after her release from the Looshais.

killed, and Captain A. Battye (2nd Goorkha Regiment) and nine men were wounded.[15] The column continued to advance into Lushai country and by the end of January the enemy declared themselves ready to treat and as a token of their intention the daughter of the planter who had been abducted in the previous year was handed over unharmed. Brigadier Brownlow continued his advance until the chiefs of the Northern Howlongs asked for peace on 18 February. The Southern Howlongs, having seen the remainder of the country seeking peace, also submitted to the Indian force. Peace having been established, the troops returned to Chittagong during March 1872. The expeditionary force, on this occasion, was formed solely from Indian Army units and this had proved highly successful.

The IGSM, together with the clasp 'Looshai', which was granted for active service during the period 9 December 1871 to 20 February 1872, was approved and issued under the authority of G.G.O. No 1295 of 1872.[16] General Brownlow issued an order commending the troops under his command during the Lushai expedition which read: '. . . to convey to the troops he

had had the honour to command his grateful sense of the uniform loyalty, courage and good conduct which all ranks displayed in contending for five months with difficulties, privations and exposure of no ordinary nature, in forcing their way through an unknown and formidable country, and bringing to a successful issue a campaign which, with an enemy more worthy of their steel, would, doubtless, have afforded opportunities of distinction to many.' Two members of the expedition were specifically mentioned in despatches. These were Major D. MacIntyre and Rifleman Inderjit Thapa, for their gallantry during the assault on the western boundary of Lal Gnura's stockade.[17]

During the Bhutan and the Lushai expeditions three awards of the Victoria Cross were made to members of the Indian Army but, like the previous awards, these were to British officers serving with the army. They were:

Lieutenant James Dundas, Royal (late Bengal) Engineers – VC promulgated in *The London Gazette* dated 31 December 1867
Major William Spottiswoode Trevor, Royal (late Bengal) Engineers – VC promulgated in *The London Gazette* dated 31 December 1867
Major Donald MacIntyre, 2nd Goorkha Rifles – VC promulgated in *The London Gazette* dated 27 September 1872

The next clasp to be awarded with the Indian General Service Medal was made to the troops who took part in the Perak Campaign of 1875-76. Perak was one of the states of Malaya (now, in 1990, part of Malaysia), with its northern border bounding on Province Wellesley. The coast line of Perak is about 100 miles long and the state, at the time of the campaign, extended about 50 miles into the interior. The Perak River intersects the central plain from north to south. The northern district of Perak, known as Laroot, was an area extensively used for tin mining and in October 1871 the Chinese tin miners, who numbered about 20,000, quarrelled among themselves. The Muntri (Chief) was unable to restore order, and in addition there were different factions attempting to place a new Sultan on the throne. The situation became serious enough to bring about British intervention which resulted in a treaty, known as the Pangkore Treaty of 1874, placing the state virtually in the hands of the British who, having then taken control of the administration, imposed a Resident and Assistant Resident to ensure that order was maintained and tin mining could continue.

The first British Resident, John Wheeler Woodford Birch, had an unpopular task to perform and, being a very determined man, he pushed through all the regulations that were to be imposed upon the Rulers and subjects of Perak, even though he knew them to be unpopular and despite various threats to his life. Birch arrived at Kota Sita and whilst there he was given a warning that trouble was brewing but he ignored the warning and even sent a telegraph to his superior just prior to leaving to go up river to Pasir Salek, reporting 'All quiet. Proclamations issued in Perak . . . Troops not required . . .'[18] Birch arrived at Pasir Salek shortly before midnight on 1 November 1875 and his

PERAK 1875~1876

One Superintendent and ten signallers, with field telegraph of 100 miles of wire
One company of Madras Sappers and Miners
Medical Officers with doolies and doolie bearers[19]

The party was despatched with camp equipment, light tents and provisions for a six-week sea voyage and ten days' land rations. The command of the expedition was given to Brigadier-General J. Ross CB, and the following staff officers were appointed:

Major M. Heathcote – AQMG
Major H. L. Hawkins, Brigade Major
Lieutenant J. J. Preston, 4th Bn, The Rifle Brigade – ADC
Captain J. R. Badcock – DAAG

The Indian contingent moved into Malaya and was ordered to occupy the northern portion of the country and marched through Laroot to Kuala Kangsar on the Perak River. The march was completed without opposition and detachments were left en route at Bukit Gantong and Kampong Boyah. The effect of the concentration of troops at Kuala Kangsar prevented the northern chiefs from joining the disaffected chiefs lower down river. On 4 January 1876 a detachment of the Indian force left

party, carried in a number of small boats, moored for the night. The next morning Birch moved his boats across the river and tied his own boat to a floating Chinese bath house. He instructed his interpreter, Mat Arshad, to post proclamations but, having posted one, a group of some fifty Malays, accompanied by Dato Sago, appeared and tore down the notice. Birch then instructed Mat Arshad to post the other copies and then went into the bath house. This act so incensed the Malays that they attacked the interpreter and then rushed the bath house and speared Birch through the walls killing him immediately. Mat Arshad was rescued from the river but died soon afterwards. This event led to what was to be known as the Perak War. An expeditionary force was immediately called for and troops were taken from Hong Kong and Singapore to move into Perak to bring the culprits to justice. To reinforce the British units, the Governor of the Straits Settlements telegraphed India asking for assistance in the form of an expeditionary force of 1,500 men. Although the British force had mainly brought the situation under control by the time the Indian contingent arrived, they were still involved in some fierce fighting in minor actions. The rapidity with which the Indian contingent was assembled and despatched to Penang Island was noteworthy as the alarm was raised on 2 November and within 25 days the reinforcements from India had arrived. The Indian contingent consisted of:

3rd Regiment of Foot (The Buffs), HQ and 600 men, under the command of Lieutenant-Colonel Talbot Ashley Cox
1st (Light Infantry) Goorka Regiment, HQ and 400 men
3rd Battery, 5th Brigade Royal Artillery (with 4 Mountain guns)

Kuala Kangsar and moved to Kota Lama. The kampong had been occupied and the Malays were disarmed without any show of resistance. Brigadier-General Ross landed with his small staff and a small escort when suddenly, out of the jungle, rushed some fifty or sixty Malays and attacked the party. The seamen in the landing party held firm and repulsed the attack. Unfortunately the Brigade Major – Major H. L. Hawkins – was killed with a spear. A contemporary account of the incident reads: '[Major Hawkins] received a frightful spear wound, the blade passing through his chest. A sailor named Sloper ran to his help, and shot two Malays who were running up to continue the attack . . . The officers who had gone on towards the river now returned, and tried to move him, but they were compelled in turn to fall back towards the river, Surgeon Townsend being the first to be assailed by three Malays with spears. One he shot with his revolver, but the man struck him down in falling, and his two companions dashed in to spear him, when they were bayoneted by a couple of seaman.'[20]

The Kota Lama opposition was overcome and the Indian contingent returned to Kuala Kangsar. The British Army column from Singapore and Hong Kong had made good progress in bringing the remaining areas of Perak under control.

Meanwhile problems had arisen in the Sungei Ujong area near Malacca, to the south, where an unspecified number of Malays were holding a pass, known as the Bukit Patus pass, and defied the authorities. A detachment of 250 men of the 1st Goorkha Regiment, together with half a battery of artillery, were despatched to clear the area of the rebel Malays. The attacking force was split into two parts, one making a move to attack from the rear while the main body of some 280 made a frontal attack. On 20 December 1875 the main party reached the foot of the pass and one officer and 25 Goorkha soldiers moved ahead to reconnoitre. They advanced through the dense jungle until they were within a short distance from the defences, and being unobserved at this time, the party rushed the stockade and quickly cleared it of its defenders. Having gained one stockade, the detachment moved in and cleared the whole area of the Malays, and in doing so lost one soldier killed and one wounded. The total casualties for this action are commemorated in a memorial which now stands in the car park on Jalan Fort, in Malacca town, and lists twelve casualties, two of whom belonged to the Indian contingent and are recorded as being:

'1st Goorkha Light Infantry.
Naik Bucktring Rav
Sepoy Duljeet Poon'

The Indian General Service Medal, 1854-1895, with clasp 'Perak'.

Major Henry Lumsden Hawkins, Bengal Staff Corps was buried at the Bukit Chandran cemetery at Kuala Kangsar, together with the casualties from the British contingent. His memorial stone reads:

'Sacred to the memory
of
Major H. L. Hawkins, B.S.C.
who fell at Kota Lama
4th Jany 1876'

The officer who led the party during the successful attack on the Malay stockade at Bukit Patus pass, Captain George Nicholas Channer, who personally led the attack and was first inside the stockade, killing at least one man with his revolver, was awarded the Victoria Cross (*The London Gazette* dated 12 April 1876.) The Malay Chiefs who had originally incited the murder of Mr Birch in Perak were tried and sentenced to death. Three were hanged and the fourth was reprieved on being declared insane.

After about six months' service in Malaya, during which time the force had operated in jungle conditions, the Indian contingent returned home. The award of the IGSM, together with a clasp 'Perak' was awarded to those who served in Malaya from 27 November 1875 to 20 March 1876 and this was promulgated by G.G.O. No 242 of 1880. The British contingent, having arrived in the theatre of operations earlier, had a qualifying start date of 2 November 1875.[21]

The grave of Major H.L. Hawkins at Bukit Chandran Cemetery, Perak.

1 Cardew, Lieutenant F. G. *A sketch of the Services of the Bengal Native Army*, 1903, pp291-292.

2 *Mecham, Captain Richard* born at Loughborough, 1826. He entered the Bengal Army as a cadet for the Artillery in 1842. He arrived in India in December of that year. He was promoted to First Lieutenant in July 1845 and to Captain in June 1858. He was on furlough from April 1858 and returned to India in July 1859 and rejoined his unit, No 3 Light Field Battery, at Bannu. In October his services were placed at the disposal of the Government of the North West Provinces. On the night of 5 November 1859, when travelling from Bannu to Kohat in a doolhi (being ill at the time), he was attacked and murdered near Latamar by a gang of Darwesh Khel Waziri tribesmen and was buried at Bannu. A monument was erected near to Latamar, and a plaque placed in the church at Kohat.
Irving, Miles, *A list of Inscriptions on Christian Tombs or Monuments in the Punjab, North-West Frontier Province, Kashmir and Afghanistan*, 1910, pp167, 171 and
De Rhe-Philipe, G. W. *Part II, Biographical Notices*, 1912, pp236-237.

3 Cardew, op cit, p292.

4 *Lumsden, Brevet Lieutenant-Colonel Harry Burnett* Ensign 1 March 1838; Lieutenant 16 July 1842; Bt Captain 1 March 1853; Captain 5 February 1854; Bt Major 6 February 1854; Bt Lieutenant-Colonel 15 May 1858. Raised the Corps of Guides Cavalry and Infantry on 13 December 1846. Was wounded by an assassin while in command of the Guides on 2 August 1860.

5 *Green, Brevet Lieutenant-Colonel George Wade Guy, CB* (late 2nd European Bengal Fusiliers). Second Lieutenant 12 June 1841; Lieutenant 26 August 1843; Captain 24 November 1853; Major 19 January 1858; Brevet Lieutenant-Colonel 24 March 1858. He was wounded slightly during the assault on Delhi, on 14 September 1857.

6 *Aytoun, Lieutenant John Marriot* commissioned into 94th Foot as an Ensign on 12 January 1855. Promoted to Lieutenant on 31 July 1857 and moved to India with his regiment in 1858. He was attached to the 2nd Punjab Infantry and during the move into the Shahur Valley he was present at the storming of Barari Tangi on 4 May 1860 and during this action he was shot through the head. He was carried to the camp at Bangiwala Kach and interred. A report of the event reads 'late in the evening the body of Lieutenant Aytoun was committed to the grave. A spot carefully selected which would be almost certain to escape observation, and by the light of the moon he was laid in his last resting place; and few soldiers sleep in a wilder spot.' (De Rhe-Philipe, op cit, pp8-9).

7 Cardew, op cit, p294.

8 *Bishop, Lieutenant St George Meadows* born at Darjeeling 23 April 1841 he entered the Bengal Army in 1857 and arrived in India in December of that year. He saw service with the 19th Foot in Fort William and accompanied that unit to the Upper Provinces. In October 1858 he was posted to the 66th (Gurkha) Bengal Native Infantry. In January 1860 he moved to serve with the 8th Irregular Cavalry and was appointed Adjutant of that unit which was retitled 6th Bengal Cavalry. In July 1861 he was appointed to a civil post being made acting Joint Magistrate at Sitapur. In January 1862 he rejoined his regiment at Peshawar where he served at various times as adjutant and acted as Second-in-Command. On 5 December 1863 he was killed whilst in command of a troop of his regiment during a gallant charge against a body of 500 Mohmand, Bajauris and other tribesmen. He was buried in

the Taikal Cemetery at Peshawar and a memorial stone was placed on his grave by his brother officers.

9 The three officers killed were:
Clifford, Lieutenant Robert entered the Bengal Army in 1853 and arrived in India in February 1854. He served with the 29th Bengal Native Infantry. In October 1858 he was appointed to do duty with the 2nd Punjab Cavalry. In April 1860 he was appointed Adjutant to 1st Punjab Cavalry, and in January 1862 was admitted into the Bengal Staff Corps and continued to serve with the 1st Punjab Cavalry. He volunteered to serve with the 3rd Punjab Infantry and accompanied that regiment on active service. He was killed in the action in Ambela Pass on 26 October 1863. He was buried at Peshawar.
Richmond, Lieutenant George Mitchell entered the Bengal Army in 1858 and arrived in India in June of that year. He saw service at Delhi with the 2nd European Bengal Fusiliers. In February 1859 he was transferred to the 23rd Punjab Infantry. In February 1860 he moved to the 8th Punjab Infantry and saw service with that unit in China, being awarded the China Medal with two clasps. He returned with his unit to India and moved to Peshawar. His unit became the 20th Punjab Native Infantry and in October 1863 he accompanied his unit on active service in the Yusafzai Field Force. On the 26 October, 'after a display of the most heroic gallantry, he fell mortally wounded in the defence of his position. He died of his wounds in camp during the following morning.' He was buried at Peshawar.
Subadar-Major Mir Ali Shah 20th Bengal Native Infantry, killed on 26 October 1863.

10 Lieutenant G. V. Fosbery was awarded the Victoria Cross in *The London Gazette* dated 7 July 1865.
Lieutenant H. W. Pitcher was awarded the Victoria Cross in *The London Gazette* dated 16 July 1864.

11 *Harding, Major George Whittail* born 1824, he entered the Bombay Army in 1841 and arrived in the autumn of that year. In January 1842 he joined 2nd Bombay Native Infantry. After a long period of leave from 1852 to 1855 he was appointed to the Oudh Irregular Force. In December 1856 he was transferred to the Punjab Irregular Force and appointed Commandant of 2nd Sikh Infantry. He remained in command of the regiment until October 1863 when he was appointed Orderly Officer to Sir Neville Chamberlain for the Ambela Expedition. On 6 November he was selected to command a detachment guarding working parties making a road to the village of Ambela and whilst on this duty the party was attacked by tribesmen and it became necessary to withdraw. The covering party being out-numbered, Major Harding organised a determined defence but early in the action was shot in the neck and seriously wounded. Whilst being carried out of action by a Gurkha sepoy he was killed during a sudden determined attack by the tribesmen who overran the position. He was buried in the Old Cemetery at Mardan.
Dougal, Lieutenant Thomas Ballard born on 25 July 1832, he entered the Bengal Army in 1852 and arrived in India at the end of that year. He joined the 33rd Bengal Native Infantry at his own request. He returned to the UK in 1855 as he had obtained a commission in the 79th Regiment of Foot (Cameron Highlanders). He remained in the UK with his regiment until August 1857 when it embarked for Bengal. He served with the regiment through the mutiny campaign and was awarded a Mutiny Medal and clasp 'Lucknow'. He was promoted to Lieutenant on 9 September 1859. In 1862 he moved with his regiment to Nowshera and then to

Peshawar. He volunteered his services for the expedition against the Hindustani fanatics and was attached to the 71st Regiment of Foot. He accompanied Major Harding with the detachment providing 'cover' for the road working party. After a day of continual attacks by the tribesmen he was killed during the afternoon in one of the furious attacks on the party. He was buried in the cemetery at Nowshera.

Murray, Ensign Charles Balfour born in 1840, he joined the 71st Regiment of Foot on 18 March 1859. He joined his regiment at Morar, Gwalior. He moved with his regiment and arrived at Nowshera in November 1862. He was with the regiment on the expedition against the Hindustani fanatics and was killed on 6 November 1863 whilst serving with a detachment guarding a working party. He was buried in the cemetery at Nowshera.

12 *Chapman, Lieutenant Henry Howard* born 25 January 1838. He joined the Bengal Army in 1856 and served with the 37th Bengal Native Infantry. He was seriously wounded during the mutiny of his regiment at Benares and as a result was sent home on furlough. He returned to India in September 1858 and joined the 67th Bengal Native Infantry. He transferred to the 6th European Bengal Regiment and when that regiment was broken up he volunteered for general service. On 30 July 1862 he was transferred to the 101st Foot (Royal Bengal Fusiliers) and joined that regiment at Multan. After service in Rawalpindi and Abbottabad he joined the Yusafzai Field Force. He saw active service throughout the operations until 18 November on which day he was killed. During one of the fierce attacks made on the British positions he was shot and although mortally wounded he attempted to dress the wounds of Captain C. F. Smith, of the 71st Foot. It was whilst he was carrying out this first aid that the enemy overran the British position and both officers were hacked to death by the tribesmen. He was buried at the Old Cemetery at Mardan.

Mosley, Lieutenant William Fielden born 1 April 1838, commissioned as Ensign 13 June 1857, promoted to Lieutenant 18 May 1858, he served in the 35th Bengal Native Infantry. At the time of his death on 19 November 1863 he was serving with the 14th Bengal Native Infantry.

Smith, Captain Charles Francis born 1828, he was commissioned into the 71st Regiment of Foot as an Ensign on 30 May 1845. He was promoted to Lieutenant on 19 March 1847 and to Captain on 29 December 1854. He joined his regiment in India, from home service, during 1858 and after returning home on sick leave in 1859 he rejoined the regiment at Sialkot in 1861. He was on active service with the Yusafzai Field Force when he was seriously wounded during the action on 18 November. Lieutenant Chapman came to his assistance but the position was overrun by tribesmen and both he and Lieutenant Chapman were killed. He was buried in the cemetery at Nowshera.

Jones, Lieutenant Thomas Sheridan Gore born in February 1836, he became an Ensign in the 37th Regiment of Foot on 7 September 1855. He served with that regiment in Ceylon and during the Mutiny campaign and exchanged into the 79th Regiment of Foot on 27 June 1860 – joining that regiment at Mian Mir. He accompanied his regiment to Ferozepore, Nowshera and Peshawar. In December 1862 he was appointed Fort Adjutant at Attock. In October 1863 he was permitted to volunteer to serve with the 71st Foot who were to take part in the operations in the Ambela Pass area. He was killed on 18 November 1863 during an attack by tribesmen. He was buried at Peshawar, but the inscription on his grave stone is incorrect as it gives the year of his death as '1865', not 1863.

13 *Alexander, Lieutenant George* born 1835, joined the Bengal Army in 1852. After service with the 16th Bengal Native Infantry, he was briefly moved to 6th Bengal NI and then to the 35th Bengal NI at Lucknow. He served through the Mutiny campaign and was given a civil appointment as District Adjutant of Police at Muzafarnagar but shortly afterwards returned to the Nasiri Battalion and was appointed Adjutant. He was admitted to the Bengal Staff Corps in February 1861 and with the disbandment of the Nasiri Battalion he served for eight months with the 2nd Battalion, The Rifle Brigade. He was appointed to the 41st Bengal Native Infantry in August 1862 and in October of that year transferred to the 23rd Punjab Native Infantry (Pioneers) and in 1863 he was employed with that unit making roads in the Simla Hills. He then accompanied the unit on active service in the Ambela Pass operations. At the close of the operations he lost his life on 16 December 1863 when he was killed during the last desperate charge of some tribesmen near the village of Ambela. He was buried in the Old Cemetery at Mardan.

14 Cardew, op cit, p313. The three officers are named as 'Captain Griffin, Lieutenant Anderson (and) Lieutenant Waller.'

15 Cardew, op cit, p321.

16 Major L. L. Gordon, in his book *British Battles and Medals*, p237, refers to some British medal awards for the clasp 'Looshai' as follows: '[Gordon states that he has] seen a medal to No 113 Pte H. Thompson, 55 Foot, Pte J. Formby, 22nd Foot and one to the 80th Foot with this bar.'

17 Shakespear, Colonel L. W. *History of the 2nd King Edward's Own Goorkha Rifles (The Sirmoor Rifles)*, 1912, p86.

18 Burns, P. L. (Editor) *The Journals of J. W. W. Birch, 1874-1875*, 1976, p36.

19 *Frontier and Overseas Expeditions from India*, Vol VI, 1911, p348.

20 McNair, Major The Hon T. F. A. *Perak and the Malays*, 1878, p387.

21 Gordon, Major Lawrence L. *British Battles and Medals*, 1962, pp237-38.

Left:
Risaldar-Major Sayyid Abdul Aziz,
5th Bengal Cavalry.

Right:
13th Bengal Cavalry, c1897.

Below:
6th Bombay Cavalry (Jacob's Horse).

Above:
A Trooper of the Scinde Horse

Left:
A Duffadar of the 1st Bengal Cavalry.

Opposite page:
Risaldar-Major Gurdath Singh, 12th Bengal Cavalry and Orderly.

Below:
4th (Prince Albert Victor's Own) Bengal Cavalry.

CHAPTER FOUR

Overseas Stations and the Malta Expedition

Following the Abyssinian campaign, the Indian army settled into a routine of drills, guard duties, training, and keeping the peace within the vast continent. One of the major problems encountered by the three armies, that is the Bengal, Madras and Bombay armies, was the seniority system that controlled the careers of the British Officers. Providing an officer was fit enough to continue his duty, he continued on active service. When an officer reached a senior rank he was generally employed on duties relating to staff, civil or police work and was thus out of touch with the problems relating to the day to day welfare of the Indian soldier.

By the 1870s the number of officers in senior posts and blocking promotion for the younger and more active officer, had become a serious problem and was the cause of some inefficiency in the Indian Army. Needless to say, there was a reluctance to retire on the part of some of the older and more senior officers and the situation was further complicated by the use of military officers filling civil posts, whereas such posts should have been filled by a member of the civil service.

An examination of the actual posts being filled by officers of the rank of Lieutenant-Colonel in the year 1871 produces a surprising result with only a little over one-third of the total being employed with regiments.

The breakdown of the figures are as follows:

Army	Serving with a regiment	Civil & Staff employment	On Furlough	Shown as serving at a Station (ie Meerut etc)
Bengal	71	88	56	39
Madras	67	66	49	3
Bombay	22	50	34	—
Totals	160	204	139	42

At this time a total of 545 Lieutenant Colonels were on the paid strength of the Indian Army and, as can be seen, a large number were on furlough but by far the greater number were being employed away from their parent regiment. Officers were employed on such diverse duties as Deputy Commissioner, Assam; Officer in charge of the Cantonment Magazine, Dum Dum; Government Agent Chepauk; General Superintendent of operations for the Suppression of Thugee & Dacoity and Political Agent Meywar. These are of course in addition to the many normal staff appointments at headquarters and garrisons.

In addition to the commitments within India, and the operational requirements brought about by actions on the frontiers, the Indian Army was required to provide garrison troops for Singapore and the Straits Settlements and Hong Kong. The garrisons had previously been provided by the armies of the East India Company and the commitment was inherited by the Indian Army when it was formed following the mutiny. In 1871 the question of manning the garrisons in the Far East was considered and, in an effort to cut costs, a plan was devised whereby a British battalion would be stationed at Hong Kong and Singapore, with an increased participation of the local volunteer force in the defence of the colonies. Plans were therefore made for the withdrawal of the Indian Army units, which departed from Singapore in 1872, and Hong Kong in 1873. This situation lasted until the turn of the century, when the war in South Africa and the Boxer Rebellion in China brought about a change in the way overseas garrisons were to be manned and the India Army once again provided units for Singapore and Hong Kong. The following units served in the garrisons, as shown, during the period 1858-73:

Singapore and the Straits Settlements
14th Regiment Madras Native Infantry
  1858-60   Singapore and Malacca
29th Regiment Madras Native Infantry
  1858   Penang
22nd Regiment Madras Native Infantry
  1859-60   Penang
40th Regiment Madras Native Infantry
  1860-63   Singapore and Malacca
20th Regiment Madras Native Infantry
  1861-64   Penang
34th Regiment Madras Native Infantry
  1863-66   Singapore and Malacca
35th Regiment Madras Native Infantry
  1864-68   Penang
8th Regiment Madras Native Infantry
  1866-69   Singapore

Top:
Sepoys cooking at Hong Kong.   ILN

A Mat shed at Hong Kong showing the living conditions of the Indian Troops stationed at Hong Kong.   ILN

The proclamation of Queen Victoria as 'Empress of India' being made at Delhi, 1877.

7th Regiment Madras Native Infantry
   1868-69   Penang
   1869-71   Singapore
19th Regiment Madras Native Infantry
   1871-72   Singapore
(departed from Singapore during March 1872)

Hong Kong
11th Punjab Infantry
   1860-61   Garrison duties 1861
19th Punjab Infantry
   1860-61   Garrison duties 1861
3rd Bombay Native Infantry
   1860-62   Garrison duties Hong Kong and Canton 1861
5th Bombay Light Infantry
   1860-63   Garrison duties Hong Kong and Canton 1861
21st Regiment Madras Native Infantry   1860-61
22nd Regiment Bombay Native Infantry   1862-65
29th Regiment Madras Native Infantry   1868-71
13th Regiment Madras Native Infantry   1871-73

On 1 January 1877, Her Majesty Queen Victoria was proclaimed 'Empress of India' and a Grand Assemblage was held at Delhi to which Indian Native Princes and foreign Government representatives were invited. To mark the occasion a distinctive medal was struck and was presented in gold and silver versions to a very wide variety of personages. The details of the medal and the list of appointments that were awarded the Silver Medal is given at Appendix B. The military featured in the awards with two main categories:

The Adjutant General of the Army and Commanders of Divisions or Corps including Volunteer Corps present at Delhi. A selected private soldier or non-commissioned officer from each regiment, European or Native, serving in India.

It would appear that the actual allocation of the medal, within each unit, was left to the discretion of the Commanding Officer and, this being the case, there appears to be no 'general order' listing those non-commissioned officers or soldiers who were awarded the Empress of India medal.

On 12 June 1882 the War Office issued a directive to the effect that the 'Delhi Imperial Assemblage Commemorative Medal should not be worn when in uniform.'

The Indian Army next became involved in an overseas expedition in 1878, which was as a result of the agreement reached between Great Britain and Turkey on 4 June 1878 which became known as 'The Cyprus Convention'. Under the terms of the treaty, Britain agreed to come to the aid of Turkey should that country be attacked. In return His Imperial Majesty, The Sultan, agreed to assign the island of Cyprus to the British who would occupy and administer the island. In order to achieve this it was planned to set up an occupation force which would consist of British and Indian troops who were to be assembled on the island of Malta. Although the Treaty was not signed until June, orders for the preparation and embarkation of the Indian contingent were issued as early as April 1878. The force which was designated the Malta Expeditionary Force, was placed under the command of Major-General J. Ross CB and consisted of the following Staff and units:

Staff

Brigadier-General J. Watson CB, Bombay Corps
    Commanding Cavalry Brigade
Brigadier-General H. T. Macpherson CB, VC,
    Bombay Staff Corps, Commanding Infantry Brigade
Major F. J. S. Adam, Bombay Staff Corps
    Assistant Quarter Master General
Major W. T. Keays, Bombay Commissariat Department
    Assistant Commissary General[1]
Captain S. D. Barrow, 10th Bengal Lancers
    Brigade Major, Cavalry
Major R. M. Lloyd, Bombay Staff Corps
    Brigade Major, Infantry
Major J. G. Watts, Bombay Staff Corps
    Brigade Major, Infantry

Deputy Surgeon General T. B. Beatty, Bombay Medical
    Establishment, Principal Medical Officer[2]

Units

M Battery, 1st Brigade, Royal Artillery
F Battery, 2nd Brigade, Royal Artillery
9th Bengal Cavalry
1st Bombay Cavalry
2 Companies (Queen's Own) Madras Sappers and Miners
2 Companies, Bombay Sappers and Miners
2nd (PWO) Goorkha Regiment (The Sirmoor Rifles)
13th (The Shekhawattee) Bengal Native Infantry
31st Bengal Native Infantry
25th Madras Native Infantry
9th Bombay Native Infantry
26th Bombay Native Infantry

All units, with the exception of 25th Madras Native Infantry, embarked at Bombay, whilst the 25th Native Infantry embarked at Cananore. The movement of the force gave the authorities a considerable problem as, apart from weapons and stores, the actual numbers embarked were, according to embarkation records:

European Officers	105
Indian Officers	126
European soldiers	342
Indian Army soldiers	5,557
Followers	2,340
Total embarked	8,470

Central India Horse family group taken at the Indore Residency, c1877.

In addition, 1,384 horses and 526 ponies were also embarked to accompany the Malta Expeditionary Force.[3]

In order that units could embark at full strength, volunteers of similar class composition were called for and those who volunteered were required to be men of good character and medically fit for field service. The regiments that provided volunteers were permitted to recruit up to their full establishment. Officers and men belonging to the units nominated for the expedition who were on furlough were recalled and their travelling expenses paid by the State. All those embarking were required to be in possession of Regulation Field Service kit and, in addition, a free issue was made to each man consisting of 'two canvas frocks, two pairs flannel drawers, two jerseys, two pairs warm socks, and one pair English boots.'[4] The followers also received a free issue of clothing on the scale of 'one blanket, one pair of pyjamas, one great coat, one lascar coat, one pair of boots, one tin canteen, one haversack, two pairs socks, and two jerseys.'[5]

Native Infantry regiments drew extra batta[6] whilst on the expedition and G.G.O. No 347 of 1878 also authorised the Native Cavalry to draw free rations or ration money during the same period.[7] Public followers received an additional 50 per cent on pay and batta, in addition to free rations. Each of the infantry regiments were provided with 50 picks, 50 shovels and 100 billhooks which were taken with complete camp equipment and quartermasters stores estimated for a three-month period. In addition, 200 rounds of ammunition were provided for each

infantryman and 100 rounds for each cavalryman. No land transport was taken on this expedition although, in anticipation of being able to obtain mules, 2,000 sets of mule pack saddles were provisioned.

The force embarked on 12 steamers towing 15 sailing ships and arrived in Malta harbour at the end of May. Disembarkation began on 27 May and whilst some units were given accommodation in barracks, other units moved out of Valletta and were accommodated in camps. G Company (Queen's Own) Madras Sappers and Miners were employed in making roads and providing additional cover for the troops in the camp at San Antonia. On 12 June the troops of the force paraded for the Governor and on 17 June all the troops in Malta were inspected by HRH The Duke of Cambridge. Following the inspection he issued a very complimentary order directed at the Indian Forces on parade which read:

His Royal Highness cannot speak too highly of their soldierly qualities. Their uniform good conduct and smartness reflects the greatest credit on all ranks. Their steadiness under arms and drill and the excellent state of their camps leave nothing to be desired.

Top left:
Commandant of the Central India Horse – Colonel J. Watson CB, VC, *photograph taken 1877.* AMOT

Below left:
The 2nd (Prince of Wales's Own) Goorkha Regiment (The Sirmoor Rifles), part of the Malta Expeditionary Force, 1878. ILN

Following the inspection, preparations were made for the force to re-embark for Cyprus with an advance party of Madras Sappers and Miners arriving off Larnaka, on the south coast of Cyprus, on 16 July. The whole of the Sapper equipment was disembarked by 19 July and the men were employed in the construction of landing stages in preparation for the main party which arrived on 23 July 1878. The combined British and Indian force was under the command of Lieutenant General Sir Garnet Wolseley and after disembarkation the troops were accommodated in temporary camps before proceeding to garrison the main towns of the island, these being Nicosia, the capital, inland; Limassol and Paphos in the south; Famagusta on the east coast; and Kyrenia on the northern coast. Whilst the Sappers were busy building camps, repairing and, on occasions, making roads, the infantry and cavalry were engaged manning the garrisons which had been established at the main towns on the island. The cavalry were also employed in providing armed escorts for officers and parties moving around the island which was mountainous, and in the hills bandits were still a major source of trouble to the authorities. Once the initial landing had been completed and, apart from the bandit problem there was no opposition to the change from Turkish to British administration, it was decided that the overall garrison could be reduced to a British battalion with supporting troops. The main

Below:
Duke of Cambridge at Malta with British and Indian Officers, 1878.

Review of Indian Troops on the Floriana Parade, Malta.   ILN

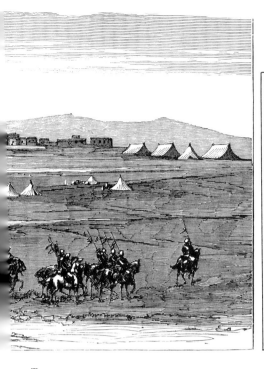

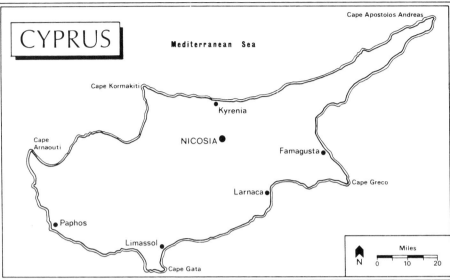

Top:
The Indian Native Cavalry camp at Malta. ILN

part of the Malta Expeditionary Force re-embarked during the latter part of August and returned to India. The force was commended by the Commander-in-Chief, Sir Garnet Wolseley, for the good work carried out. The Sappers and Miners remained in Cyprus until the end of October and, prior to embarkation, were thanked for their work, which had been difficult and undertaken often in severe weather conditions. The following is the extract from a General Order dated Monastery Camp, Nicosia, 31 October 1878.

The Madras and Bombay Sappers and Miners being about to embark for India, the Lieut-General cannot allow them to leave the Command without placing upon record his sense of the valuable work they have done in this Island. He will not fail to bring to the notice of the Government of India his appreciation of the services they have rendered.

By order of His Excellency the Commander-in-Chief

In addition, a Brigade Order was published by Brigadier-General Macpherson CB, VC dated 28 August 1878 which commended the whole force and included the following:

[My] very best thanks for the admirable discipline that has been maintained throughout the expedition, under circumstances of no ordinary temptation. The highest authority in the army has represented to Her Most Gracious Majesty his high appreciation of their soldierlike bearing, in terms of which every individual of the Indian Contingent must feel justly proud.[8]

Although the force was not required to engage in any military action there were a number of military casualties, both in Malta

Song sheet to commemorate the acquisition of Cyprus, 1878.

Presentation of Indian Officers to the
Duke of Cambridge in the
Governor's Palace, Malta.   ILN

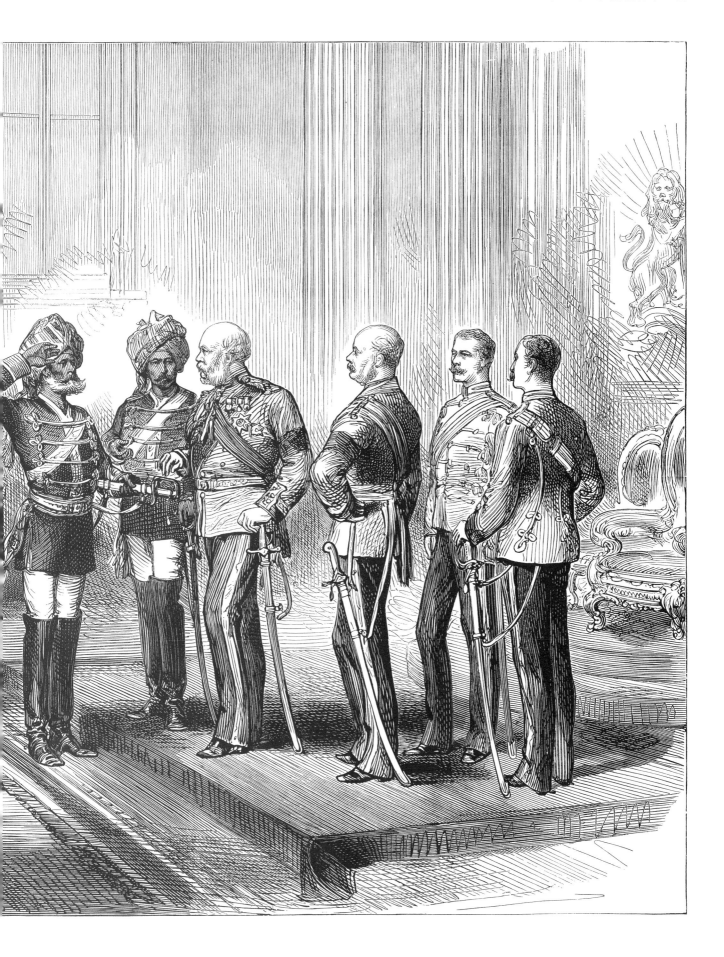

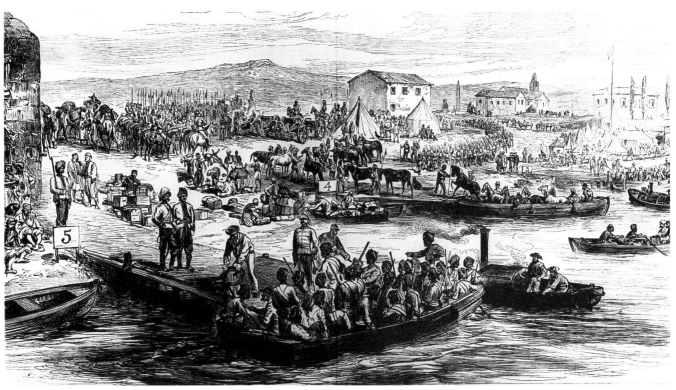

General view of the landing place at Larnaca, Cyprus, with Indian troops disembarking. ILN

A gravestone at Pembroke Barracks, Malta, to mark the death of two of the soldiers of the Indian Expeditionary Force whilst serving at Malta. This memorial has recently been saved from destruction during a rebuilding programme due to the intervention of the Maltese authorities. (1990)

and in Cyprus, due to fever which was prevalent on both islands. The Sappers and Miners lost two European non-commissioned officers, three Indian other ranks, and three followers[9] during the six months that the force was serving outside India. As the whole operation was concluded peacefully no campaign medal or clasp was issued for the Malta-Cyprus operation. Although this operation was probably classed as a 'major' operation, with over 8,000 troops taking part, a smaller number of troops were involved in an action outside India when they served with a British force in Malaya in the Perak campaign of 1875-76.[10] The events in this action, for which medals and a clasp were issued, are covered in the previous chapter which deals with the campaigns for which the Indian General Service Medal (1854-95) and clasps were issued.

1   *Keays, Major William Tufnell*, Bombay Staff Corps. The officer is incorrectly shown in *Frontier and Overseas Expeditions from India*, Vol VI, 1911, p23 as Major W. *F.* Keays.

2   *Beatty, Deputy Surgeon-General Thomas Berkeley*, Bombay Medical Establishment, served as the Principal Medical Officer. He is incorrectly shown as '*J.* Beatty' in the Staff list given at p23 of the above reference. T. B. Beatty was appointed D.S.G. from 21 October 1876.

3   *Frontier and Overseas Expeditions from India*, Vol VI, 1911, p24.

4   *Frontier and Overseas Expeditions from India*, op cit, pp21-22.

5   *Frontier and Overseas Expeditions from India*, op cit, p22.

6   *Batta* – an allowance made to officers, soldiers, or other public servants, when in the field, or on other special grounds. (*Hobson-Jobson*, Yule H. and Burnell, A. C. 1903, p72)

7   Cardew, Lieut F. G. *A Sketch of the Services of the Bengal Native Infantry*, 1903, p326.

8   Roe, Lieutenant-Colonel C. H. *Historical Record of the 2nd 'Queen's Own' Sappers and Miners, 1790-1909*, 1909, p109.

9   Vibart, Major H. M. *The Military History of the Madras Engineers and Pioneers*, 1883, p493.

10 Gordon, Major Lawrence L. *British Battles and Medals*, 1962, pp237-38.

Top: Sepoys on duty at the East Gate, Nicosia, Cyprus, 1878.   ILN

Serving rations to Indian Troops at Larnaca, Cyprus, 1878.   ILN

Above:
2nd Madras Lancers.

Right:
5th Cureton's Multanis,
1897.

Left:
11th Bengal Lancers
(Probyn's Horse),
c1897.

18th Bengal Lancers.

19th Bengal Lancers.

11th Bengal Lancers (Probyn's Horse), c1897.

Risaldar-Major Ali Muhammed Khan, 2nd Bengal Lancers.

CHAPTER FIVE

The Second Afghan War, 1878–80

Probably the one major campaign in which the Indian Army was involved during the latter half of the 19th century was the conflict with Afghanistan which became known as the Second Afghan War 1878-80. The war involved both the British and the Indian armies and the events brought a high casualty rate to both armies. A medal was issued with six clasps for the actions as follows:

Ali Musjid	21 November 1878
Peiwar Kotal	2 December 1878
Charasia	6 October 1879
Kabul	10-23 December 1879
Ahmed Khel	19 April 1880
Kandahar	1 September 1880

The history of the Second Afghan War is far too complex to be dealt with in a book of this nature and the subject has been covered in many well researched and written books and two such works which give a very detailed account are *The Afghan Campaigns of 1878-1880* by Sydney H. Shadbolt and *The Second Afghan War 1878-80 – Abridged Official Account* which was produced by the Intelligence Branch of the Army Headquarters in India,[1] and to support these two reference works the *Casualty Roll of the Second Afghan War 1878-1880* compiled by Anthony Farrington[2] will give the reader a virtually complete story of the war. However, in order to give a complete coverage of the campaigns of the Indian Army in the 19th century it is necessary to include a brief description of the events.

The background to the war started in 1873 when the boundaries between Afghanistan and India were settled by an agreement between the British and Shere Ali, the Amir of Afghanistan, and for this agreement he was to be paid a substantial subsidy. However, the relations between Shere (or Sher) Ali, his son Dost Muhammad, and the Indian Government had gradually deteriorated through the hostility and ingratitude of the Amir himself. Shere Ali had been able to gain the throne mainly due to the help given to him by the British, but for this favour and numerous concessions he gave nothing in return. The situation took a serious turn when he refused to have a British Resident in Kabul and, in addition, raised an army and actively promoted ill feeling against the British between the border tribes, who were only too willing to have the opportunity to fight the British.

In August 1878 the Amir signed a treaty with Russia giving

that country his guardianship and the right to defend Afghanistan against any aggression, this being mainly aimed at any threat to Afghanistan from India. The final insult was when he refused entry to an advance party of a British Mission to Kabul, which was led by Sir Neville Chamberlain. The party, which had left Peshawar on 21 September 1878, was turned back at Ali Masjid and when an ultimatum was sent on 28 October requesting a reply by 20 November, this was ignored by the Amir.

During the period of waiting for a reply to the ultimatum the combined British and Indian forces were being organised into

Far left:
The Afghan War – the 10th Bengal Lancers in the Jugdulluk Pass. ILN

Left:
Quarter Guard of the 3rd Goorkhas (The Kemaoon) Regiment. ILN

Below:
Commissariat area showing elephants and oxen used for transportation of stores.

three columns which were to take to the field should it be necessary and by the time the ultimatum had expired and a state of war declared, the three columns had almost completed their preparations. The three Field Force columns were made up as follows:

PESHAWAR VALLEY FIELD FORCE
Commanded by Lieutenant General Sir Samuel J. Browne, KCB

1st Division
Cavalry
10th (Prince of Wales's Own) Royal Lancers (2 Squadrons)
11th (Prince of Wales's Own) Bengal Lancers
Corps of Guides (Queen's Own) Cavalry
Artillery
4 Batteries Royal Artillery
No 4 Mountain Battery, Punjab Frontier Force
Engineers
Headquarters and 4 companies of the Bengal Sappers and
  Miners
Infantry
  1st Brigade
  4th Battalion, The Rifle Brigade (The Prince Consort's Own)

Attack on Fort Ali Masjid (21 November 1878).

20th (Punjab) Native Infantry
4th Goorkha Regiment
2nd Brigade
1st Battalion, 17th Foot
Corps of Guides (Queen's Own) Infantry
1st Sikh Infantry
3rd Brigade
81st Foot (Loyal Lincoln Volunteers)
14th (The Ferozepore) Bengal Native Infantry
27th (Punjab) Native Infantry
4th Brigade
51st King's Own Light Infantry Regiment
6th Bengal Native Infantry
45th (Rattray's Sikhs) Bengal Native Infantry

2nd Division
Cavalry
9th (The Queen's Royal) Lancers
10th (the Duke of Cambridge's Own) Bengal Lancers
13th Bengal Lancers
Artillery
2 batteries of horse and one of field artillery
Infantry
  1st Brigade
1st Battalion 25th Foot (King's Own Borderers)
24th (Punjab) Native Infantry
Bhopal Battalion

2nd Brigade
1st Battalion, 5th Foot (Northumberland Fusiliers)
2nd (Prince of Wales's Own) Goorkha Regiment (The Sirmoor Rifles Mhairwara Battalion[3]

The force assembled for service in the Kuram Valley was under the command of Major-General F. S. Roberts, CB, VC and was titled the Kuram (Kurram) Valley Field Force and consisted of the following units:

Cavalry – Under command of Colonel H. H. Gough
10th Hussars (one squadron) 12th Bengal Cavalry
Artillery
A battery and a half of Royal Artillery
Nos 1 and 2 Mountain Batteries, Punjab Frontier Force
Engineers
One company of Bengal Sappers and Miners
Infantry
  1st Brigade
  2nd Battalion, 8th Foot (The King's)
  29th (Punjab) Native Infantry
  5th Bengal Native Infantry

2nd Brigade
72nd Foot (Duke of Albany's Own Highlanders
21st (Punjab) Native Infantry
5th Goorkha Regiment (The Hazara Goorkha Battalion)
23rd (Punjab) Native Infantry (Pioneers)[4]

The third column was originally designated the Kandahar Column, but was later changed to the Southern Afghanistan Field Force and consisted of two divisions made up as follows:

1st (Mooltan) Division – Under command of Lieutenant-General D. M. Stewart

Cavalry
15th (King's) Hussars
8th Bengal Cavalry
19th Bengal Cavalry
Artillery
10 Batteries of Royal Artillery with a siege-train
Engineers
3 companies of Bengal Sappers and Miners
Infantry
1st Brigade
2nd Battalion, 60th Rifles
15th (The Loodianah) Bengal Native Infantry
25th (Punjab) Native Infantry

2nd Brigade
59th Foot (2nd Nottinghamshire)
1st Goorkha Regiment
3rd Goorkha (The Kemaoon) Regiment

2nd (Quetta) Division – Under command of Major-General M. A. S. Biddulph
Cavalry
1st and 2nd Punjab Cavalry
3rd Sindh Horse (3rd Punjab Cavalry)
Artillery
1 Field and 1 Mountain Battery
No 3 (Peshawar) Mountain Battery
Engineers
1 Company of Bengal Sappers and Miners
Infantry
1st Brigade
70th Foot
19th (Punjab) Native Infantry
30th Bombay Native Infantry
2nd Brigade
26th (Punjab) Native Infantry
1st Punjab Infantry (Punjab Frontier Force)
29th Bombay Native Infantry

32nd (Punjab) Native Infantry (Pioneers)) Not Brigaded
2nd (or Hill) Sikh Infantry[5]   )

General Roberts and his staff.

With the intention of taking the stronghold of Ali Masjid, the Peshawar Valley Field Force moved into the Khyber (Khaiber) Pass on the evening of 20 November 1878 but was met with stiff opposition and, with the initial loss of two officers and 14 men killed as well as a number wounded, the attack was not pressed and the force withdrew to await a more favourable opportunity. However on the following day the Afghans evacuated the fort at Ali Masjid which was then occupied without further opposition. The Afghan commander and his force, having evacuated the fort, blundered into the troops under the command of Brigadier-General A. M. Tytler and were made prisoner.

In the meantime, the Kurram Valley Field Force, under command of General Roberts, moved out on the outbreak of hostilities. They moved slowly due to the terrain and frequently had to build roads for the artillery, and so were under the watch of the Afridis who were waiting to attack. The fort at Kurram was reached on 26 November where General Roberts left his sick under guard of a small garrison to cross the Peiwar Kotal some twelve miles away. The weather conditions were adverse with intense cold and snow but over the next three days careful reconnaissance showed that the enemy were in strength with field guns in position to cover the pass. A feint attack was made on Peiwar Kotal whilst a part of the force moved along Spin Gawi (White Cow Pass) which led to a ridge which the Field Force could work along so as to make a flank attack on the enemy position. General Roberts accompanied the flanking force which included, apart from the British unit and Punjab Regiment PFF, the 21st and 29th (Punjab) Native Infantry and the 5th Gurkha Regiment, supported by a mountain battery and a four-gun elephant battery, and advanced along the ridge. Brigadier-General A. H. Cobbe prepared to make the frontal attack with the 8th Foot, 5th Bengal Native Infantry and the 12th Bengal Cavalry. The group on the ridge, which had advanced during the night, succeeded in reaching the summit while it was still dark and when the general advance was made at 6am, the leading troops found themselves confronted by barriers of felled trees, from which the Afghans opened fire. The 5th Gurkha Regiment, together with the 72nd Foot, charged the enemy in the half-light of early morning and cleared the position. At 7.30am General Roberts heliographed a message to Brigadier Cobbe that the flanking force was now on the summit.

Five guns had been moved forward under the cover of darkness so as to engage the enemy batteries, which they did, and at 6am the 8th Foot and 5th Bengal Native Infantry began a direct attack on the enemy positions. After three hours they were gradually advancing through the dense pine forest and drove the enemy from the first ridge. They then pressed on to take the second ridge, but during this action Brigadier-General Cobbe was severely wounded and the resistance put up by the enemy was such that the advance slowed and by 2.30pm only the 8th Foot and some 40 or 50 men of the Indian regiments were able to make any progress. They eventually crossed a deep chasm and then covered 1½ miles of rocky track, under heavy enemy fire. The combined British and Indian party reached a

Left: The Afghan War, a Punjaub Regiment on the march. ILN

Methods of carrying mountain guns.

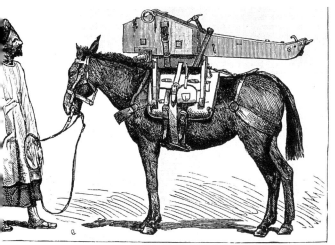

Camp of the 3rd Goorkhas in the snow at Sultan Mohammed. ILN

An attack in the Khooram Valley.

position about 800 yards from the enemy position which, eventually, they were able to clear by concentrated fire.

General Roberts ordered his force to advance if the enemy showed signs of wavering but although the enemy held firm, the 8th Foot charged the Afghan positions with fixed bayonets and at that stage the enemy withdrew, leaving their guns and tents in the hands of the Field Force. It was estimated that the Afghans had been about 4,000 strong but had been defeated at the cost of four officers and 90 men killed or wounded.

On 6 December General Roberts advanced to Ali Khel and two days later reached the Shutargardan Pass. The Field Force then commenced its return march to Kurram, at the same time exploring the southern route through the Mangiar defile. The units taking part in this operation were No 1 Mountain Battery, the 23rd Punjab Native Infantry (Pioneers), 5th Gurkha Regiment and a wing of the 72nd Foot. The main body negotiated the defile without trouble but the rearguard and baggage were suddenly attacked by the Mangal Pathans. The situation was saved by the 'steadiness and gallantry of the 5th Gurkha Regiment' who repelled every attack made by the large number of tribesmen who had massed to attack the force. The fighting lasted for five hours but the baggage was saved without any loss of kit and equipment although two officers were injured during the encounter. They were Captain F. T. Goad, Assistant

Superintendent of Transport, and Captain C. F. Powell of the 5th Gurkha Regiment. Both had been seriously wounded during the attack and subsequently died of their wounds.[6]

The headquarters reached Fort Kurram on 14 December. During January 1879 General Roberts continued with his plan to occupy the Khost district and on 6 January the fort at Matun was given up without resistance, but on the same day several thousand Mangals gathered to attack Roberts's force. On the following day General Roberts took the initiative and the enemy were dispersed by a group led by Colonel H. H. Gough, which consisted of the cavalry, supported by No 2 Mountain Battery and the 28th Punjab Native Infantry; and a second party led by Colonel F. B. Drew who had under his command No 1 Mountain Battery, a troop of the 5th Punjab Cavalry, the 21st Punjab Native Infantry, and the British regiment, the 72nd Highlanders. This action was followed by the troops surveying the district returning to Fort Kurram on 31 January. The remainder of the winter and early spring passed without any further major incident in the Kurram Valley.

The Kandahar Column, under Lieutenant-General D. M. Stewart, captured the city of Kandahar on 8 January without having to fire a shot. The place had been abandoned by the Afghan army who fled to Kabul and on entering the city the population greeted the troops without any hostility, and the

The Kojak Pass on the road to Candahar. ILN

Hindu population 'crowded round the troops with every manifestation of delight'.[7] The Field Force camped outside the city walls and the actual occupation was made by a token force of half a battalion of infantry in the central square and the placing of guards at each of the city gates.

The final major skirmish of this first phase of the war occurred on 27 March when a detachment of the 30th Bombay Native Infantry, under the command of Major F. T. Humfrey, together with half a troop of the 1st Punjab Cavalry, were attacked by a body of some 1,600 Barechi insurgents. The attack, which took place at Saiadbud, was repulsed with an estimated loss of over a hundred of the tribesmen.

The Amir, Sher Ali Khan, died at Mazar-i-Sharif on 21 February and his son, Yakub Khan, succeeded to the throne and indicated that he was willing to negotiate with the British, and a treaty was drawn up at Gandamak on 26 May 1879. The northern Field Force was at once ordered to withdraw, but unfortunately the hot weather was at its height and whilst they were in the Khyber area cholera broke out. The troops suffered greatly during the outbreak, which resulted in many regiments having a high casualty rate. Fortunately, the Kandahar Field Force was ordered to remain in position during the hot weather and so generally missed the devastating effect of the cholera epidemic.

Cardew, in his history of *The Services of the Bengal Native Army* records that 'The thanks of Both Houses of Parliament were voted to the Viceroy, to the Commander-in-Chief in India, and to all engaged in the campaign (G.G.O. No 185 of 1879); a special medal was granted to all troops employed in Afghanistan between the 21st November 1878 and the 26th May 1879, with clasps for the actions of Ali Masjid and Paiwar Kotal . . . Six months' batta was granted to all ranks by G.G.O. No 804 of 1879.'[8]

The treaty which had been signed on 26 May placed the affairs of Afghanistan under British control and guaranteed the country from aggression, this being generally aimed at stopping Russian interference. It also provided for a British Resident at Kabul and for the British to have control over the Khyber Pass. These terms permitted the British Resident to proceed to Kabul and Major Sir P. L. N. Cavagnari, KCSI, was appointed to that post. He proceeded to Kabul with an escort of 25 sowars and 50 sepoys of the Queen's Own Corps of Guides, under the command of Lieutenant W. R. P. Hamilton, VC, and the party arrived at Kabul on 24 July 1879. As early as 6 August hostile actions towards the members of the Mission became obvious and the situation gradually deteriorated, but on 2 September Sir Louis Cavagnari despatched a telegram to the Viceroy of India to the effect that all was well at the Embassy. This was not the

Major Cavagnari arranging with the Shinwarries for the protection of the road from Dakka to Lundi Khana. (Published in The Illustrated London News *of 25 January 1879.)*

case, as on the following morning Afghan Troops who had paraded at the Bala Hissar, the citadel of Kabul, rioted when their pay arrears were not forthcoming. The majority of the British Mission and guard were at their Embassy building at the Bala Hissar, with the exception of seven troopers who were out on the plains beyond the city collecting fodder with a party of grass cutters. As soon as the rebellious Afghan troops broke away from their parade, some went to the arms kote whilst some attacked the stables used by the British Mission. The gates of the courtyard were immediately closed but within a very short time the Residency was besieged. Despite Sir Louis Cavagnari sending a message to the Amir, who responded by sending his son and the Commander-in-Chief of his forces, Daud Shah, to bring the Afghan troops under control, the Amir made no other attempt to relieve the besieged party.

The small force defended the Residency hour after hour with no hope of relief and a little before noon, three of the British officers, at the head of a party of 25 Guide Sowars, charged the Afghans. This was followed later by two other desperate charges, but all failed. A fourth and last charge was made by a gallant Sikh Jemadar, all the British officers having been killed by this time, but that too failed to bring to a halt the attack on the British Residency. The gates of the courtyard were broken open and the mob fired the building in which the members of the

Mission were making their final stand. The building eventually started to collapse and the mob were then able to gain access and overran the last defenders of the small garrison. Sir Louis Cavagnari, his staff, and the gallant sowars and sepoys of the escort were killed.[9] The news reached India of the massacre and immediate orders were issued to invade Afghanistan and re-establish control and to punish those who had murdered the British Resident and his staff and escort.

The Viceroy summoned the Council on 5 September, the news having only reached him late on the previous night and, acting with promptitude, the troops began to move into position so as to prepare for the advance towards Kabul. The major problem was the long line of communication and supply that would be required to sustain a force in Afghanistan and to this end the Government were urged to 'use every endeavour to collect, purchase or otherwise, some 20,000 camels' which would be required to maintain the British force in Kabul.

On 6 October advance cavalry patrols discovered large numbers of Afghans in occupation of the hills and defile between the towns of Charasiah and Kabul. The cavalry dismounted and engaged the enemy and held them until the arrival of the main party, which included the 23rd Punjab Native Infantry (Pioneers), 5th Punjab Native Infantry, and the 5th Gurkha Regiment, as well as 72nd Foot (Highlanders) and a detachment of the 92nd Highlanders led by Major G. S. White. The gallant attack made by the combined British and Indian troops overran the Afghan positions and they retreated leaving twenty guns and a great number of casualties. The combined Field Force lost Jemadar Khanimulla, 5th Punjab Native Infantry, and 19 men killed; and three British officers and 64 men wounded.

In this important battle at Charasiah less than half of General Roberts's force had routed the entire army of Kabul and had captured almost all of its artillery.

On 8 October the expeditionary force advanced on Kabul and preparations were made to attack the enemy on the following day, but during the preceding night the enemy left their positions, leaving behind them stores, ammunition and artillery. On 12 October, General Sir Frederick Roberts formally took possession of the Bala Hissar. Vast stores of powder and ammunition were found in the arsenal and, despite precautions being taken, an explosion occurred on 16 October in which a number of lives were lost. The General gave orders for the Bala Hissar to be demolished, partly as a precaution and partly to be seen as a punishment to the occupants of the city who had permitted the murder of the British Resident and his staff. The work was put in hand immediately and this action did have an effect on subsequent events, as the destruction of the building was taken as an insult by the Afghanis. Amir Yakub Khan expressed his determination to abdicate and he was deported to India on 1 December. In the meantime, Sir Frederick Roberts was promoted to Lieutenant-General and was nominally in command of the Government in Afghanistan. The Khyber route was open and the Shutargardan was abandoned for the winter and the garrison withdrawn. The 21st Punjab Native Infantry retired to Ali Khel, and No 1 Mountain Battery, together with two squadrons of the 9th Lancers and the 3rd Sikh Infantry, accompanied Brigadier-General H. H. Gough on his return to Kabul. Minor actions continued to take place as the combined army continued to seek out enemy resistance and to consolidate the line of communication through the North West Frontier Province, and the Khyber Pass to Kabul.

Hostility towards the British continued, inflamed by the continued occupation of their country and by the destruction of Bala Hissar and the deportation of the Amir to India. It was easy for the 'mullas' to rouse the tribes against the British and a 'jehad' against foreign invaders. The call to arms was eagerly taken up by the tribesmen and a scheme was planned to overwhelm the British force at Kabul and Sherpur. Measures were immediately taken to defeat the enemy plans.

Early in December an attempt was made by two columns to bring the enemy into a trap but, unfortunately, a force of 500 men under the command of Brigadier-General W. G. D. Massy moved by a shorter route than was planned and was therefore unsupported and came under fire from a large group of Afghans, which have been estimated to be as many as 'nearly 10,000 in number' whilst other accounts give the number as being 4,000. Whichever figure is correct, Massy's force was completely outnumbered. A number of guns were lost but were later recovered by the Gurkhas and the situation was saved by the arrival of General Sir Frederick Roberts and his men. The Afghan force was now under the control of Muhammad Jan, a leader of experience, and under his command the enemy gained some advantage by taking some heights from which an attack could be mounted on Kabul. The enemy force at this time was thought to be in the region of 45,000 strong and, this being so, General Roberts abandoned his plan for an offensive and withdrew his troops from the more isolated positions in order to concentrate his force within the protection of the Sherpur cantonment, a mile outside Kabul. This site gave a strong defence position in which the troops could be concentrated, including the cavalry with their horses, transport animals, supplies and stores. The defence works were strengthened and abattis constructed on all sides, and the Engineers closed the gap between the western face of Behmaru Heights and the western end of the Sherpur cantonment. The cantonment was comprised of a rectangular enclosure 1½ miles long and more than two-thirds of a mile in width. The British and Indian force had all assembled by 15 December, and for a week no actual attack was made although some sniping did take place causing several casualties. On 16 December the post at Lataband, which was being held by the 28th Punjab Native Infantry and a wing of the 23rd Punjab Native Infantry (Pioneers), was attacked by about 1,000 Afghan tribesmen but was able to repulse the attack with considerable loss. The men inside the Sherpur cantonment learned that an attack would be made on 23 December and preparations were made. When the time came the force stood fast and held back an attack by a body of about 60,000. The 5th Punjab Cavalry were used in a counter-attack from the flank and this caused the enemy to withdraw and by 1pm the firing had almost ceased. By the following day the enemy had completely withdrawn. The garrison remained undisturbed at Kabul until Spring 1880, with General Roberts keeping in touch with his forces by heliograph and telegraph. Supplies were brought in from Peshawar, through the Khyber Pass, using a combination of animals to maintain the supply train, including camels, oxen, mules and ponies. The loss of life of these baggage-animals was enormous, with one authority quoting a figure of 80,000 animals having perished.[10]

A force, commanded by General Sir Donald Stewart, moved out from Kandahar to occupy Ghazni on 29 March 1880 and for three weeks marched northwards without meeting opposition but as all the villages beyond Kalat-i-Ghilzai were deserted, problems arose as there were difficulties in obtaining supplies. On the morning of 19 April the force had been on the march for about two hours when a strong Afghan party of about 15,000 was encountered on an undulating ridge near Ahmad Khel (Ahmed Kheyl), which is about 23 miles from Ghazni. The enemy attacked Stewart's troops with great determination and succeeded in driving back the British line. In the centre and right, the attack was pressed home by Afghan swordsmen that even case-shot, at a distance of 50 yards, failed to stop. The situation became critical and the enemy's advance was only checked by the effective fire by the 3rd Gurkha Regiment on the left, and the 2nd Sikh Infantry in the centre. On the right, the enemy were charged by the 19th Bengal Lancers and the 2nd Punjab Cavalry. At this point the enemy began to retreat, using the cover of villages and orchard walls and they kept up firing until they were routed by the Indian cavalry units. The Ghazni Field Force (as they had been titled) lost 17 killed and 115 wounded. It was estimated that the enemy lost 1,000 killed and more than 2,000 men wounded.

After a rest of two hours, the march was resumed and Ghazni was captured without any defence being put up by the Afghans, and the advance toward Kabul resumed. On 25 April the Ghazni Field Force, which at this time became the Third Division of the Kabul Field Force, met an army of about 6,000 tribesmen and, after a fierce fight which lasted less than an hour, the Afghans retreated with a loss to the Field Force of two killed and eleven wounded.

On 2 May, Sir Donald Stewart and his men entered Kabul and took control of the political affairs, and troops were deployed around the country to ensure that the roads were kept open and the supplies could still reach the Field Force now in the area of Kabul. During the months April to August 1880 the Khyber area continued to be unsettled and raids and disturbances were frequent. Throughout the spring and summer, negotiations were being held with the Kabuli sardars with a view to establishing Abdur Rahman Khan as the Amir. Ayoub Khan, the brother of the Yakoub Khan the claimant to the Afghan throne, was busy rallying considerable numbers of tribesmen to his standard and marching from Herat with a large force of regular Afghan cavalry and infantry, together with 36 guns which were under the control of a number of Russian artillery officers, towards the British force under the command of Brigadier-General G. R. S. Burrows, who took to the field with native troops supplied by the Wali of Kandahar. The combined force moved out with a total strength of 2,300 men and six guns. On 14 July the native troops supplied by the Wali mutinied but were dispersed by the cavalry and artillery, leaving only a small force consisting of E Battery Royal Horse Artillery; a smooth-bore battery of 6-pounders, taken from the Wali's troops and manned by an officer and 42 men of the 66th Foot; and from the Indian Army the 3rd Sind Horse, a detachment of Sappers and Miners, the 1st Native Infantry (Grenadiers), and the 30th Bombay Native Infantry (Jacob's Rifles).[11] On 27 July the Afghan army made a flank move, which was screened from the British by hills, and made their way completely undetected to a position on a range of hills overlooking the British camp. General Burrows, with his depleted force, believing the enemy to be three miles away at Maiwand, ordered his troops to advance and some cavalry skirmishes took place as the Field Force moved into battle positions. Ayoub Khan deployed his regiments in the centre with a number of his guns, and on his right were 400 of his cavalry, whilst on his left he had 2,000 Ghazis. The Afghan cavalry made an attack and then quickly retreated, whereupon General Burrows dispatched two of his guns and a squadron of cavalry to follow the retreating Afghan force. He then ordered his line to advance to support that move and fell into the trap that the enemy had set. He moved from an advantageous position to an area of a ruined fort and village with undulating ground which gave the enemy the opportunity of advancing, being sheltered from the fire of the Field Force. Although Burrows's rifled 9-pounder guns were superior to the smooth bore guns used by the Afghans, that advantage was lost once the enemy was able to get in under their effective range of 1,000 yards. General Burrows organised his defence with the 66th Foot in the centre, the 30th Bombay Native Infantry on his left and the 1st Bombay Grenadiers on the right. A charge of Afghan regular cavalry on the British left, which coincided with a fanatical attack by the Ghazis on the front and right of the line, caused the 1st Bombay Grenadiers and the 30th Bombay NI to fall back under the extreme pressure of the attack. Two of the British guns were captured and, even after a counter-attack, only one was retaken.

During the heavy fighting the Field Force position became a triangle with the 66th Foot at the apex; the two Indian regiments which defended the sides suffered badly, many casualties being caused by the Afghan artillery on the flanking heights. In an attempt to counter this, Burrows sent out skirmishing parties into the hills to silence the guns, but these parties were beaten back. In the meantime, the Ghazis moved round to the rear of the depleted force and attacked the rearguard. The baggage and stores were saved but at the high cost of 100 men killed and wounded. By 1pm the remaining men of the 66th Foot, now under fire from more than 4,000 enemy and some 30 guns, fell back in good order by alternate wings, twice having to form a square when attacked by the enemy cavalry. Unfortunately, the 30th Bombay Native Infantry were thrown into disorder by the continued fierce attack by hordes of Ghazis and moved to the rear of the 66th Foot. Stragglers from the 66th Foot, together with the 30th Bombay Native Infantry and the 1st Bombay Grenadiers (1st Bombay Native Infantry (Grenadiers)), put up a stiff resistance from a small enclosure until their ammunition ran out and then fought the enemy in a desperate hand-to-hand struggle. General Burrows succeeded in extricating some of the infantry and attempted to withdraw along the Kandahar Road, but the troops were badly disorganised and the situation was complicated by the presence of hundreds of camp-followers who milled around completely terrified. The cavalry were still making charges to try to relieve the situation and the artillerymen continued to serve the guns until only one gun was left firing but they were finally cut down by the attacking tribesmen who were by then at close quarters. About 100 officers and men of the 66th Foot made a determined stand in a garden surrounded by almost all the Afghan force, until only eleven men were left, with the regimental pet, a small white dog. With all the ammunition gone, this small party charged out of the garden and stood in the open, back to back, until the last

Headquarters Staff. AMOT

man had been killed. The final stand of the 66th Foot at Maiwand is graphically depicted in a painting entitled 'The Last Eleven at Maiwand', prints of which were published in London in 1884.

Throughout the battle of Maiwand (as it became known) General Burrows set a fine example to his men, having had two horses shot from under him and, with the final stand of the 66th Foot, he gathered the few survivors and made a fighting retreat along the 16 miles to Kandahar. The remaining survivors of the 3rd Sind Horse continued to make repeated charges to slow down the enemy who were following the survivors of the disaster. Seven miles west of Kandahar a relief force met with the survivors and covered their retreat to Kandahar. The Field Force lost 1,302 men and two Victoria Crosses were awarded for the action.[12] Two senior officers were court-martialled but were honourably acquitted. Brigadier-General Burrows was removed from the Brigade staff as it was considered to be his lack of judgement that caused the disaster at Maiwand.

Following the defeat of the British at Maiwand, the troops of Ayub Khan and those of the Wali Sher Ali Khan of Kandahar now besieged the fortified town of Khandahar. It was imperative to relieve the garrison at Khandahar and to restore British prestige in Southern Afghanistan. On 3 August orders were given for the immediate despatch of a strong relief force from Kabul, under the command of Lieutenant-General Sir Frederick Roberts, GCB, VC, CIE, which consisted of the following units:

Cavalry Brigade
9th Lancers
3rd Bengal Cavalry
3rd Punjab Cavalry
Central India Horse
Artillery
No 6 Battery, 8th Brigade, Royal Artillery
No 11 Battery, 9th Brigade, Royal Artillery
No 2 Mountain Battery
Infantry
1st Brigade
92nd Highlanders
23rd (Punjab) Native Infantry (Pioneers)
24th (Punjab) Native Infantry
2nd Gurkha Regiment
Commanded by Brigadier-General H. T. Macpherson
2nd Brigade
72nd Highlanders
2nd Sikh Infantry
3rd Sikh Infantry
5th Gurkha Regiment
Commanded by Brigadier-General T. D. Baker
3rd Brigade
2nd 60th Rifles
15th (Sikh) Native Infantry
25th (Punjab) Native Infantry
4th Gurkha Regiment
Commanded by Brigadier-General C. M. MacGregor[13]

Loading camels in the camp of the 19th Bombay Native Infantry, 1879.

The combined British and Indian Force, which was given the title of 'The Kabul-Kandahar Field Force' was formed and all preparations completed during the first week of August. On 8 August they assembled at Bini Hisar and on the following morning the march commenced that was to become recognised as one of the famous military achievements of the British in India.

The march has long been taken as an example of what can be achieved by good organisation, energy and determination. The British and Indian regiments, supported by as much transport and supplies as could be procured from Kabul, commenced a march of over 320 miles which was completed in 22 days. The army, which consisted of 10,000 men and about 8,000 followers, set off through territory which was under the control of the new Amir and thus encountered no hostilities, but the remaining two-thirds of the march were through enemy or hostile country. That the march was a success was entirely due to good planning and organisation and to the conscientious work carried out by all ranks from the General downwards.

They moved through the Logar valley, in order to take advantage of the crops available there, and arrived at Ghazni on 15 August, having completed a 98-mile march in seven days. The Field Force then continued through a rough and treeless terrain, all being exposed to the sun, and following each day's march the troops had to make camp, provide picquets, and the following morning move off for another full day's march. The

force continued its daily advance and reached Kalat-i-Ghilzai on 23 August, having then completed 232 miles in 15 days. A one-day halt was made to give the troops a well-earned rest and on 25 August the advance was resumed and on 27 August heliographic communication was established with the Kandahar garrison by a detachment of the cavalry brigade at Robat. During the evening of that day several officers garrisoned at Kandahar joined the force, as the seige of the garrison had been lifted by the Afghan army who were now entrenched north-west of the town. General Roberts gave his troops a day's rest at Robat and then marched the last 18 miles to Kandahar by two stages so as to ensure that his men would be able to give a good account of themselves in the forthcoming battle. The main body reached Robat on 28 August, having covered a distance of 303 miles in only 20 days.

Whilst General Roberts was completing his memorable march from Kabul to Kandahar, another strong force had been assembled at Quetta, under the command of Major-General R. Phayre, which included the 3rd, 4th and 17th Bengal Native Infantry, and moved out to approach Kandahar from the south.

Kandahar was finally reached on 31 August and the army camped on the plain to the west of the city and cantonment. The 2nd and 3rd Brigades occupied the hills overlooking Kandahar

Arrival of the Commissariat stores for the Quetta Column at the camp at Mian Meer.   ILN

and during the afternoon a reconnaissance established that the Afghan force, led by Ayub Khan, was holding the village of Pir Paimal and the Baba Wali Kotal, to the north-west of the Field Force. Having established the position of the enemy, Sir Frederick Roberts prepared for an attack on the Afghan positions on the morning of 1 September. The Field Force had, by this time, been reinforced by the garrison of Bombay troops that had been at Kalat-i-Ghilzai. The plan was to use the Bombay force to threaten the left flank of the Afghans and, with the whole of the infantry of the Kabul-Kandahar Field Force, to attack the right. The cavalry were to attempt to threaten the enemy from the rear. The combined Field Force moved into their positions early on the morning of 1 September, but during the night the Afghans had also planned to take the offensive and had occupied two villages, which necessitated a change in the British plan. The 1st Brigade was now required to drive the Afghan force from the village of Gandi Mulla Sahibdad and then advance to the low hill beyond the village. Shortly after 9.30am the combined British and Indian offensive began with the commencement of a bombardment from the artillery. General Macpherson advanced with the 2nd Gurkha Regiment and the 92nd Foot (Gordon Highlanders) and after a short battle the village of Gandi Mulla was secured. Meanwhile,

General Baker advanced with the 2nd Sikh Infantry and the 72nd Foot (Duke of Albany's Own Highlanders), both of which sustained heavy casualties, and eventually carried their advance through the enemy positions and drove the Afghan force back to Pir Paimal. The 1st and 2nd Brigades were then able to unite and commenced to sweep the enemy before them until they reached the Afghan entrenched positions on the far side of the Baba Wali Kotal. At this point the Afghans made a desperate stand but were broken by the continued pressure from General Roberts's force which at this point was led by the 92nd Foot (Gordon Highlanders). It was expected that the Afghans would regroup and make a further stand but when the British advance was resumed it was found that Ayub Khan's camp had been deserted and that the whole of the Afghan army was in flight. The action during the morning of 1 September was fierce and the casualties were recorded as being:

3 British officers, one native officer and 33 men killed and 10 British officers and 4 native officers and 202 men wounded – making a total loss on the two days of 40 killed and 228 wounded, of the latter of whom more than 20 afterwards succumbed to the injuries they had received.[14]

The battle of Kandahar brought about the relief of the

garrison and an end of the war. Troops were withdrawn from Kabul and plans were made to withdraw the armies from Southern Afghanistan, with the exception of a small garrison which was to be maintained at Kandahar. The troops were to maintain that small garrison for only one year, after which they returned to Indian territory behind the frontier as agreed by the treaty concluded at Gandamak.

The medal for the Second Afghan War (1878-1880) was awarded to all those who took part in the campaign, and who had not received the award for the earlier phase of the war. Under the authority of G.G.O numbers 673 of 1880 and 472 of 1881, clasps were awarded for the actions at 'Charasia' (6 October 1879), 'Kabul' (10-23 December 1879), 'Ahmad Khel' (19 April 1880) and 'Kandahar' (1 September 1880), also the medal 'Kabul to Kandahar Star', which was granted to those troops who took part in that operation during the period 9-31 August 1880. The award of the Kandahar Clasp to the Afghan War Medal was also made to those officers and men who took part in the reconnaissance of Kandahar on 31 August 1880 but did not take part in the defeat of the Afghan army on the following day.[15]

In October 1880 a small expedition was sent against the Marri tribes who had been particularly active since the disaster at Maiwand. Brigadier-General C. M. MacGregor and a small force consisting of a Mountain Battery, the 3rd Punjab Cavalry, together with 4th and 5th Gurkha Regiments, 2nd and 3rd Sikh Infantry, and the 2nd Battalion, 60th Foot (King's Royal Rifle Corps) advanced into the Marri area and, although the terrain was extremely difficult, they met with little opposition and reached Kahun, the chief town of the tribes. At a meeting with the chiefs the terms set out by the Government were accepted and the Field Force withdrew in November 1880. The final phase of the Afghan and frontier operations was concluded in May 1881 when an expedition was mounted against the Mahsud Waziris who had been originally incited by the Afghans but who had continued to raid and disrupt the line of communications in the Kurram Valley. The expeditionary force, led by Brigadier-General T. G. Kennedy, consisted of part of the Peshawar Mountain Battery, supported by detachments of the 1st and 4th Punjab Cavalry and the 8th Company of Sappers and Miners. The infantry column was made up from detachments from 32nd (Bengal) Native Infantry (Pioneers), 1st and 4th Sikh Infantry, and 1st, 2nd, 4th and 6th Punjab Infantry. In addition, a reserve column was assembled at Bannu under command of Brigadier-General J. J. H. Gordon, consisting of No 1 Battery, 8th Brigade Royal Artillery and No 1 Mountain Battery (two guns) together with the 18th Bengal Cavalry, the 6th Company Bengal Sappers and Miners, with infantry support provided by the 14th, 20th, 21st and 30th (Bengal) Native Infantry and the 5th Punjab Infantry. Prior to the main advance, most of the tribes submitted and it was only the Nana Khel section holding out. The force advanced without too much opposition until 3 May when the enemy launched a major attack on the Field Force near Shah Alam Ragza, but the attack was driven off by a determined stand by the 1st Sikh Infantry. The advance

The Second Afghan War Medal.

Second Afghan War Medal (left). Kabul to Kandahar Star (right).

continued and on 11 May they reached Makin. In the meantime, the Bannu Field Force advanced up the Khaisora valley and reached Razmak on 9 May. After some skirmishing, and having established the British presence, the remaining tribes agreed to the peace settlement. Following completion of the operation, the force withdrew to British territory, having lost eight men killed and 24 wounded.

The Second Afghan War brought awards of two medals, with six bars and, in addition, the Indian Government made two grants of six months' batta to all ranks engaged in the campaign; the second grant was authorised by G.G.O. No 459 of 1880. The descriptions of the two medals that were issued are as follows:

Second Afghan War Medal

Obverse The crowned and draped head of Queen Victoria and legend 'Victoria Regina Et Imperatrix'.

Reverse A scene of troops on the march with an elephant carrying a gun in the centre. Around the top is the word 'AFGHANISTAN' and in the exergue the dates '1878-79-80'.

Size 31mm diameter.

Ribbon 32mm wide. Green with crimson stripes on each edge.

Kabul to Kandahar Star

Obverse A five-pointed star with a ball between all the points except the top two. In the centre is the monogram 'V.R.I.' around which is a raised circular border. On this in raised letters is 'KABUL TO KANDAHAR' with the year '1880' in the centre at the bottom. The star is surmounted by a crown. The suspension loop is attached to the crown.

Reverse Plain except for the recipient's name which is engraved around the hollow centre.

Size Maximum width 45mm. Height 62mm (excluding suspension ring).

Ribbon 38mm wide in a rainbow pattern of red, white, yellow, white and blue.

In addition to the campaign medals and clasps to members of the forces who had taken part in the operations, a number of gallantry awards were made. Details of these awards are given in the book *The Second Afghan War 1878-1880 Casualty Roll* but a list of such awards to members of the Indian Army is given below. At this time the award of the Victoria Cross had still not been approved for members of the Indian Army, other than to British officers serving with the army:

Victoria Cross

Adams, Rev James William
    Bengal Ecclesiastical Establishment
    The London Gazette, 26 August 1881.
Cook, Major John
    5th Gurkha Regiment, *The London Gazette*, 18 March 1879.
Hamilton, Lieutenant Walter Richard Pollock
    Guides Cavalry, *The London Gazette*, 7 October 1879.
Hammond, Captain Arthur George
    Guides Infantry, *The London Gazette*, 18 October 1881.

Vousden, Captain William John
    5th Punjab Cavalry, Punjab Frontier Force
    The London Gazette, 18 October 1881.[16]

Although at this time Indian other ranks were ineligible for the Victoria Cross, gallantry was recognised by the award of the Indian Order of Merit, the Military Division of which had been originally instituted by the Honourable East India Company in 1837. The award to 'all ranks for "conspicuous gallantry in the field"' was authorised under General Order by the Governor General of India No 94 dated 1 May 1837 which set out the rules and regulations.[17] The awards in the Military Division of the Indian Order of Merit to men in the units listed were for gallantry during the Second Afghan War:

Unit	Indian Order of Merit		
	3rd Class	2nd Class	1st Class
Serving with E/4 Royal Artillery	1	–	–
1st Bengal Cavalry	1	–	–
10th Bengal Lancers	1	–	–
11th Bengal Lancers	1	–	–
14th Bengal Lancers	2	–	–
18th Bengal Cavalry	1	–	–
19th Bengal Lancers	16	–	–
14th Bengal Native Infantry	7	–	–
21st (Punjab) Bengal NI	2	–	–
23rd (Punjab) Bengal NI	12	1	–
24th (Punjab) Bengal NI	6	–	–
27th (Punjab) Bengal NI	8	–	–
28th (Punjab) Bengal NI	3	–	–
29th (Punjab) Bengal NI	6	–	–
45th Bengal NI	4	–	–
2nd Gurkha Regiment	8	–	–
5th Gurkha Regiment	13	1	1
(Sepoy Kishnbiar Nuggurkoti awarded 3rd Class GGO 89 of 24 Jan 1879; 2nd Class (as Kissen Beer Nuggerkoti) GGO 1260 of 26 Dec 1879 and 1st Class (in the rank of Naik) GGO 251 of 23 Apr 1880.)			
1st Punjab Cavalry	8	1	–
2nd Punjab Cavalry	3	–	–
3rd Punjab Cavalry	1	–	–
4th Punjab Cavalry	1	–	–
5th Punjab Cavalry	11	1	–
Corps of Guides	21	1	–
No 2 Mountain Battery	4	–	–
2nd Sikh Infantry	7	–	–
3rd Sikh Infantry	5	2	–
4th Sikh Infantry	1	–	–
1st Punjab Infantry	4	–	2
Mhairwara Battalion	3	–	–
3rd Bombay Light Cavalry	2	1	1
(Ressaidar Dhowkul Sing was promoted to 2nd Class and 1st Class under GGO 59 of 4 Feb 1881.)			
Poona Horse	9	–	–
3rd Sind Horse	11	–	–
(Sowar Syud Imman Ali awarded 3rd Class posthumously GGO 689 of 17 Dec 1880.)			
No 2 Coy, Bombay Sappers & Miners	3	–	–
1st Bombay Native Infantry	2	–	–

19th Bombay NI   2   –   –
(Privates Elahi Bux and Sounak Tannack awarded 3rd Class posthumously by GGO 689 of 17 Dec 1880.)

29th Bombay NI   3   –   –

30th Bombay NI   8   –   –
(GGO 356 of 23 Jun 1882 awarded a three-year pension to the widows of Private Goolan Mahomed and Bugler Suddu Sing and, as a special case, the daughter of Havildar-Major Brindaban from 27 July 1880. Had the three men, who were killed in action, lived they would have been 'admitted to the 3rd Class'.)

A list of the Indian Army units that served during the Afghan War is given in Appendix at end of this Chapter.

1 *The Second Afghan War, 1878-80*, produced in the Intelligence Branch, Army Headquarters, India (John Murray, 1908).

2 Farrington, Anthony, *The Second Afghan War 1878-1880, Casualty Roll*, 1986.

3 Cardew, Lieutenant, F. G. *A Sketch of the Services of the Bengal Native Army*, 1903, pp337-338.

4 Cardew, op cit, p343.

5 Cardew, op cit, p345.

6 Cardew, op cit, p344.

7 Shadbolt, S. H. *The Afghan Campaign of 1878-1880*, 1882, p33.

8 Cardew, op cit, p347.

9 Shadbolt, op cit, p41.

10 Featherstone, Donald, *Colonial Small Wars 1837-1901*, 1973, p125.

11 *The London Gazette*.

12 The two Victoria Crosses awarded for gallantry during the action at Maiwand were awarded to: Sergeant P. Mullane, Royal Horse Artillery, *The London Gazette*, 16 May 1881. Gunner J. Collis, Royal Horse Artillery, *The London Gazette*, 16 May 1881. (Gunner Collis forfeited his VC under Royal Warrant of 18 November 1895.)

13 Cardew, op cit, pp370-371.

14 Cardew, op cit, p374.

15 Gordon, Major Lawrence L. *British Battles and Medals*, 1962, p214.

16 Farrington, op cit, pp155-158.

17 Tamplin, J. M. A. & Abbott, P. E. *British Gallantry Awards*, 1971, pp181-184.

APPENDIX TO CHAPTER FIVE

List of Corps and Regiments of the Indian Army which served in Afghanistan during the years 1878-81

Corps	Regiments, Battalions or Battery	Commanding Officer	Date
Native Artillery (Mountain Batteries)	*Punjab Frontier Force Artillery* No 1 (Kohat) Mountain Battery	Captain J. A. Kelso) Captain H. N. Jervois) Bt Major H. R. L. Morgan)	1878-80
	No 2 (Derajat) Mountain Battery	Major G. Swinley) Major A. Broadfoot) Captain H. F. Smyth)	1878-80
	No 3 (Peshawar) Mountain Battery	Major J. Charles	1878-79
	No 4 (Hazara) Mountain Battery	Major E. J. de Latour	1878-79
	No 5 (Kohat) Garrison Battery	Captain H. F. Smyth	1879
		Lieut R. A. C. King	1879-81
	Bombay No 1 Mountain Battery	Captain J. D. Snodgrass	
	No 2 Mountain Battery	Major R. Wace	1878-81
Royal Engineers	*Bengal Sappers and Miners* (Lieut-Col E. T. Thackeray RE VC)	–	
	No 1 Company		
	No 2 Company	Lieut J. C. L. Campbell RE)	
	No 3 Company	Captain H. Dove RE)	1878-80
	No 4 Company	Captain P. Haslett RE)	

Corps	Regiments, Battalions or Battery	Commanding Officer	Date
	No 5 Company	Lieut E. S. Hill RE)	
	No 6 Company	Lieut W. F. H. Stafford RE)	
	No 7 Company	Lieut P. T. Buston RE)	1878-80
	No 8 Company	Lieut H. P. Leach RE)	
	No 9 Company	Lieut M. C. Barton RE)	
	No 10 Company	Major L. F. Brown RE)	
	Madras Sappers and Miners		
	(Lieut-Col Ross Thomson RE		
	Lieut-Col C. A. Sim RE)		
	A Company	Lieut C. H. Darling RE	
	B Company	Lieut W. B. Connor RE	
	C Company	Lieut A. R. F. Dorward RE	
	E Company	Captain T. H. Winterbotham MI	
	I Company	Lieut A. E. Dobson RE	
	K Company	Lieut C. C. Rawson RE	
	Bombay Sappers and Miners		
	No 1 Company	Lieut-Col John Hills CB	
	No 2 Company	Lieut G. H. W. O. Sullivan RE	
		Lieut G. T. Jones RE	
	No 3 Company	–	
	No 4 Company	Lieut W. Coles RE	
		Lieut W. A. E. St Clair RE	
	No 5 Company	Captain W. W. B. Whiteford RE	
		Lieut E. C. Spilsbury RE	
		Lieut E. H. Bethell RE	
Bengal Cavalry	1st Bengal Cavalry	Major A. R. Chapman)	1878-80
		Colonel R. Jenkins)	
	3rd Bengal Cavalry	Lieut-Col A. R. D. Mackenzie	1879-80
	4th Bengal Cavalry	Lieut-Col M. M. Prendergast	1880
	5th Bengal Cavalry	Major H. A. Shakespear	1880-81
	8th Bengal Cavalry	Colonel B. W. Ryall)	1878-80
		Lieut-Col H. Chapman)	
	10th Bengal Lancers	Lieut-Col O. Barnes)	1878-80
		Major A. England)	
	11th Bengal Lancers	Lieut-Col R. E. Boyle)	1878-79
		Lieut-Col A. H. Prinsep)	
	12th Bengal Cavalry	Lieut-Col H. A. McNair)	1878-80
		Lieut-Col J. H. Green)	
	13th Bengal Lancers	Lieut-Col R. C. Low CB)	
		Major W. H. Macnaghten)	1878-80
		Lieut-Col C. R. Pennington)	
	14th Bengal Lancers	Lieut-Col R. C. W. Mitford)	1879-80
		Colonel T. G. Ross CB)	
	15th Bengal Cavalry	Colonel G. A. Prendergast	1879
	17th Bengal Cavalry	Lieut-Col T. J. Watson)	1879-80
		Major E. G. Newnham)	
	18th Bengal Cavalry	Major T. R. Davidson)	1879-81
		Major H. C. Marsh)	
	Bengal Lancers	Colonel W. Fane CB)	
		Colonel P. S. Yorke)	1878-80
		Lieut-Col A. G. Owen)	

Corps	Regiments, Battalions or Battery	Commanding Officer	Date
Bengal Infantry	1st Bengal Infantry	Lieut-Col L. H. P. De Hochepied Larpent	1880
	2nd Bengal Light Infantry	Colonel T. N. Baker	1879
	5th Bengal Light Infantry	Colonel E. Venour	1880
	6th Bengal Light Infantry	Colonel G. H. Thompson) Major W. Atkins)	1878-79
	8th Bengal Infantry	Colonel G. A. Williams) Lieut-Col R. Smith) Lieut-Col H. De Brett)	1879-80
	9th Bengal Infantry	Colonel T. E. Webster	1880
	11th Bengal Infantry	Colonel P. H. F. Harris	1879-80
	12th (Kalat-i-Ghilzai) Regiment	Colonel W. Macdonald	1878-79
	13th Bengal Infantry	Colonel J. T. Watson) Colonel W. Playfair)	1879-81
	14th (Ferozepore) Sikhs	Colonel L. H. Williams	1878
	15th (Loodianah) Sikhs	Lieut-Col G. R. Hennessy	1878-80
	16th (Lucknow) Regiment	Colonel R. S. Moseley	1879-81
	19th Punjab Infantry	Colonel E. B. Clay) Lieut-Col A. Copland)	1878-80
	20th Punjab Infantry	Colonel R. G. Rogers CB) Lieut-Col H. W. Gordon)	1878-79
	21st Punjab Infantry	Lieut-Col F. W. Collis	1878-80
	22nd Punjab Infantry	Colonel J. J. O'Bryen) Colonel B. T. Stafford)	1879-80
	23rd Punjab Pioneers	Colonel A. A. Currie CB) Lieut-Col H. Collett CB)	1878-80
	24th Punjab Infantry	Colonel F. B. Norman CB	1878-80
	25th Punjab Infantry	Colonel J. W. Hoggan CB	1878-80
	26th Punjab Infantry	Colonel M. G. Smith	1878-79
	27th Punjab Infantry	Lieut-Col C. J. Hughes	1878-81
	28th Punjab Infantry	Colonel J. Hudson CB	1878-80
	29th Punjab Infantry	Colonel J. J. H. Gordon CB	1878-80
	30th Punjab Infantry	Colonel T. W. R. Boisragon CB	1879-80
	31st Punjab Infantry	Lieut-Col F. Tweddell	1879-80
	32nd Punjab Pioneers	Lieut-Col H. Fellowes) Lieut-Col A. C. W. Crookshank)	1878-80
	39th Bengal Infantry	Colonel G. W. Fraser) Major F. Gellie)	1878-79
	41st Bengal Infantry	Colonel H. S. Obbard	1880-81
	45th Rattray's Sikhs	Lieut-Col F. M. Armstrong CB	1878-80
Gurkha Regiments	1st Gurkha Light Infantry	Colonel J. S. Rawlins) Colonel R. Sale-Hills CB)	1878-80
	2nd Gurkha Regiment	Colonel D. MacIntyre VC Lieut-Col A. Battye CB)	1878-80
	3rd Gurkha (Kamaon Battalion)	Colonel A. Paterson) Colonel H. H. Lyster VC)	1878-80
	4th Gurkhas	Lieut-Col J. P. Turton) Lieut-Col F. F. Rowcroft) 44th Bengal Native Infantry)	1878-80
	5th (Hazara) Gurkhas (P.F.F.)	Lieut-Col A. FitzHugh CB) Lieut-Col J. M. Sym)	1878-80

Corps	Regiments, Battalions or Battery	Commanding Officer	Date
Punjab Cavalry (PFF)	1st Punjab Cavalry	Lieut-Col C. S. Maclean, CB	1878-80
	2nd Punjab Cavalry	Colonel T. G. Kennedy CB, Commandant)	
		Punjab Frontier Force)	1878-80
		Lieut-Col F. Lance)	
	3rd Punjab Cavalry	Lieut-Col A. Vivian	1880
	5th Punjab Cavalry	Lieut-Col B. William	
		Lieut-Col F. Hammond	
Corps of Guides (PFF)	Guides Cavalry) Col F. H. Jenkins CB	Lieut-Col G. Stewart)	
	Guides Infantry)	Lieut-Col R. B. P. P. Campbell)	1878-80
Sikh Regiments (PFF)	1st Sikh Infantry	Lieut-Col A. G. Ross)	
		Lieut-Col H. C. P. Rice)	1878-79
	2nd Sikh Infantry	Lieut-Col J. J. Boswell CB	1878-80
	3rd Sikh Infantry	Lieut-Col G. Noel-Money CB	1879-80
Punjab Infantry (PFF)	1st Punjab Infantry	Lieut-Col F. J. Keen CB	1878-79
	2nd Punjab Infantry	Lieut-Col H. Tyndall CB	1878-79
	4th Punjab Infantry	Colonel H. P. Close	1879
	5th Punjab Infantry	Lieut-Col J. W. McQueen CB	
		Lieut-Col H. M. Pratt	1878-80
Central India Horse	1st Regiment (wing)	Lieut-Col C. Martin CB	1880
	2nd Regiment (wing)		
Native Contingents	Bhopal Battalion	Colonel H. Forbes	1878-79
	Mhairwarra Battalion	Lieut-Col F. W. Boileau	1878-79
	Deoli Battalion	–	
Madras Cavalry	1st Regiment Madras Cavalry	Lieut-Col E. M. Cherry	1880-81
Madras Infantry	1st Madras Infantry	Colonel F. Dawson)	
		Lieut-Col G. Tyndall) 4th Madras Infantry	1879-80
	Lieut-Col G. C. Hodding	1879-80	
	15th Madras Infantry	Colonel G. Hearn	1879-80
	21st Madras Infantry	Major T. B. Middleton	1879
	30th Madras Infantry	Colonel T. C. Georges	1878-80
Bombay Cavalry	2nd Bombay Cavalry	Lieut-Col A. W. Macnaughten	1880
	3rd Bombay Light Cavalry	Major A. P. Currie	1880
	Poona Horse	Colonel C. D'U. La Tonche	1880-81
	2nd Regiment Sind Horse	Major M. M. Carpendale)	
		Captain C. A. de N. Lucas)	1878-81
	3rd Regiment Sind Horse	Colonel J. H. P. Malcolmson CB	1878-80
Bombay Infantry	1st Grenadiers	Colonel H. S. Anderson	1878-80
	4th Infantry Rifles	Colonel W. Bannerman	1880
	5th Light Infantry	Colonel F. Roome)	
		Colonel R. A. C. Hunt)	1880
	8th Infantry	Colonel S. Fellows	1880
	9th Infantry	Major V. Birch)	
		Lieut-Col L. H. Sibthorpe)	1880

Corps	Regiments, Battalions or Battery	Commanding Officer	Date
	10th Light Infantry	Colonel H. H. James) Lieut-Col A. Durand)	1880
	16th Infantry	Colonel T. W. W. Pierce) Lieut-Col F. S. Iredell)	1880-81
	19th Infantry	Colonel W. Creagh) Colonel C. T. Heathcote CB)	1878-81
	23rd Light Infantry	Colonel J. Harpur	1880-81
	24th Infantry	Colonel J. H. Henderson) Lieut-Col R. M. Chambers)	1880-81
	27th (1st Baluch) Infantry	Major Hogg) Colonel T. Bell)	1878-81
	28th Infantry	Colonel J. R. Nimmo) Lieut-Col W. H. Newport)	1880-81
	29th (2nd Baluch) Infantry	Lieut-Col G. Nicholetts) Colonel O. V. Tanner CB)	1878-81
	30th (Jacob's Rifles) Infantry	Colonel W. G. Mainwaring CIE	1878-80
Contingents of Sikh Feudatory States	Patiala – Infantry (battalion), Cavalry Bahwalpur – Infantry (wing), Cavalry (squadron) Jhind – Infantry (battalion), Cavalry (2 squadrons) Nabha – Infantry (battalion), Cavalry (2 squadrons)	Kapurthala – Infantry (wing) Cavalry (squadron) Maler Kotla – Infantry (2 companies) Cavalry (troop) Faridkot – Infantry (2 companies), Cavalry (troop) Nahan Infantry (2 companies)	

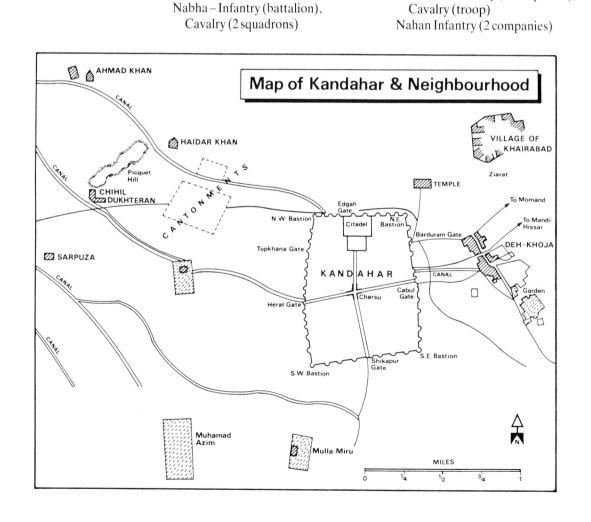

Map of Kandahar & Neighbourhood

CHAPTER SIX

Frontier Campaigns of 1875–78

Whilst the Indian army was involved in the second Afghan War during the years 1878-80, two other minor campaigns (by comparison with the Afghan War) involved troops of the Indian army. Troops taking part in the two campaigns were awarded the Indian General Service Medal (1854-1895) with the appropriate clasp.

Previously there had been problems with the Naga tribes on the Assam frontier when, during early 1875, a survey party under the command of Lieutenant W. A. Holcombe (Bengal Staff Corps) was massacred at Ninu.[1] On 2 February 1875 a small expedition was raised under the command of Colonel J. M. Nuttall CB, which was made up of detachments of the 42nd and 44th (Bengal) Native Infantry. The party, which had a total strength of 308 all ranks, departed from Dibrugarh, the station of the 44th Bengal NI, on 27 February and advanced through the thickly populated country and, after a short engagement with the Naga tribesmen, captured the large village of Ninu on 19 March. Having taken the main village, Colonel Nuttall despatched detachments into the surrounding countryside to destroy the villages of those known to have taken part in the murder of the survey party. When this action had been completed, and a number of the tribesmen who had been implicated were captured, the force moved back to their own cantonment at Dibrugarh, arriving there on 11 April 1875. Despite the retaliatory action taken by the Indian Government, the Naga tribes again attacked a survey party during December 1875 and on this occasion Captain John Butler (Bengal Staff Corps)[2] was mortally wounded. No immediate action was taken against the Nagas for this attack, but during the next two years the Naga tribes became openly aggressive and carried out a number of attacks on Indian property. Eventually it was decided that a second expedition would be mounted against the offending tribes and in December 1877 a force of 200 men of the 42nd (Bengal) Native Infantry, under the command of Captain William Brydon, departed from Gowhatty. The small party reached the village of Mozima on 8 December which it captured and then destroyed but, due to the small size of the party, it was virtually trapped in that area by the hostile tribes until 9 January 1878 when a relief force of 100 men from the 43rd (Bengal) Native Infantry arrived and relieved the situation. The Nagas then sued for peace and the force withdrew to its cantonment.

The situation remained quiet for a few months until 14 October 1879, when the Nagas again carried out an unprovoked attack on the Local Commissioner, a Mr Damant, who was killed together with Jemadar Prem Singh and ten Sepoys of the 43rd (Bengal) Native Infantry. A number of Sepoys and policemen were wounded.[3] Once again the Indian Government were compelled to send a force into the Naga territory to bring order to this area. The force was made up of a 'small party of the 34th, a detachment (300 men) of the 43rd and the whole of the 44th Native Infantry with two mountain guns'.[4] The two guns were, in fact, 7-pounder mountain guns which were carried by coolies and 'worked' by a detachment of the 44th (Bengal) Native (Light) Infantry under the command of Lieutenant A. Mansel (Royal Artillery).[5] The Field Force was commanded by Brigadier-General J. L. Nation and, having taken to the field a detachment of the 43rd (Bengal) Native (Light) Infantry, under Major H. M. Evans, attacked and secured the village of Sephima on 15 November. On 21 November the Field Force prepared to attack the Naga stronghold at Konoma on the following day. It had been believed that there would be only minimal resistance but when the assault was mounted the Indian troops, having been split into several assault parties, encountered a very determined opposition. The Gurkhas of the 44th Native Infantry attacked with great determination and gallantry, led by their Adjutant, Lieutenant R. K. Ridgeway,[6] who was awarded the Victoria Cross for his gallant conduct during the battle.

They made some headway and secured a few positions which they held until nightfall. The artillery detachment used all its ammunition during the day-long fight and although the force prepared for another major assault on the following day, the Nagas evacuated Konoma during the night, retreating to entrenched positions about a mile away. During the conflict Subadar-Major Narbir Sahi of the 44th Native Infantry and 17 men were killed; and four British Officers, two Indian Officers and 27 were wounded, two of the British officers and three Indian other ranks mortally.

Brigadier-General Nation moved back to Sachima, leaving a garrison force to hold Konoma, and on 27 November the Naga village of Jotsoma was attacked and destroyed. Little progress was made during December as supplies and reinforcements were awaited. A wing of the 42nd (Bengal) Native Infantry arrived at the end of December and operations were resumed with the successful attack on the villages of Cheswejuma and Pollongmai. A wing of the 18th (Bengal) Native Infantry arrived

14th Bengal Lancers, c1881.

on 12 March, and with these additional troops the operation drew rapidly to a close with the Naga tribes suing for peace. During the operation a total of two Indian officers and 44 sepoys were killed, as were two British officers who were serving with the Indian Army. They were Major Charles Richard Cock, who was employed as a Deputy Assistant Adjutant General, and Lieutenant H. H. Forbes, of the 44th (Bengal) Native (Light) Infantry. At the close of the long running campaign against the Naga tribes the troops who took part in the expedition were awarded the Indian General Service Medal, with a clasp 'Naga 1879-80', for service in the area during December 1879 and January 1880. The bar was also awarded to the troops who took part in the early expedition of 1875.[7]

In August 1877, during the time of the Naga expedition, led by Captain William Brydon (1877-78), it became necessary for the Indian Government to mount another expedition to punish the Jowaki Afridis for a series of raids into British territory. The tribal area was between Peshawar and the Kohat Pass in the North West Frontier region, where there had been no major trouble until the Indian authorities decided to construct a road through the territory. A force was made up of No 1 Mountain Battery, together with detachments from the 2nd Punjab Cavalry and 1st, 3rd and 4th Seikh Infantry, the 6th Punjab Native Infantry and the Guides Infantry. The expedition, under the command of Colonel D. Mocatta, advanced into Jowaki

country on 29 August and, separating into three columns, attacked and destroyed several villages and then withdrew, having lost one man killed and one officer and nine men wounded.

Unfortunately this attempt to subdue the Jowaki Afridis failed and once Colonel Mocatta's force had withdrawn they continued to make forays into the adjacent territory and attacked peaceful villages, destroyed them and murdered many of the inhabitants. This resulted in the reformation of the expeditionary force and on this occasion two columns were formed, both to move into the Jowaki territory. One column, under command of Brigadier-General C. P. Keyes, consisted of Nos 1 and 4 Mountain Batteries, the 29th (Bengal) Native Infantry, with detachments of No 2 Mountain Battery, 2nd Punjab Cavalry, the Guides Infantry, 1st and 3rd Seikh Infantry, 4th, 5th and 6th Punjab Native Infantry and the 5th Gurkha Regiment. The Peshawar column was under the command of Brigadier-General C. C. G. Ross, and had half of 1/C Battery RHA, No 4 Hazara Mountain Battery, 2 and 3 Companys of the Bengal Sappers and Miners, together with a detachment of No 4 Company; the 14th, 20th, 22nd and 27th Bengal Native Infantry, which were supported by three British Army battalions (9th and 51st Foot and 4th Battalion, The Rifle

Signalling with the heliograph – Jowaki 1877-1878.

Brigade). The force under Brigadier-General Keyes advanced into Jowaki territory on 9 November, moving in three columns, attacking and occupying Paiah and Kahto. On 12 November the enemy attacked the third column but were repulsed by a company of the 5th Punjab Native Infantry. The Field Force then concentrated at Paiah and were compelled to remain there for the next two weeks due to excessive rainfall. On 1 December an advance was made into the Jamu valley where enemy opposition was encountered but the Force then occupied Bagh. On 7 December the village of Ghariba was captured and destroyed. Meanwhile the Peshawar column had been delayed at Peshawar due to the incessant rain. On 4 December it was at last able to move out. The two passes leading to the Bori valley were occupied and a number of villages taken and destroyed. The destruction of tribal villages was one of the few measures that were open to the Indian authorities to bring some form of retribution to dissenting tribes. Unless the offenders were known and captured, the tribesmen, having made a stand against an expeditionary force, generally withdrew into the hills. When the Indian force withdrew from their territory the tribes came out of the hills to rebuild the village. It was then planned that the two columns would advance from the north and south and occupy the Pastaoni valley. The village was taken on 31 December by the Peshawar column under General Ross, and during the next three weeks the Indian troops moved through Jowaki territory without encountering too much opposition. On 23 and 24 January 1878 the Jowaki tribesmen sued for peace and the expeditionary force withdrew after what was a ten-week operation. During that time 11 sepoys had been killed and one officer and 50 men wounded. G.G.O. Nos 143 and 285 of 1880 authorised the award of the Indian General Service Medal together with the clasp 'Jowaki 1877-8' to the officers and men who took part in the operation.

It was during 1878 that two other minor expeditions were mounted to deal with refractory tribes but, because of the short duration, no medal award was made to the troops taking part. They were however purely Indian army operations with no British army support. The first of the two operations commenced in March 1878, when a small force consisting of the Hazara Mountain Battery, with the Corps of Guides Cavalry and Infantry, commanded by Major R. B. P. P. Campbell,[8] was ordered to deal with the Swati tribe of Ranizais who were at the village of Skakot. The troops marched out of Mardan, the Guides' 'home', on the evening of 13 March, reached the village at 2am and surrounded it before daybreak. The tribesmen, finding that resistance was almost impossible, surrendered. The troops established their 'presence' in the area and returned to Mardan.

During the building of the Swat Canal, tribesmen of the Utman Khels attacked a party of unarmed labourers and massacred many of the workers. A detachment 280-strong was despatched from the Corps of Guides' headquarters at Mardan, under the command of Captain Wynyard Battye, and advanced towards the village of Sapri. The detachment of Guides reached the objective in February and surprised the enemy. During the

attack the leader of the raiders was killed. The other Utman Khel villages refused to submit and it became necessary for a further force to be despatched to bring the tribes under control. The second force, which was also made up from the Corps of Guides, under the command of the Commandant, Lieutenant-Colonel F. N. Jenkins,[9] marched out of Mardan on 20 March and crossed into the Utman Khel territory on the following day. On this second occasion little opposition was encountered and the refractory villages submitted to the commander of the Guides and having achieved their objective they returned to Mardan the same evening.[10]

There were other clasps to the Indian General Service Medal, awarded for operations ranging from Sikkim, the Black Mountains and Burma during the period from the end of the Second Afghan War in 1880-95 but these actions will be dealt with in later chapters in chronological order. The next campaign in which troops of the Indian army were involved was the Egyptian campaign, where the Indian units served alongside units of the British army and for this service were awarded the Egyptian Medal (1882-89) and the appropriate clasps.

1   *Lieutenant William Alexander Holcombe* commissioned as Ensign 29 November 1867, promoted to Lieutenant on 17 February 1870. Served with the 6th Regiment of Foot in the Hazara Campaign of 1868 and in the operations in the Black Mountains.

2   *Captain John Butler* born 27 December 1842 at Burpetah, Kamroop, Lower Assam. Became an Ensign on 7 June 1861, promoted to Lieutenant 16 July 1862, and Captain 7 June 1873. He was appointed Personal Assistant to the Commissioner of Assam on 4 December 1868. He became Assistant Commissioner First Grade as Agent for the Naga Hills from 20 May 1873 and became Deputy Commissioner from 15 December 1874. The General report on Topographical Surveys 1874-75, and 75-76, p24 records: 'John Butler, Political Agent, was killed by a spear wound in the right breast whilst leading a survey party through the Naga Hills. Ambushed on 25 December 1875, near Pangtim 28 miles South east of Golghat resulting in Butler's death on 7 January 1876. He was buried at Gologhat Cemetery. Hodson Index, National Army Museum.'

3   Cardew, Lieutenant F. G. *A Sketch of the Services of the Bengal Native Army*, 1903, p327.

4   Ibid.

5   *Frontier and Overseas Expeditions from India*, Vol IV, North and North-Eastern Frontier Tribes, 1907, p213.

6   *Captain Richard Kirby Ridgeway*, Bengal Staff Corps, was commissioned 8 January 1868, promoted Lieutenant 14 February 1870, was awarded the Victoria Cross for the action at Konoma on 22 November 1879. The award was promulgated in *The London Gazette* dated 11 May 1880.

7   Gordon, Major L. L. *British Battles and Medals*, 1962, pp238-239. The clasp for the Naga Hills Expedition was authorised by G.G.O. No 344 of 1881.

8   *Major Robert Byng Patricia Price Campbell*, Corps of Guides. Commissioned 4 September 1855; Lieutenant 2 September 1857; Captain 4 September 1867; Major 4 October 1875. He continued to serve with the Corps of Guides during the Second Afghan War.

9   *Lieutenant-Colonel Francis Howell Jenkins*, Corps of Guides. Commissioned 20 December 1851; Lieutenant 15 November 1853; Captain 20 December 1863; Major 20 December 1871; Lieutenant-Colonel 20 December 1877, and commanded the Corps of Guides during the Second Afghan War (1878-1880).

10   Cardew, op cit, p326.

Lieutenant-Colonel C.R. Pennington, c1880.

Pipers of the 1st Sikh Regiment at Dakka, 1878.

Left:
Subadar-Major Jiwand Singh Bahadur, 45th Sikhs.

Below:
45th Rattray's Sikhs, c1897.

Following pages:
Left:
14th Sikhs.

Right:
36th Sikhs, c1897 (above).
3rd Sikh Regiment, 1897 (below).

CHAPTER SEVEN

The Egyptian Campaigns 1882 and 1885

The year 1882 saw the start of a series of campaigns in Egypt which brought Indian troops into contact with a number of British units with whom they had not previously served. The outbreak of hostilities in Egypt were as a result of tension which had been building up over a number of years and it was in 1875 that the Khedive sold his shares in the Suez Canal to the British Government, after which a state of financial chaos followed, during which time the Khedive gradually lost all authority. In 1881 the Egyptian Army mutinied for more pay but serious trouble was averted by the intervention of the British and French Ministers. In July of that year Sheik Mohammed Ahmed of Dongola proclaimed himself Mahdi, 'Guided by God', or 'The Directed One', and began to stir up trouble in the Sudan. In September 1881 the Egyptian Army, led by Ahmed Arabi Pasha, again revolted for more pay and as the situation deteriorated rioting broke out in Alexandria, where Arabs began attacking all Europeans. In May 1882 a combined British and French Naval Squadron arrived off the coast at Alexandria and, in a quest to bring about stability, the Allies demanded the resignation of Arabi Pasha, who had by this time been appointed Minister for War. The situation deteriorated when the Egyptians began arming the forts guarding the harbour and on 11 June 1882 a rebellion broke out which the Egyptian Government could not contain and as a result a number of civilians were killed. Following various demands from the British Admiral, which were ignored, the British Fleet opened fire on the morning of 11 July. In the meantime the French Fleet had withdrawn and took no further part in the action at Alexandria. During the following night the town was set on fire by the Egyptians who also freed all the prisoners in the gaols, allowing them to murder and plunder within the city. The next morning a white flag was flown over the city but when the British landing party arrived they found that the city had been abandoned by Arabi Pasha and the Egyptian army, which was by now under his control. By this time the Khedive had lost control of the situation and looked to the British to restore order and dismiss Arabi Pasha from his post.

It became obvious that an expeditionary force would be required to restore and maintain order and to bring the mutinous Egyptian army under control. The French now declined to assist in any way and it was therefore left to the British, who ordered a combined expeditionary force to be formed under the command of Lieutenant-General Sir Garnet

Colonel Frederick Knowles, 2nd Bengal Cavalry.

Wolseley. The British army provided units from various overseas stations as well as from the United Kingdom. Meanwhile, in India orders were issued and units began to assemble prior to embarkation to Egypt. The Indian Division of the Egyptian Expeditionary Force was under the command of Major-General Sir H. T. Macpherson VC, KCB and was made up of the following units that had been warned for active service on 6 July:

2nd Bengal Cavalry
6th Bengal Cavalry
13th Bengal Lancers
7th Bengal Native Infantry

20th Bengal (Punjab) Native Infantry

29th Bombay Native Infantry

A and I Companies, Madras Sappers and Miners.[1]

The Indian Division embarked with full supporting services from the Telegraph Train, Ordnance, Commissariat, Pay, Medical and Veterinary departments. In addition, the 4th and 31st Madras Native Infantry were despatched to Aden to be held as reserve units.[2]

The artillery unit for the division was the 7-1st Battery, Royal Artillery, who embarked with four 40-prs and two 6.3 howitzers and a total strength of 6 British officers, 112 British other ranks, 158 Indian other ranks, and 127 followers and 300 mules.

The Indian cavalry and infantry were to embark as near their field service strength of 550 and 832 respectively, as possible. They were not permitted to call for volunteers from other units, although the one exception was the 29th Bombay Native Infantry who were given a company of the 27th Bombay (Baluch) Native Infantry to bring them up to strength. Ambulance transport was also provided for the Division in three columns of 23 doolies and 74 dandies.[3] The Division was rationed from India and Aden and one month's rations were shipped when embarking, together with three months' supply of rations for land service.

In addition to the Indian units in the division, two British Army units who had been stationed in India and Aden were included; these were the 1st Battalion Manchester Regiment and the 1st Battalion Seaforth Highlanders stationed in Aden but reinforced from their 2nd Battalion which was stationed at Lucknow. The total number embarked for the expedition has been officially given as:

British Officers	221
British WOs, NCOs and men	1,778
Indian Army all ranks	5,323
Followers	7,315

In addition a figure of 104 was given for 'departmental subordinates'

Horses 1,896; Ponies 724; Mules 4,816

It had been planned to take mule transport but the Indian Government had been advised that there were plenty of camels for hire at Suez and a requisition was sent for 750 camels. However, when the division arrived at Suez only 13 camels were available for the force. The actual embarkation took place over the period 21 July to 12 September, all embarking from Bombay with the exception of the 20th and 29th Bombay Native Infantry who boarded at Karachi, and the 4th and 31st Madras Native Infantry who sailed from Madras for Aden. The division assembled at Ismailia on the Suez Canal and then part of the 13th Bengal Cavalry were despatched to Kassassin where they encountered the dis-affected Egyptian army which was repulsed; however, they lost one killed and one wounded. The troops who had arrived in Egypt were moved into position and the infantry were attached to the 2nd Division, and the cavalry became the Second Brigade of the Expeditionary Force's Cavalry Division.

After dusk on 12 September camp was struck and the troops moved to their pre-arranged positions by 1.30am on 13 September, and then advanced. At daybreak the infantry engaged the enemy and, after a short fierce action, carried the enemy entrenchments while the 2nd Cavalry Brigade moved round to the left of the enemy and were able to harass the retreat of the Egyptians. Pushing on to the railway station at Tel-el-Kebir, a train full of fugitives was captured. The Indian Infantry Brigade marched from Kassassin at 2.30am and, moving along the south side of the Freshwater Canal, engaged the enemy at about dawn and succeeded in taking their positions south of the canal. The main body of infantry halted at Tel-el-Kebir but the Indian Brigade continued their advance and reached Zag-a-zig at 6pm capturing ten railway engines and 100 carriages. The Indian contingent lost one man killed and three wounded during the day's action. On 14 September a large portion of the Egyptian army surrendered at Abbassieh, and that evening the British entered Cairo, occupied the citadel, and Arabi Pasha was imprisoned. Following the victory at Tel-el-Kebir, the Indian contingent remained as part of the garrison at Zag-a-zig

Officer of the Sikh Infantry.

29th Bombay Native Infantry, c1886.

and Abbassieh. Early in October the withdrawal of troops from Egypt commenced and by the end of October all the Indian units, which had formed the Indian Division, had returned to Bombay. For their services in the Egyptian campaign of 1882 the Egyptian Medal (1882-89) together with the Khedives Egyptian Star 1882, was awarded to all ranks and for those who took part in the battle of Tel-el-Kebir the clasp 'Tel-el-Kebir' was awarded with the Egyptian Medal. These awards were authorised by G.G.O. Nos 578 and 665 of 1882.

In the action at Tel-el-Kebir on 13 September 1882 the casualties of the 'Indian Contingent' were recorded as being one soldier killed and nine wounded.[4] During the whole operation the total casualty figures have been recorded as being:

Indian Officers   1 died of wounds; 1 died of fever
Indian Other ranks   4 killed, 6 died of fever; 15 wounded

Soon after the British had secured Cairo, the Khedive dissolved his army and appointed Sir Evelyn Wood VC as the commander of a new army, which was reformed with the help of seconded British Officers. In the meantime trouble was developing in the Sudan where thousands of men joined the Mahdi in what he regarded as a Holy War. After a number of clashes with the Egyptian army during 1882 and 1883, the Mahdi's army annihilated the Egyptian force under the command of Colonel William Hicks (known as Hicks Pasha) at Kashgil on 3-5 November 1883. In the following year, on 1 February, another Egyptian force, this time led by General Valentine Baker, was defeated by the Mahdi's army led by Osman Digna who, following the success, moved on to place the port of Suakin on the Red Sea under siege, but this was raised after a combined military and naval force defeated the enemy. Unfortunately the British Government decided to abandon the Sudan and left the area very much still in the control of the Mahdi and his followers. The situation continued to deteriorate and with the failure to relieve General Gordon and his small force at Khartoum and the murder of General Gordon on 26 January 1885, the British Government was forced to take action, if for no other reason than to quell the unrest at home over the news of the death of Gordon.

Early in 1885 the Indian Government was requested to form another expeditionary force to join the British Army in Egypt and Suakin. Prior to this request being received, the Government in India had issued instructions to change the titles of all regiments in the three armies, so that from 1 January 1885 the word 'Native' would be removed from regimental titles. Therefore regiments would in future be known as 'Bengal Infantry' etc. The G.G.O. was issued on 14 February 1885 appointing Major-General J. Hudson as the commander of the Indian expeditionary force and the following units were placed under his command and embarked from India on the dates shown:

15th Bengal Infantry (Loodianah Sikhs)	– 22 February
9th Bengal Cavalry (equipped as lancers)	– 23 and 27 February
17th Bengal Infantry	– 24 February
28th Bombay Infantry	– 28 February and – 1 March
1 Company, 2 Queen's Own Sappers & Miners	– 2 March

A special scale of pay was authorised for Indian other ranks taking part in the expeditionary force and the Indian Government was also responsible for the supply of grain and fodder for the Indian contingent. The force was destined to act as part of the garrison at Suakin and by 14 March the whole Indian contingent had landed.

Initially the Indian army units were employed in defence work but during this time they were subjected to continual night attacks during which a number of sentries were killed or wounded. On 19 March a combined British and Indian force moved out through difficult country covered with bush which enabled the enemy to hide and fire on the troops as they advanced. No major action took place on that day but on the following day the enemy were engaged and during the action in the bush-covered terrain the 9th Bengal Cavalry lost Ressaidar Shibdeo Singh and 11 men killed and 15 wounded. The force withdrew to Suakin the same evening. On Sunday, 22 March, the Indian contingent infantry moved out from Suakin together with the 9th Bengal Cavalry and a number of British Army units to a position some eight miles south-west of the port. The force under the command of Major-General Sir J. C. M'Neill had,

Soldier of the Bombay Infantry.

due to the difficult terrain, only covered six miles in four hours when it was decided that a halt should be made at a place called Tofrek. At 2.40pm, when the sappers and men of the Berkshire Regiment were cutting down the thick bush around the position, a large force of Arabs suddenly attacked. The unfinished defences were manned in the west by the 15th Bengal Infantry (Sikhs), in the south by the 17th Bengal Infantry and in the north by the 28th Bombay Infantry. However the main attack came from the south-west and the suddenness of the onslaught, together with the confusion as the Indian cavalry returned from scouting, enabled the enemy to break through the defence and a considerable number reached the centre of the position. The 17th Bengal Infantry lost a number of its men and followers, and as the enemy had reached the baggage animals there was considerable difficulty in restoring the position. The 15th Bengal Infantry held the position on the west despite a sustained effort to break the line by the enemy and 'by their steadiness and gallantry did much towards preserving the whole force from disaster'.[5] By 3.30pm the enemy withdrew, having suffered many casualties, and the combined British and Indian force completed their work on the defence position and, leaving the 15th and 17th Bengal Infantry to man it, the remainder of the men returned to Suakin. The Indian contingent lost one officer[6] and 29 men killed, and one officer and 45 men wounded.

Throughout March the troops at Suakin were employed on escort duties to the various positions in the surrounding countryside and, apart from the occasional long range shoot, no actual fighting took place. On 31 March a cavalry patrol reported that a strong enemy force was at Tamai, and two days later a Field Force set out from Suakin which included a large part of the Indian contingent. On 3 April the column reached Tamai and, finding the village deserted, burned all the huts. During this operation the enemy kept up skirmishing fire from the bush. The column returned to Suakin the following day without any major incident. The next major move in the campaign was on 2 May, when Lord Wolseley arrived at Suakin and made preparations for a major sortie out of the port. A two-pronged attack was then made on the strong enemy position at Thakul, some 18 miles west of Suakin. The Suakin Column included the 9th Bengal Cavalry, and the second column moving from Otao included the 15th Bengal Infantry. The enemy were taken by surprise and were driven from their camp, which the combined British and Indian force then destroyed. The active operations in the Suakin area then drew to a close and the Indian force moved back to India, with the exception of one Squadron of the 9th Bengal Cavalry and the 15th and 17th Bengal Infantry which were retained in Suakin as garrison troops until November.

The Egyptian Medal 1882, with the clasp 'Suakin 1885' was awarded to troops who took part in the campaign between 26 March 1884 and 14 May 1885, and those officers and men who took part in the battle of Tofrek on 22 March 1885 were also awarded the clasp 'Tofrek' under the authority of G.G.O. No 655 of 1885. In addition, all the troops who were employed at Suakin were awarded the Khedive's bronze star.[7]

The Egyptian Medal

Obverse – The diademed head of Queen Victoria and the legend 'VICTORIA REGINA ET IMPERATRIX'.

Reverse – The Sphinx on a pedestal with the word 'EGYPT' above. In the exergue is the date '1882' for those who were awarded the medal for the first campaign of that year. Later issues have a plain exergue.

Size – 36mm diameter.

Ribbon – 32mm wide with three bright blue and two white stripes of equal width.

Khedive's Egyptian Star (1882-91)

Obverse – In the centre is the Sphinx with three pyramids behind. Around is a raised circle on which is embossed the word 'EGYPT' followed by the date or dates.

Reverse – The Khedive's monogram 'T.M.' within a raised circle.

Size – The maximum width of the star is 48mm.

Ribbon – 39mm wide. Plain dark blue.[8]

Egypt Medal (left).
Khedive's Egyptian Star.

The Indian contingent which had been sent to take part in the operations in and around Suakin had proved to be efficient and well-disciplined, and the final despatch written by Lord Wolseley, dated 15 June, recorded his appreciation of their work as follows. 'The Indian contingent, under Brigadier-General Hudson CB, showed high soldier-like qualities, and was of the utmost value in the operations round Suakin.' Sir Gerald Graham, in his despatch of 30 May, commented, 'The 15th Sikhs on several occasions displayed their splendid marching powers . . . the force was composed of the British troops of Her Majesty, and of the native soldiers of her Army in India . . . but though the troops were drawn from so many different sources all were animated and bound together by a firm determination to preserve untarnished the reputation of the British Army.'[9]

1   *Frontier and Overseas Expeditions from India*, Vol VI, Expeditions Overseas, 1911, pp47-51. The Embarkation return for the Egypt Expeditionary Force, 1882.

2   *Frontier and Overseas Expeditions from India*, op cit, p26.

3   *Dhooly, Doolie* – a covered litter – consisting of a cot, suspended by the four corners from a bamboo pole and carried by two or four men. *Dandy, Dandi* – a kind of a vehicle used in the Himalayas consisting of a strong cloth slung like a hammock to a bamboo staff, and carried by two (or more) men. The Traveller can either sit sideways, or lie on his back. (Yule, Colonel H, & Burnell A. C. *Hobson-Jobson*, 1903, pp296 & 313)

4   Maurice, Colonel J. F. *Military History of The Campaign of 1882 in Egypt*, 1887, p198.

5   Cardew, Lieutenant F. G. *A sketch of the Services of the Bengal Native Army*, 1903, p383.

6   *Von Beverhoudt, Major James Mandeville Wood*. Commissioned as a Second Lieutenant 8 March 1864 in the 90th Foot. Promoted Lieutenant on 28 September 1869. He transferred to the Bengal Staff Corps and was promoted Captain 8 March 1876. He served with the 17th Bengal Native Infantry and was promoted to Major on 8 March 1884. (Hodson Index, National Army Museum)

7   Cardew, op cit, p384.

8   Gordon, Major Lawrence L. *British Battles and Medals*, 1962, p218-28.

9   *Frontier and Overseas Expeditions from India*, op cit, p64.

CHAPTER EIGHT

The Burma Campaigns

By the mid-1880s the Indian Army had gained considerable experience in action, having been involved in the war in Afghanistan, the continuing frontier wars on the North West and North East frontiers, and in overseas operations. The Indian Army had gained a reputation for being well disciplined and an effective fighting force under differing conditions with its participation in the conflict in Egypt in the west, and under difficult conditions in the Malayan jungle in the east during the Perak War. Individual members of the army had, during these various actions, acted with courage and in many instances had been awarded for their gallantry, but by the outbreak of the Third Burmese War in 1885 no Indian officer or soldier had been awarded the coveted Victoria Cross. The Indian army was made up of many martial races, covering the whole of the subcontinent, with men being recruited from the Pathans in the north to Tamils in southern India, all of which made recruiting and the composition of regiments difficult. However by the late 19th century the problem was gradually resolved and recruiting was, generally, restricted to the groups as shown:

Pathans from the North West Frontier district and the tribal territories;
Baluchis and Brahuis from Kelat and British Baluchistan;
Sikhs, Jats, Dogras, and Muslims from the Punjab;
Garhwalis, Kumaonis and Gurkhas from the Himalayan area;
Rajputs, Brahmans, and Muslims from the Delhi and Hindustan areas;
Rajputs, Jats, Mers and Muslims from Rajasthan and central India;
Marathas and Deccani Muslims from western India;
Christians, Muslims, Tamils and Untouchables from the Southern area of India.[1]

The Third Burmese War was brought about by the violations of the Treaties between Britain and Burma which were virtually ignored by King Thebaw, who acceded to the throne in 1879. There were many acts of aggression on the frontier and instances of 'outrage and injustice' to British traders. In addition to his obvious anti-British attitude, the King began secret negotiations with France concerning the rights in Upper Burma. In 1885 the King arbitrarily imposed a ruinous fine on a British trading company which they were obviously unable to pay. The Burmese refused to take the matter to an impartial enquiry and when an ultimatum was sent to the Court of Mandalay it was met with an evasive reply and open hostility. It then became obvious that war between Britain and Burma was inevitable and orders were issued on 30 October 1885 for the despatch of a field force to Burma as soon as possible.[2]

The Field Force was placed under the command of Major-General H. N. D. Prendergast CB, VC and was made up of six batteries of artillery; six companies of sappers and miners; seven regiments of Indian infantry, together with three British Army Regiments and a Naval Brigade. The Indian army element was made up of the following units:

> No 4 Mountain Battery, Punjab Frontier Force
> No 1 Bombay Mountain Battery
> Nos 4 and 5 Companies Bengal Sappers and Miners
> B, D and H Companies, Madras Sappers and Miners
> No 2 Company, Bombay Sappers and Miners
> 1st Madras Pioneers

The infantry were brigaded as follows:

1st Brigade (Brigadier-General H. H. Foord)
21st and 25th Madras Infantry
2nd Battalion, King's Liverpool Regiment
2nd Brigade (Brigadier-General G. S. White, CB VC)
12th and 23rd Madras Infantry
2nd Battalion, Hampshire Regiment
3rd Brigade (Brigadier-General F. B. Norman CB)
2nd (Queen's Own) and 11th Bengal Infantry
1st Battalion, Royal Welsh Fusiliers

The Chief Commissioner of Burma in reply to a request for river transport, which was the only means of advancing the 300 miles to Mandalay from the coast, sent the following telegram:

For the despatch of troops up the river, partly from Rangoon, and partly from Prome Terminus, to frontier, and thence onward, we can hire ample steamers and flats (of the Irrawaddy Flotilla Company) at rates of existing contract; their rates are high, but cannot be changed now.[3]

The whole force arrived at Rangoon between 5 and 11 November and moved up-river in a fleet of steamers and flats provided by the Irrawaddy Flotilla Company to Thyetmyo and then the advance was made into hostile territory on 14 November. A number of small towns were occupied without resistance although it was expected that the Burman forces

Soldier of the 25th Madras Infantry.

(11th Bengal Infantry) and three men were killed, and four officers and 23 soldiers wounded. Two Italians, who had been employed to train the Burmese Army, surrendered to the Field Force and the advance continued without encountering any great opposition. Pagan was evacuated by the enemy, Ava and Sagain fell on 27 November without any resistance at all, and on the following day the force reached Mandalay. On landing, the town and palace were occupied and King Thebaw made a prisoner. On 29 November he was 'sent down river under escort' and later was deported to India. News reached Major-General Prendergast that the Chinese were massing on the frontier with the intention of taking advantage of the situation in Burma to seize the town of Bhamo. A small party set off for the frontier on 18 December, proceeded up the Irrawaddy and occupied Bhamo on 28 December without any opposition.

The campaign was a difficult one as movement generally had to be made by river, which was easily defensible and ideal for sniping and ambushes. When the troops were 'on land' the paths were narrow and ideal for ambush and, had the Burmese put up a more determined resistance, the combined British and Indian force would have had a far higher casualty figure. All members of the expeditionary force suffered greatly from heat-apoplexy and malaria. The high temperature and humidity took its toll, and equipment, and even the men's boots, were subject to deterioration and fell to pieces in the excessive heat.

With the end of the campaign to take control from King Thebaw, the British Government then proceeded to annex Upper Burma and although there was no major action, the occupation force, which is what the Field Force had become, was troubled by skirmishes and attacks from dacoits.

It was unfortunate that when the Burmese army was disbanded the soldiers were permitted to disperse all over the country, many still armed, and to add to the ever growing problem, a number of pretenders to the throne appeared and local leaders incited their people to rebel against the British occupation. It soon became evident that the occupation army was inadequate and that reinforcements were required to keep control of the situation.

Accordingly the following reinforcements were despatched from India:

> 7th Bengal Cavalry
> 26th Bengal Infantry
> 27th Bengal Infantry
> 43rd Bengal Infantry

Major-General Prendergast handed over command to Brigadier-General G. S. White CB, VC on 1 April 1886 who was given the local rank of Major-General.[5]

Throughout the summer of 1886 with attacks from bands of dacoits and insurgents in all districts, the army was kept fully occupied. In the area of Pagan, Myingyan and Meiktila, the 11th Bengal Infantry were continually engaged not only repulsing attacks, but in manning the numerous posts that had been established, hopefully to keep control of the area. During one such attack Lieutenant Forbes of the 11th Bengal Infantry[6] was

would make a determined defence at the forts of Gwe-gyaung-Kampo and Minhla which, being on opposite banks of the river, provided an effective block on the river. A simultaneous attack was made on the two forts on the morning of 17 November and although Gwe-gyaung-Kampo was the stronger fortification, the defenders put up only a token resistance. The fort on the opposite side was defended stubbornly and when the Indian troops advanced from their landing point at Malun, some four miles from Minhla, they came under fire from the enemy who were hiding in thick jungle. The 2nd (Queen's Own) and 11th Bengal Infantry advanced rapidly and stormed the stockade of the village adjacent to the fort which then remained to be taken. The two Bengal units split and, making an encircling move whilst under fire from the fort and the jungle, finally rushed the defences. It was during this final attack that Lieutenant Wilkinson[4] (12th Madras Infantry) who had joined the 11th Bengal Infantry, fell and was immediately attacked by some of the Burman defenders. Although severely wounded, his life was saved by the determined advance of the men of the 11th Bengal Infantry. The fort of Minhla was taken, but Lieutenant Dury

13th (Duke of Connaught's) Lancers.   Scouting.

Opposite page:
Top left: Officer of the 7th Bombay Lancers,
1897.
Top centre: Officer of the 4th Bengal Cavalry,
1897.
Top right: Officer of the 7th Bengal Cavalry,
1897.
Below: 3rd Madras Light Cavalry, Review
Order, 1891.

Top: Corps of Guides, Cavalry and Infantry.
Right: Colour of the 24th Regiment Madras
Native Infantry.

Left: 14th (Ferozepore Sikh) Regiment of Bengal Infantry.
Below left: Troops engaged in the Indian Frontier 'Rising'.
Below right: 45th (Rattray's Sikh) Bengal Native Infantry.

Right: 1st Bengal Cavalry, Review Order, 1891.
Below: The Madras Army and Troops under the Government of India.

Above: 29th Bombay Native Infantry (Duke of Connaught's Own) Belooch Regiment, 1890.
Right top: Types of the Bombay Army.
Right below: Types of the Bengal Army.

10th Bengal Lancers, Field Service Kit, 1890.

General White and staff – Burma campaign.

killed and seven sepoys wounded whilst on convoy duty on 21 April. Operations continued in the Bhamo district and the 26th Bengal Infantry and the Hazara Mountain Battery were involved in action at Katran, which they captured after stiff resistance although this small force had nine men wounded during the attack. Due to the lack of supplies, they had to retire but another small force returned to the area and secured Katran without further opposition. During the summer, detachments of the 4th, 42nd and 44th Bengal Infantry moved from Manipur and secured Tammu in the Kubo Valley after some resistance and, eventually, during the autumn the enemy were driven from the Kubo Valley.

In the meantime Salin, a large walled town six miles from the Irrawaddy and about 40 miles north of Minbu, was the focal point of many disturbances and in June 1886 the town was threatened by a large number of dacoits. The area was under the control of the 2nd (Queen's Own) Bengal Infantry and on 12 June, whilst dealing with an attack outside the city walls, one of its officers, Captain Dunsford, was killed.[7] Six weeks later, the dacoits besieged the town which was defended by the small garrison which, fortunately, was able to hold out until relieved on 31 July, by which time all the ammunition had been used and food supplies were almost exhausted. In the western part of the District the Deputy Commissioner, Mr R. Phayre, was attacked and killed at Padaing on 8 June. A small force under the command of Major J. A. D. Gordon, 2nd (Queen's Own) Bengal Infantry, advanced into the area and captured Ngape, a large village at the foot of Aeng Pass, on 19 June with the loss of six men killed and 25 wounded. Unfortunately the climate of Ngape was so unhealthy at that time of the year that the small garrison had to retire from the village on 1 August.

At the end of the summer it became necessary to send further reinforcements which included 18th Bengal Infantry, 3rd Gurkha Regiment and the 5th and 12th Bengal Infantry.[8] In addition, a number of cavalry units were brought into the force and these included the 1st Madras Lancers, who arrived at Rangoon over the period 22-27 September 1886; 3rd Hyderabad Contingent Cavalry, who arrived during the period 4-9 October; also the 1st Bombay Lancers who reached Rangoon on 1 and 2 October 1886.[9] The field force was divided into six brigades and one independent command, with the whole being placed under the command of Sir Herbert Macpherson, Commander-in-

Chief of Madras. Unfortunately, before he could put his plans into operation, Sir Herbert Macpherson died of fever on 26 October 1886 near Prome. As a result of this sudden loss to the field force the Government of India requested that General Sir Frederick Roberts VC, then Commander-in-Chief in India, be given command of the force in Burma and, on assuming command, he transferred his headquarters to Burma.

Over the following year a number of actions took place which, by the end of April 1887, saw the end of the campaign to bring Burma under control. A number of these actions are worthy of mention, although the whole campaign is fully documented in the book *Frontier and Overseas Expeditions from India*, Volume V (Burma), which was published in Simla in 1907.

A column was despatched from Mandalay during October to bring order in the hill area east of the town. After some minor skirmishing, during which time one soldier was killed and three wounded, the column continued to scour the hills looking for insurgents and dacoits. On 20 November Captain Pulley with a detachment of the 3rd Gurkha Regiment, marched from Lamaing and on 25 October attacked and secured a strongly defended position at Zibyubin, during which time he and six men were wounded. Also in the First Brigade area the 7th Bengal Cavalry continued to pursue the dacoit leader Hla-u during the month of December. In March 1887 a mixed column, which included part of the 27th Bengal Infantry, succeeded in attacking and capturing the enemy stockade at Hmawaing.

The Second Brigade, which included detachments of the 7th Bengal Cavalry, and details of the 1st, 12th and 26th Bengal Infantry, secured Wuntho and the inhabitants were disarmed.

There was considerable activity in the Third Brigade area and in January a column, which included detachments from the Hampshire Regiment and the 3rd Gurkha Regiment from the 1st Brigade, marched on the Shan States and brought that area under control although there was little opposition to this combined force.

Hmawaing, which was in the Fourth Brigade area, was attacked by a mixed force which included a detachment of the 27th Bengal Infantry, who after several days of jungle fighting, stormed the village, took possession of it and destroyed the place. The force then withdrew but this decisive action made a good impression on the local inhabitants who saw that the British were determined to bring stability to Burma.

The Fifth Brigade were engaged in successful operations in the area of the Ruby Mines and although some skirmishing took place, no real resistance was encountered.

Two dacoit leaders, Boh Shwe and Oktama, were the main objects of the operations in the Sixth Brigade area. A strong column advanced from Minbu under the leadership of Brigadier-General Low which consisted of detachments of artillery, 1st Madras Lancers, 1st Battalion The Rifle Brigade, the 2nd Bengal Infantry and the 3rd Hyderabad Infantry. Little opposition was encountered until the force reached Paeng, at the foot of the Arakan range, and during the skirmish at that place the force lost one man killed and seven wounded.

Moveable columns were formed and the country patrolled, although there were very few encounters with the enemy.

Meanwhile, on the Chindwin River the dacoits still remained a problem and during October 1886 there were a number of actions which resulted in a few casualties. On 28 October the Assistant Commissioner of the District, Mr Gleeson, was attacked at Yu and his escort of 20 men of the 18th Bengal Infantry put up a determined defence and, although Mr Gleeson

Mountain Mule Battery at Drill for the Burma campaign.

was killed, they eventually beat off the attackers and brought Mr Gleeson's body back to Tandwin. The small party of 20 lost one man killed and five were wounded.[10] Once again the steadiness under fire showed that the men of the Indian army were a well trained and disciplined force.

With the main conflict now considered to be at an end, General Sir Frederick Roberts handed over command of the Burma Field Force to Major-General Sir George White CB, VC

and on 1 April the whole force was reduced, with the result that the Brigades were reduced from six to four. Fifth Brigade was amalgamated with the Second, and the Sixth Brigade with the Fourth. During the autumn of 1887 and spring of 1888 detachments of the 7th Bengal Cavalry, together with the 1st, 5th, 10th and 33rd Bengal Infantry, were frequently engaged in conflict with bands of roving dacoits. Other units, including No 1 Mountain Battery and the 12th Bengal Infantry, were employed in operations against the Kachins and although these services were difficult and some losses occurred, there were no other actions of note and a decision was made, at command level, to reorganise the Burma force.

The redistributed force, under Major-General Sir George White, was allocated to districts as follows with the Headquarters being at Mandalay, Myingyan and Meiktila:

1st Brigade
No 1 Bengal Mountain Battery, and half 42nd Bengal Infantry
2nd Brigade
Half 10th Bengal Infantry and 33rd Bengal Infantry
Bhamo Command
No 2 Bengal Mountain Battery
12th Bengal Infantry
Ruby Mines Command
Half 42nd Bengal Infantry
Chindwin Command
Half 10th Bengal Infantry

Later in the year, the Burma Force was reinforced by the 17th and 44th Bengal Infantry.[11]

Officers and men of the Indian Army were awarded the *Indian General Service Medal*, with the clasp 'Burma 1885-7' for service between 14 November 1885 to 30 April 1887, which was

authorised by G.G.O 434 of 1887. For the Campaign of 1885-87 a bronze medal was issued to non-combatants and this practice continued up to, and including, the award of the clasp 'North West Frontier 1908'. Bronze editions of the medal ceased with the accession of King George V.[12]

Although the major campaign was at an end, the Burma Force continued to be involved in minor incidents during the remainder of 1887 and into 1888. Generally the country was peaceful and the occupation was satisfactory except in the frontier area, where the tribes began to encroach on the Burmese who had settled into a peaceful existence under British rule. It became necessary to mount an operation to bring the various hostile tribes under control and a plan was drawn up for operations in the Chin, Mogoung, Eastern Karenni, Ruby Mines and Bhamo districts.

The most important of these operations was against the tribes in the Chin Hills, who throughout the summer of 1888 carried out attacks on peaceful villages etc. Two columns were sent into the Chin Hills and moved to Tokhlaing (which was afterwards named Fort White), after numerous posts manned by the Bengal regiments had been attacked. The force moved out and on 5 February 1889 attacked the enemy at that location and, having secured the position, set up headquarters. A small force of 75 of the 42nd Bengal Infantry and 100 men of the 44th Bengal Infantry, supported by two guns, moved against the

3rd Bengal Cavalry, c1885.

1st Bengal Cavalry, c1885.

Kanhau Chins. Between 8 and 22 March the Indian troops inflicted severe casualties on the Chin tribesmen and destroyed their villages. On 4 May a detachment, including men of the 42nd Bengal Infantry, moved against the village of Tartan which was strongly defended. The attack on the enemy stockades was fiercely resisted to such a degree that the combined British and Indian Force had to retire with the loss of one officer and three men killed. This was the only occasion on which the enemy were able to defeat the British. During the whole of the operations in the Chin Hills the loss to the Bengal Force was nine men killed and 27 wounded.[13]

In the meantime, in January 1889 another expedition was mounted by the Burma Force against the Lepei Kachins and the only contribution made by the Indian Force for this operation was the provision of two guns from No 2 Bengal Mountain Battery in support of a detachment of the 1st Battalion, Hampshire Regiment. The operation was successful, as was a similar small expedition mounted against the Eastern Karenni, and in this action the Indian army participation was to provide two guns from the No 1 Bengal Mountain Battery. The total casualties for the two operations were six killed and 35 wounded, of which six were British Officers; one of these was

Lieutenant William Carmichael Hawker of the Hampshire Regiment.

In the Ruby Mines area an uprising took place in January 1889 when a body of some 800 rebels threatened the town of Momeit. A number of skirmishes took place during which another officer of the Hampshire Regiment, Lieutenant Walter Thomas Henry Nugent, was killed. During this time various parties were sent out to deal with bodies of rebels and although the composition of such parties was generally British infantry, the support came from the artillery units of the Indian Army. In February 1889 a small force made up of two guns of the No 2 Bengal Mountain Battery, and 150 men of the 17th Bengal Infantry, with a detachment of the Hampshire Regiment, set out from Bhamo against a body of rebels in the Sinkan valley. The enemy had taken up a position at Malin and were only defeated after a sharp engagement on 7 February, during which time Second Lieutenant George Robert Douglas Stoddart of the Suffolk Regiment and two men of the 17th Bengal Infantry were killed, and ten men were wounded. In the following month a detachment of the 17th Bengal Infantry attacked and defeated parties of the enemy in the Mansi area without any loss. During April 1889 the Indian troops continued to be involved in action and a force despatched from Bhamo, consisting of 150 men of the 17th Bengal Infantry and 100 men of the 42nd Bengal

Infantry, together with four guns of No 2 Bengal Mountain Battery, successfully completed the task that they had been set. During the same month the force in Burma was again reorganised so as to meet the changed circumstances and the command was then given to Major-General B. L. Gordon.

Upper Burma was divided into two districts which were Mandalay and Myingyan. Mandalay district included Bhamo, Ruby Mines and Shwebo and was controlled by Nos 1 and 2 Bengal Mountain Batteries and the 17th Bengal Infantry. The Myingyan District included the Chin Field Force which was made up of the 10th, 33rd and 42nd Bengal Infantry.

Under the authority of G.G.O. No 31 of 1890 the award of the Indian General Service Medal, with the clasp 'Burma 1887-89', was made to all officers and men who served in Burma up to 31 March 1889. Those who had previously qualified for the medal and the clasp were granted the additional clasp for their service.[14]

During the cold weather of 1888-89 an expeditionary force was mounted and despatched into the Lushai territory with the object of punishing the tribes for raids carried out by them, which included the murder of a British officer carrying out surveying duties. The force was under the command of Colonel V. Tregear, and included detachments of 250 men from the 2nd and 9th Bengal Infantry and a wing of the 42nd (Goorkha Light Infantry). They assembled at Demagiri in February and during the following month the Shendu country was visited when the village of Howsata was destroyed as a reprisal for the villagers' involvement in the murder of the officer on surveying duties. The force was unopposed but the expedition was an extremely arduous one due to the nature of the country through which they had to pass, which was largely trackless jungle. They withdrew from the Lushai territory in April 1889. In the meantime another expedition was mounted under the command of Brigadier-General W. P. Symons, which was given the title the Burma Column. This Column was divided into three sections:

Northern Column – A wing of 10th Bengal Infantry; a detachment of the 38th Bengal Infantry and a wing of the 42nd (Goorkha Light Infantry).

Southern Column – No 1 Bengal Mountain Battery, and a wing of the 2nd 4th Goorkha Regiment.

Other units in the force included Nos 5 and 6 Companies Madras Sappers and Miners, 2nd Madras Infantry together with the 1st The King's Own Scottish Borderers, and detachments of the Norfolk Regiment and the Cheshire Regiment, some of which made up the third column as garrison and line of communication troops.

The Northern Column advanced in November and established posts along the Burmese frontier to guard against raids from the Chin tribesmen. During these operations the force met with considerable opposition from the Kanhau and Siyin Chins and in the encounters the column received a number of casualties. The Southern Column which advanced towards Haka encountered such difficult jungle terrain that it took 66 days to reach its objective instead of the anticipated 12 days. Little opposition was encountered from the Chins but the troops suffered very severely from malarial fever.

The two operations continued until 30 April 1890, when the whole Chin Lushai operations came to an end and the field force was disbanded. Those who took part in these operations were awarded either the Indian General Service medal, with the clasp 'Chin Lushai 1889-90' or, if they were already in possession of the medal, they were just awarded the clasp. The issue was authorised by G.G.O. No 275 of 1891 which granted the award for service during the period 15 November 1889 to 30 April 1890.

During the various operations in Burma in 1889 two Surgeons were awarded the Victoria Cross for their gallantry. Surgeon J. Crimmin of the Bombay Medical Services was awarded the Cross for his gallantry at Nga Kyaing, during the capture of Sawlon on 1 January 1889. His award was published in *The London Gazette* of 17 September 1889.[15] Surgeon F. S. Le Quesne of the British Medical Staff won his award for his actions with the Chin Field Force on 4 May 1889 and his award was promulgated in *The London Gazette* of 29 October 1889.[16]

1 Heathcote, T. A. *The Indian Army, The Garrisons of British Imperial India 1822-1922*, London 1974, p94.
2 Cardew, Lieut F. G. *A Sketch of the Service of the Bengal Native Army*, 1903, p385.
3 *Frontier and Overseas Expeditions from India*, Volume V, Burma, Simla, 1907, p137.
4 *Wilkinson, Lieutenant Henry Thomas Diedrick*, commissioned as Second Lieutenant 22 January 1881, promoted to Lieutenant 1 July 1881. He served in the Essex Regiment and at the time of his death was serving on probation with the 12th Madras Infantry.
5 Cardew, op cit, p387.
6 *Forbes, Lieutenant William Greenlaw*, commissioned into the South Staffordshire Regiment as a Lieutenant from 10 May 1882, was serving with the 11th Bengal Infantry at the time of his death.
7 *Dunsford, Captain William George*, commissioned into the 108th Foot as a Second Lieutenant on 28 October 1871, promoted to Lieutenant 28 October 1871, and serving with the 2nd Regiment Bengal Native Infantry at the time of death.
8 Cardew, op cit, p389.
9 *Frontier and Overseas Expeditions from India*, Vol V, p242.
10 Cardew, op cit, p391.
11 Cardew, op cit, p392.
12 Gordon, Major Lawrence L. *British Battles and Medals*, 1962, p239-40.
13 Cardew, op cit, p398.
14 Cardew, op cit, p400.
15 Smyth, Brigadier Sir John *The Story of the Victoria Cross, 1856-1963*, p127, and *The London Gazette* dated 17 September 1889.
16 Smyth, op cit, p127, and *The London Gazette* dated 29 October 1889.

CHAPTER NINE

The Frontier Campaigns of 1888–95

The reputation of the Indian Army continued to be enhanced by the conduct of its units in both major and minor conflicts, during which time many of its members were awarded the Indian Order of Merit, Military Division. During the second and third decade of its existence the Indian Army was subjected to a number of changes in its organisation, some of which were welcomed. One such change was the cessation of the secondment system whereby officers were loaned to the Civil authorities to serve as deputy commissioners of districts, magistrates etc. In 1876 military officers were no longer accepted for civil posts in Bengal, the Central and North West Provinces and Oudh. Other areas followed this principle although not immediately, with the Scinde in 1885, the Punjab in 1903; but this was not effective in Assam until 1907. Because of the unusual nature of the conditions in the North West Frontier Province military officers continued to be used to fill civil posts in the still dangerous tribal areas. The advantage of reducing the number of officers on loan to the civil authorities meant that regiments were no longer having to function with an under-manning of British Officers due to long furlough and seconded service. An

Colonel H.W. Webster and British officers of the 30th Punjab Infantry, 1887.

British and Indian officers of the 29th Punjab Infantry at Paloosi, on the right bank of the Indus, c1888.   AMOT

examination of the service of Majors serving in the Bengal Army in 1874 shows that of the 176 officers on establishment, 73 were serving with the civil authorities, on headquarters staffs, or had been loaned to such organisations as the Revenue Survey Department, or as Fort Adjutants, or Station Staff Officers. Forty-nine were on long furlough, thus leaving only 54, or approximately one-third, actually on regimental duty. With more regimental officers serving continuously with their parent regiment, the relationship between the officers and soldiers improved and this, in turn, was reflected in the efficiency of the regiment.

The period under review also brought changes to the total establishments of the three armies when, in 1882, a reduction of the number of regiments was ordered. The regiments affected by this economy were:

16th and 17th Bengal Cavalry	These two cavalry units had not been converted to 'Lancer' regiments.
3rd Scinde Horse 34th, 35th, 36th, 37th and 41st Bengal Native Infantry	The junior cavalry regiment. The question as to why these units were selected for disbandment has been the subject of speculation, but it would seem probable that they were fairly junior regiments and stationed in peaceful stations in the plains. Other higher numbered regiments were Gurkha units, and the 45th was a Sikh regiment. (neither units had acquired battle (honours.
4th Punjab Cavalry 3rd Punjab Infantry 34th to 41st Madras Native Infantry 6th, 11th, 15th and 18th Bombay Native Infantry	The eight junior regiments. The reason for the selection of these 'old faithful' regiments was given as being that none had been engaged in any campaign since the Second Maratha War.[1]

Quarters of Colonel Pratt CB at Paloosi, 1888. AMOT

In the autumn of 1885 the 16th and 17th Bengal Cavalry were reformed and at that time the strengths of the regiments of Bengal Cavalry were increased by adding a fourth squadron. In the following year, second battalions were added to the 1st, 2nd, 4th and 5th Goorkha regiments, and two Mountain batteries were raised. In 1887, five new battalions of Bengal Infantry were raised, two of which were Sikhs and one of Dogras, and these took the place of the disbanded 34th, 35th, 36th and 37th Bengal Infantry units whilst the fifth, Garhwalis, became the 2nd Battalion of the 3rd Goorkha Regiment. At the same time an additional squadron of Guides Cavalry was formed. At the time that the two Bengal Cavalry units were reformed, the Bombay Army was increased by one cavalry regiment which was given the title the 7th Bombay Cavalry; this unit filled the gap left by the previous disbandment of the 3rd Scinde Horse. At the same time the Poona Horse, and the 1st and 2nd Scinde Cavalry were renumbered 4th, 5th and 6th Bombay Cavalry.[2]

Following the reductions in 1882 in the Madras Army, the next regimental change took place in the following year 1883, when on 13 June the 1st and 4th regiments were made Pioneer Corps and were given the title of 1st Madras Native Infantry (Pioneers) and 4th Madras Native Infantry (Pioneers). It was just prior to this change, on 17 May 1883, that the Madras Army relinquished the old type of dress and adopted a new pattern of clothing which included the issue of:

> 1 serge zoave jacket
> 1 serge knickerbockers
> 1 pair of khakee (*sic*) gaiters
> 1 khakee blouse
> 1 khakee knickerbockers and gaiters
> 1 khakee turband with band of the colour of the regimental facings, and a fringe of the same colour as the turband.[3]

Although the campaign in Burma was continuing, the Indian Army had to deploy troops to deal with other problems. At the close of 1887 the Sikkim Rajah infringed the treaty of 1861 when he established a force of Tibetans at the fort of Lingtu, and this was seen as a threat to peace and a small force was organised to

13 Mountain Battery.

deal with the situation. The force consisted of four guns of No 9 Battery, 1st Brigade Northern Division Royal Artillery, 200 men of the 2nd Battalion, Derbyshire Regiment, and a wing from each of the two Indian Army units – the 13th Bengal Infantry and the 32nd Bengal Infantry (Pioneers), all of which was under the command of Colonel T. Graham, RA. Whilst half the force remained at Padong, the remainder advanced and on 20 March attacked and secured a stockade near Lingtu. On the

following day the fort at Lingtu was occupied without resistance. The casualties to the combined British and Indian force were small, with one officer and four men slightly wounded. The force then established an entrenched camp at Gnathong which was attacked by a strong body of Tibetans on 22 May. The enemy pressed home their attack but were eventually driven off by the superior weapons of the Field Force. Despite this, the Tibetans continued to build up their troops in the area and, due to the increased numbers arriving in the Jalep Pass, Colonel Graham requested additional troops in order to keep the situation under control. By the end of August

then continued their advance to Tumlong, the capital of Sikkim. The small force met with no opposition but in fact were 'met with cordiality by the inhabitants'. The detachment moved back to Gantok on 5 October. This concluded the military operation and although the artillery and the Derbyshire Regiment moved back to India before the winter, the remainder of the troops remained in Sikkim until October 1889.

Those that took part in the operations at Sikkim between 15 March and 27 September 1888 were granted the Indian General Service Medal with the clasp 'Sikkim 1888', which was authorised by G.G.O. No 431 of 1889.[4]

There was another operation being conducted during the time that the latter part of the Sikkim disturbances were being dealt with. The second expedition, in the Black Mountain area, was brought about by an attack on a party of 5th Goorkha Regiment, Punjab Frontier Force, by the tribesmen of the Black Mountain region. Major L. R. Battye, together with Captain H. B. Urmston of the 6th Punjab Infantry, left Abbottabad on 16 June 1888 to visit a detachment of the regiment, and early on 18 June the two officers departed from the outpost to explore the Black Mountains and to search for possible water supplies in the area. The route taken was along the Agror border between British territory and the independent tribal area. The main party moved along below the crest, but Major Battye and an advance guard travelled along the crest and, on reaching a small hamlet named Chappra, were met with a hostile reception. Although fired upon from tribesmen hiding in the wooded area through which they were passing, Major Battye refused to be drawn into a fight and would not even allow his men to open their ammunition. The Gujar tribesmen continued to harass the party from the rear but Major Battye continued to hold fire. The numbers of the enemy increased as they grew more determined and the Goorkha party still did not open fire. Inevitably the situation deteriorated so that the party was forced to withdraw from the ridge, leaving a small rear-guard under Havildar Garbu Sing Thapa, whilst the remainder moved down towards the village of Atir. Havildar Garbu Sing Thapa was wounded soon after the withdrawal had begun and Major Battye, accompanied by Captain Urmston and Subadar Kishanbir Nagarkoti, returned to the ridge to help the rearguard. Unfortunately, during the retreat communication was lost with the larger party and when the tribesmen observed that the two British Officers were only accompanied by a Subadar, a Naik, three sepoys and a bugler, they used the trees for cover and quickly made a determined attack. Both officers were severely wounded in close-quarter fighting. Subadar Kishanbir and his three remaining men put up a gallant fight to defend the two wounded officers, with the Subadar killing several of the tribesmen with his pistol. Major Battye was then killed with a shot through the neck and almost immediately Captain Urmston was also killed. Subadar Kishanbir and his two remaining men withdrew to Atir and he then led a party back up the wooded hillside and recovered the bodies of the two British Officers.[5] Three of the rearguard were killed in addition to the two officers, these being Naik Dhansing Saru, Sepoy

his Field Force at Gnathong had increased to 1,700 men, which included the addition of 514 men from the 2nd Battalion, 1st Goorkha Regiment. The Tibetans continued to build up their strength and defences in the Jalep Pass and on 24 September Colonel Graham assumed the offensive and attacked, and succeeded in taking the Tibetan advance positions and driving the enemy back over the Nimla Pass. With this success he pressed on and on 26 September reached Chambi. Finding the enemy disorganised and beaten, he withdrew his troops to Gnathong on 28 September. Meanwhile a detachment of 150 men of the 13th Bengal Infantry moved to occupy Gantok and

Chandarbir Thapa and Bugler Kalu Nagarkoti. The Havildar, Garbu Sing Thapa, who had been wounded at the outset of the fighting, died soon after the withdrawal from the ridge had begun. Of the three survivors of the rear party, two – Sepoys Indarbir Thapa and Motiram Thapa – were admitted to the Third Class of the Indian Order of Merit. Subadar Kishanbir Nagarkoti, who had already been successfully admitted to the Third and Second classes of the Order of Merit as a Sepoy, and to the First Class as a Naik, was granted the pay of the First Class of the Order in the rank of Subadar, and was given a special award of a 'Gold Bar' to be worn on the ribbon of the Order.[6]

The attack on the detachment of the Indian army could not be ignored and in retaliation the Black Mountains Expedition was mounted under the command of Brigadier-General J. M. McQueen. The expeditionary force was made up into four columns and moved into the tribal territory against the Hassanzais, Akazais and Chagarzais from a base established at Ughi (also spelt Oghi). The composition of the force was as follows:

First Column
Commanding – Colonel J. M. Sym
No 4 (Hazara) Mountain Battery – Two Gatling guns
Half of No 3 Company, Bengal Sappers and Miners
3rd Sikh Infantry
1st Battalion, 5th Goorkha Rifles
plus a British Army battalion – 2nd Northumberland Fusiliers

Second Column
Commanding – Colonel R. H. O'G. Haly
No 3 Battery, 1st Brigade South Irish Division RA (four guns)
A wing of the 34th Bengal Infantry (Pioneers)
40th Bengal Infantry
45th Bengal Infantry (Rattray's Sikhs)
plus a British Army battalion – 1st Suffolk Regiment

Third Column
Commanding – Lieutenant Colonel M. S. J. Sunderland
No 3 Battery, 1st Brigade South Irish Division RA (two guns)
Half of No 3 Company, Bengal Sappers and Miners
14th (the Ferozepore Sikhs) Bengal Infantry
24th Bengal Infantry (Punjab)
plus a British Army battalion – 2nd Royal Sussex Regiment

Fourth Column
Commanding – Colonel A. C. Crookshank, CB
No 2 Battery, 1st Brigade Scottish Division RA
  'and some Gatling guns'
29th Bengal Infantry (Punjab)
A wing of the 34th Bengal Infantry (Pioneers)
4th Punjab Infantry, Punjab Frontier Force
plus a British Army battalion – 2nd Royal Irish Regiment

In addition, a 'Field Reserve' was built up at Abbottabad consisting of the 15th Bengal Cavalry, 2nd (or Hill) Sikh Infantry and the 2nd Battalion, Seaforth Highlanders. The reserve was also strengthened by a contingent of the troops of the Maharajar of Kashmir and the Khaibar (Khyber) Rifles. Three columns moved out from Ughi on 1 October and the Fourth Column which had been concentrated at Darband, moved to Chamb on 2 October and on the 4 October advanced to Kotkai. At Shingri the enemy were encountered, and during the ensuing clash Subadar-Major Chattar Singh of the 34th Bengal Infantry was mortally wounded. The 34th Bengal Infantry and 4th Punjab Infantry covered the advance, and the guns opened fire on the enemy positions. This action was followed by a charge of the 2nd Royal Irish Regiment.

19th Punjab Infantry in heavy marching order.

Far right: 2nd Punjab Cavalry.
AMOT

However, a party of about 200 fanatics, who had been hiding in a ravine, made a desperate attack on the British line, but were repulsed by a gallant stand by detachments of the 29th and 34th Bengal Infantry who, together with the Royal Irish Regiment, succeeded in killing the whole of the enemy force. Soon after this attack the enemy withdrew and the Fourth Column moved into and occupied Kotkai. The Column lost four killed and 12 wounded, and among those killed was Captain C. H. H. Beley

DSO, of the 25th Bengal Infantry (Punjab), who was serving as an Assistant Quartermaster General.[7] He was one of the first officers to be awarded a Distinguished Service Order, which had been instituted by Royal Warrant dated 6 September 1886.[8]

On 5 October a reconnaissance party set out from Kotkai towards Kunhar but quickly came into contact with the enemy. Colonel Crookshank, who was with the party, received a severe wound which necessitated the amputation of his leg. He died as

a result of his wound on 24 October and the command was given eventually to Colonel H. M. Pratt who then continued to carry out reconnaissances. Brigadier-General Galbraith, who had the overall command of the Third and Fourth Columns, organised an attack on the enemy fort and settlement at Maidan which, having been taken, was destroyed. The Third and Fourth Columns then met and kept order in the area following the destruction of the fort.

In the meantime the other columns had moved into the three separate areas where they met with very little opposition. On 5 October the summit of the Black Mountain was reached and the advance then continued towards Seri which was then taken and destroyed on 9 October. The force continued to advance and destroy other villages of the hostile tribes until, on 13 October, the Third Column reached Kunhar.

The advance of the Expeditionary Force, and their swift retaliatory action against hostile villages had a marked effect on the tribes and on 19 October the Akazais tendered for peace. On 30 October the Hassanzais also ceased fighting. The Pariari Saiads and Tikariwals remained to be brought under submission and General McQueen used the First and the Fifth (Reserve) Column against these two tribes and, apart from a very weak defence, they also submitted and the campaign effectively finished with the fall of the enemy position on the Chaila ridge.

The Expeditionary Force withdrew to British territory and the campaign ended on 9 November. The troops engaged in the operation were awarded the Indian General Service Medal, together with the clasp 'Hazara 1888' under the authority of G.G.O. No 413 of 1889.[9]

The main problems during the latter part of the 1880s were, apart from Burma, centred on the frontiers, and in particular the North West Frontier where conditions were far from settled and the hill tribes continued to harass British outposts. At the close of the year 1890 an expedition was mounted in the North West Frontier area to enter the Zhob Valley with the dual purpose of exploration and the subjection of some sections of the Kidarzai Sherani tribe. The force, under the command of Major-General Sir George White, was known as the Zhob Valley Force and had one Bengal unit under its command which was the 18th Bengal Lancers. A second column, moving out from Derajat under Colonel A. G. Ross, had detachments of No 1 (Kohat) and No 7 (Bengal) Mountain Batteries, as well as the 1st and 3rd Punjab Cavalry, together with half-battalions of the 1st and 2nd Sikh Infantry. The operations were carried out in difficult terrain and, although the climate was also against the field force, progress was made and there was little opposition from the tribesmen. The work on this operation was concluded on 3 December 1890 and the two columns were disbanded and the regiments returned to their normal stations. No medal awards were made for this very short and relatively minor operation.

Moving on to 1891, there were four expeditions during that year, three of which brought additional clasps to the Indian General Service Medal. The three expeditions overlapped and officially took place during the following dates:

Samana 1891 – 5 April to 25 May 1891
Hazara 1891 – 12 March to 16 May 1891
N.E. Frontier 1891 – 28 March to 7 May 1891

Dealing with the campaigns in order of the date of commencement of the operation, the first expedition was mounted on 1 March 1891 when a force was concentrated at Darband and Oghi to move against some of the tribes of the Black Mountain region in Hazara who, despite the treaty of 1888, had opposed a British party passing through the area in October 1890. The second Black Mountain Expedition was under the command of Major-General W. K. Elles CB, and consisted of two columns and a few additional troops. The columns were:

Left (or River) Column
Commanding – Brigadier-General R. F. Williamson
No 1 Mountain Battery, RA
Three guns of the No 2 (Derajat) Mountain Battery
A wing of the 32nd (Punjab) Regiment of Bengal Infantry (Pioneers)
37th (Dogra) Regiment of Bengal Infantry
(Queen's Own) Corps of Guides Infantry
4th Sikh Infantry
plus a British Army battalion – 2nd Seaforth Highlanders
Right (or Tilli) Column
Commanding – Brigadier-General A. G. Hammond VC, DSO
No 9 Mountain Battery RA
11th Regiment of Bengal Infantry

A wing of the 32nd (Punjab) Regiment of Bengal Infantry (Pioneers)
2nd Battalion, 5th Gurkha (Rifle) Regiment
Khaibar Rifles
plus a British Army battalion – 1st Royal Welsh Fusiliers

The additional troops were:

One squadron of 11th (Prince of Wales's Own) Regiment of Bengal Lancers
4th Company, Bengal Sappers and Miners.

The two columns advanced into tribal territory on 12 March and until 19 March little opposition was encountered. However, just before daybreak on 19 March a sudden attack was made on one of the advance posts, at Ghazikot, by a party of Hindustani fanatics and Black Mountain tribesmen. The post was manned by the Dogra Company of the 4th Sikh Infantry, and was held by the gallant and determined action of the Dogras who, during the fierce attack, lost one Jemadar and three men killed, and 19 wounded, which included one British and one Indian officer. A number of minor engagements followed but on 16 May the column withdrew from the Black Mountain area, leaving a small token force to restrain the tribesmen.

For this short campaign the troops taking part were awarded by G.G.O. No 258 of 1892 the Indian General Service Medal and the clasp 'Hazara 1891'.

Whilst the Black Mountain expedition was underway on the North West Frontier area, problems were developing on the North Eastern Frontier area which led to the Manipur Expedition. A revolution took place in Manipur in September 1890 which resulted in the abdication of the Maharaja. In March 1891 Mr Quinton, the Chief Commissioner of Assam, together with an escort of 400 men of the 42nd and 44th Gurkha (Rifle) Regiments of Bengal Infantry under the command of Colonel C. McD Skene, marched to Imphal for the purpose of settling the unrest and arresting and deporting Tikandrajit Bir Singh, the brother of the late ruler who was implicated in the plot to overthrow the Maharaja. He was holding the post of 'Senapati', or Commander-in-Chief of the Manipur Army, and when the attempt was made to arrest him on 24 March he and his followers resisted and the British were forced to withdraw. They were driven back to the grounds of the British Residency. During this confrontation 40 officers and men were killed, including Lieutenant R. B. Berkeley[11] and two Subadars. Later that day, in the evening, Mr Quinton, Colonel Skene and Lieutenant W. H. Simpson of the 43rd Gurkha (Rifle) Regiment of Bengal Infantry,[12] went to the Maharaja's palace to attend a meeting but were seized and then killed by the orders of the Senapati and other leaders of the revolution. The enemy immediately opened fire on the troops in the Residency who, being low in ammunition, made their escape during the night and made their way in small parties to Kohima, Cachar and Tammu.

A detachment of the 43rd Gurkha (Rifle) Regiment of Bengal Infantry at Langthobal, four miles from Imphal, held the post until the following day and then withdrew in good order to Tammu. On 27 March they joined forces with a detachment of the 12th Madras Regiment (2nd Burma Battalion) under the command of Lieutenant C. J. W. Grant and the two detachments, amounting to some 83 'rifles', advanced towards Manipur in the hope of saving Mr Quinton and his party as, at this time, it was not known that they had all been murdered. At Thobal, Lieutenant Grant and his party were confronted by several thousand Manipuris. The small detachment held the enemy at bay until ordered to retire to Tammu on 9 April. The enemy followed his small party but when confronted by another detachment under the command of Captain E. R. J. Presgrave, also of the 12th Madras Regiment, it withdrew. For his very gallant conduct Lieutenant Grant was awarded the Victoria Cross, which was promulgated in *The London Gazette* of 26 May 1891 and, in addition, he was given the Brevet rank of Major. At this time Indian-born personnel serving in the army were still excluded from being awarded the Victoria Cross and therefore the Indian Officers with Lieutenant Grant's party were admitted to the Order of British India and 'every non-commissioned officer and man was decorated with the Indian Order of Merit.'[13]

Following the disastrous attempt to bring the situation in Manipur under control, it became obvious that a full-scale expedition would have to be mounted in order to secure peace in the state. An expeditionary force was organised and assembled

31st Punjab Native Infantry on the Hazara Expedition.   AMOT

31st Punjab Native Infantry, c1891. AMOT

at Kohima, Cachar and Tammu and, despite numerous difficulties with regard to the provision of transport, the three columns moved out at the end of April 1891. The force comprised the following units:

Kohima Column
Commanding – Brigadier-General H. Collett CB
No 8 (Bengal) Mountain Battery – three guns
Detachment of 100 of 13th (The Shekhawati) Regiment of
    Bengal Infantry
    400 men of 42nd Gurkha (Rifle) Regiment of Bengal Infantry
    400 men of 43rd Gurkha (Rifle) Regiment of Bengal Infantry
    300 men of 44th Gurkha (Rifle) Regiment of Bengal Infantry
plus 200 men of the Assam Military Police

Silchar (Cachar) Column
Commanding – Lieutenant Colonel R. H. F. Rennick
No 8 (Bengal) Mountain Battery – two guns
Detachment of 370 of 18th Regiment of Bengal Infantry
    103 men of 42nd Gurkha (Rifle) Regiment of Bengal Infantry
    282 men of 43rd Gurkha (Rifle) Regiment of Bengal Infantry

    114 men of 44th Gurkha (Rifle) Regiment of Bengal Infantry
1st Battalion, 2nd (Prince of Wales' Own) Gurkha (Rifle)
    Regiment
Detachment of 50 men of the Calcutta Volunteer Rifles
plus 207 men of the Surma Valley Military Police

Tammu Column
Commanding – Brigadier General T. Graham CB
No 2 Mountain Battery RA – four guns
2nd Battalion, 4th Gurkha (Rifle) Regiment
12th Regiment Madras Infantry (2nd Burma Battalion)
plus a wing of the 4th Battalion, The King's Royal Rifle Corps

The three columns reached Imphal on 27 April, having met with little opposition from the enemy with the exception of one fierce clash on 25 April, when the 12th Madras Infantry and the 2nd 4th Gurkha (Rifle) Regiment encountered opposition from a strong force of Manipuris. The result of this encounter was the almost complete destruction of the enemy force with one Jemadar and one sepoy killed, and six officers and seven men wounded. Imphal was occupied without any resistance from the enemy and it was found that the palace had been burned and that the Senapati, Prince Angeo Sana, and others implicated in the original revolt and the murder of Mr J. W. Quinton and his party, had all fled. They were all apprehended during May, and the Senapati was tried and executed as was 'the Tongal General' (who was reputed to have been an ex-mutineer of the 34th Bengal Native Infantry).[14] Others implicated in the disturbances were exiled to the Andaman Islands.

    The troops taking part in the Manipur Expedition were granted, by G.G.O. No 652 of 1892, the award of the Indian General Service Medal with the clasp 'N.E. Frontier 1891'.[15]

    Meanwhile in the North West Frontier area there were still many disturbances and in January 1891 a force was formed at Kohat to move against the Orakzai clans who repeatedly raided the Miranzai valley. The first expedition into the valley was under the command of Brigadier-General Sir W. S. A. Lockhart KCB, and consisted of the following units:

No 3 (Peshawar) and No 4 (Hazara) Mountain Batteries
5th Punjab Cavalry, Punjab Frontier Force – two squadrons
5th Company, Bengal Sappers and Miners
22nd (Punjab) Regiment of Bengal Infantry
23rd (Punjab) Regiment of Bengal Infantry (Pioneers)
29th (Punjab) Regiment of Bengal Infantry
3rd Sikh Infantry
1st, 4th and 5th Punjab Infantry, Punjab Frontier Force

The expeditionary force, which was divided into three columns advanced into the area of the hostile tribes on 26 January and, in an attempt to subdue the tribesmen, destroyed forts and towers and moved to the Samana Range established posts. There was no opposition from the enemy who, in their usual manner, retreated into the hills as the Miranzai Expedition advanced, only to move back into their own territory once the force withdrew back to Kohat in the middle of February. The situation had not been resolved and the tribesmen attacked the posts on the Samana Range on 4 April, which necessitated the formation of a second expeditionary force and on this occasion the troops, once again under the command of Sir William Lockhart, assembled at Hangu and Darband on 16 April. The force consisted of the following units:

No 3 Mountain Battery RA
No 2 (Derajat) Mountain Battery – three guns
Punjab Garrison Battery – three guns
19th Regiment of Bengal Lancers
5th Punjab Cavalry – two squadrons
No 5 Company, Bengal Sappers and Miners
15th (The Ludhiana Sikh) Regiment of Bengal Infantry
19th (Punjab) Regiment of Bengal Infantry
27th (Punjab) Regiment of Bengal Infantry
29th (Punjab) Regiment of Bengal Infantry
3rd Sikh Infantry
1st, 2nd and 6th Punjab Infantry, Punjab Frontier Force
1st Battalion, 5th Gurkha (Rifle) Regiment

In addition, the 1st Battalion, King's Royal Rifle Corps, and half a battalion of the 2nd Battalion, Manchester Regiment joined the expedition.

The force split into three columns and moved out from Hangu and Darband on 17 April and on the following day, after a number of short but fierce conflicts, succeeded in driving the enemy from the Samana Range. The enemy continued to put up resistance and it was not until 16 May that the army had completed its task of bringing all the tribes under control. The latter were led by a fanatical priest Syed Mar Basha who had declared the conflict to be a 'jihad'.[16] Although the actual fighting had been confined to small skirmishes there were 28 members of the Second Miranzai Expedition killed, including Jemadar Hashim Ali of the 19th (Punjab) Bengal Infantry. Seventy-three were wounded, including five officers, although many men became ill due to the great hardships endured during the first expedition when the weather was severe, and during the second expedition as a result of the difficult terrain that had to be covered. The Second Miranzai Expedition returned to base on 25 May and was then disbanded as a force.

The troops taking part in the operations between 5 April and 25 May 1891 received the Indian General Service Medal with the clasp 'Samana 1891'. This award was authorised by G.G.O. No 61 of 1892.

At the close of the year 1891 further disturbances occurred in the territories of Hunza and Nagar. The Gilgit agency became involved in the dispute when tribesmen continually attacked road-making parties and Lieutenant Colonel A. G. A. Durand, together with a small Indian Army force, supported by two detachments of the 1st and 2nd Kashmir Infantry, set out to stop the recurring raids. The expedition was made up as follows:

The Miranzai Expedition. The 4th Punjab Infantry searching the village of Saidan Shah.

Champion shooting team of the 26th Punjab Infantry.

No 4 (Hazara) Mountain Battery – 76 men
No 4 Company, Bengal Sappers and Miners – 6 men
20th (the Duke of Cambridge's Own Punjab) Regiment of
    Bengal Infantry – 30 men, although Gordon, in his British
    Battles and Medals, gives the number as 28
5th Gurkha (Rifle) Regiment – 188 men
Peshawar and Unorganised Transport – 159 men

In addition, there were 12 Native signallers, and the Maharajah of Kashmir provided 257 men from the 1st and 404 men from the 2nd Kashmir Imperial Service Infantry. The small semi-independent states of Hunza and Nagar are in the extreme north of the State of Kashmir and are divided by the Hunza River. These two small states are approached through a narrow defile in the Karakoram Range. They are ruled over by Chiefs, or Mirs, and were hereditarily hostile to each other. Colonel Durand's force left its base on 1 December and, having crossed the Hunza River, attacked and secured the fort of Nilt on the following day. The short, but fierce, conflict caused the loss of three men killed, and 27 wounded, including Colonel Durand. There was another clash on the following day, after which the small force continued to advance and the work culminated with

an attack on an almost inaccessible position which was taken by the Indian troops. On 21 December the Mir of Nagar surrendered and this was followed by the surrender of Hunza. The two states, being under the nominal control of the Maharajah of Kashmir, took steps to bring peace to the area. He agreed to pay both the Mirs an annual payment on the understanding that their tribesmen kept the peace. By way of acceptance of his conditions they made their tributes to him, which were merely of a token variety: 'twenty ounces of pure gold which had been panned from the Hunza river together with two dogs and two horses' from the Mir of Hunza; and the Mir of Nagar paid 'ten ounces of gold obtained from the same source and baskets of apricots'. The troops taking part in this small expedition were awarded the Indian General Service Medal together with the clasp 'Hunza 1891', although Army Order No 168 dated 1 September 1892 stated: 'The Queen has been pleased to command that the India Medal of 1854, with a clasp inscribed "HUNZA 1891", shall be granted to all troops employed in the late Hunza-Nagar Expedition between 1st and 22nd December, 1891, both dates inclusive.' The troops of the Kashmir Army were also awarded the medal and clasp and, in addition, the Maharajah of Jummoo and Kashmir awarded a bronze badge: the 'Hunza Nagar Badge, 1891'. The badge,

Elephants, artillery and infantry on manoeuvres, 1892.

which is rectangular (53mm × 26mm), has a fort-capped hill, with three soldiers in the foreground and with 'Hunza-Nagar 1891' in the lower right-hand corner on the obverse. Originally, the reverse had a brooch fitting, but later some were adapted to be worn with a ribbon, 45mm wide.[18]

During the years 1892 and 1893 three minor expeditions were mounted against tribesmen on the numerous frontiers. The first was in the Black Mountain area when the tribes, contrary to the conditions agreed after the conflict in 1891, harboured a banished chief from the Khan Khel Hasanzais, Hashim Ali Khan, and refused to surrender him to the British authorities, or expel him. He was one of the prime movers of the disturbances in 1891 and, in order to break the deadlock, Major-General Sir William Lockhart formed an expeditionary force at Darband and on 1 October 1892 was prepared to move the following troops into the Black Mountain area:

Nos 3, 8 and 9 Mountain Batteries RA
No 1 (Kohat) Mountain Battery
Nos 4 and 6 Company Bengal Sappers and Miners

11th (Prince of Wales's Own) Regiment of Bengal Lancers – two Squadrons
25th (Punjab) and 30th (Punjab) Regiments of Bengal Infantry
4th Sikh Infantry
1st and 2nd Battalions, 5th Gurkha (Rifle) Regiment

The troops also included two British battalions, which were the 1st Battalion, Bedfordshire Regiment and 1st Battalion, King's Royal Rifle Corps. They reached Baio on 6 October but found the place deserted as the tribesmen had again carried out their usual tactic of withdrawing into the hills until the expeditionary force had departed. The combined force destroyed all the towers and defences and withdrew to Darband. Further disturbances took place on the Gilgit frontier in March 1893, which resulted in the loss of Major A. Daniell of the 1st Punjab Infantry during a short engagement between a fort garrison of about 300 men of the Kashmir Imperial Service Infantry and a mixed group of some 1,200 tribesmen. The enemy were driven from the village they had occupied but with the loss of Major Daniell and 19 men.

The Indian Army was also required to keep the peace along its other borders and in May 1893 it was necessary to mount a small expedition, when the people of the Kuki village of Mongham (about 20 miles east of Imphal) carried out a raid on a Naga village and killed nearly 300 of the inhabitants. The 43rd Gurkha (Rifle) Regiment of Bengal Infantry provided a detachment of 100 men who advanced to Mongham, arrested the leaders of the raid and destroyed the village. The small force also visited other villages which were implicated in the raid and punished those involved. The detachment finally returned to Manipur during mid-June having successfully carried out its mission.

A party of 100 men of the 44th Gurkha (Rifle) Regiment of Bengal Infantry was sent on another minor expedition in January 1894 against the Abors. The force was also made up of police and by the time that the small party returned to base it had lost 41 killed and 45 wounded in a number of clashes with the enemy. Despite these losses no medal or clasp was issued for this small campaign. A bar was issued for 'Abor' much later when trouble again broke out in that area in 1911-12.

The final clasp to be issued to the Indian General Service Medal (1854) was the clasp 'Waziristan 1894-95' which covered the operations from 22 October 1894 to 13 March 1895. The problem arose through the adoption of the treaty entered into with the Amir of Kabul in 1893 and during the autumn of 1894, the delimitation of the Waziri-Afghan Boundary. The Mahsud Waziris were openly hostile and it became necessary for the boundary commission to be accompanied by a 'strong escort'. For this purpose Brigadier-General A. H. Turner was given the command of the following troops which were to make up the escort:

No 3 (Peshawar) Mountain Battery
No 2 Company, Bengal Sappers and Miners
1st Punjab Cavalry – one squadron
20th (the Duke of Cambridge's Own Punjab) Regiment of
    Bengal Infantry
1st Battalion, 1st Gurkha (Rifle) Regiment
3rd Sikh Infantry

The escort assembled at Dera Ismail Khan on 1 October, and on 18 October it met up with the Boundary Commission. By 27 October it was near Inzar Kotal, near Wana. Although during the march no actual attack had been made, it was obvious that the Mahsuds were openly hostile to the force. Adequate safeguards were taken when camping and it proved to be a very wise precaution, as just before daybreak on the morning of 3 November a Mahsud force of about 3,000 men attacked the

Commanding officer's bungalow of the 30th Punjabis.

11th Bengal Lancers.

camp. The enemy had taken full advantage of the broken terrain and had concentrated near to the camp and made a determined attack. Because of their numbers and the surprise of the assault they were able to gain access, and hand-to-hand fighting took place in a number of areas until the attackers were driven back by bayonet attacks. During the encounter the Field Force lost Lieutenant Macaulay,[18] Royal Engineers, and Subadar Padam Sing Rana and Jemadar Khark Sing Nagarkoti, both of the 1st/1st Gurkha (Rifle) Regiment, 18 men and 24 followers killed. Seventy-five were wounded, including Lieutenant R. D. Angelo, 1st Gurkha (Rifle) Regiment, who later died of his wounds. This unprovoked attack quickly brought about the formation of the Waziristan Field Force which was placed under the command of Lieutenant-General Sir William Lockhart KCB, who had the following units placed at his disposal:

Nos 1 (Kohat), No 3 (Peshawar) and No 8 (Bengal) Mountain Batteries
No 2 and No 5 Company, Bengal Sappers and Miners
1st Punjab Cavalry – two squadrons
2nd Punjab Cavalry – one squadron
3rd Punjab Cavalry

20th (The Duke of Cambridge's Own Punjab) Regiment of Bengal Infantry
33rd (Punjab) Regiment of Bengal Infantry
38th (Dogra) Regiment of Bengal Infantry
1st Battalion 1st Gurkha (Rifle) Regiment
1st Battalion 5th Gurkha (Rifle) Regiment
1st and 3rd Sikh Infantry
2nd, 4th and 6th Punjab Infantry

In addition, the 2nd Battalion, The Border Regiment, and a Maxim Gun detachment from the 2nd Battalion, The Devonshire Regiment, joined the Field Force. The Field Force was divided into three brigades which were formed at Wana, Jandola and Mirian, and as by 17 December the Mahsuds had failed to meet the demands placed on them, the force moved out. The Field Force reached its three objectives, Kaniguram, Makin and Razmak. They were then formed into smaller parties and searched out the area for the tribesmen and, whilst visiting the numerous villages, destroyed towers and any other defence position they came across. The cattle, sheep and goats

A party of the 23ᴿᴰ Bombay L.I. capturing a Pagoda held by dacoits near Phailingdan. 1887.

23rd Bombay Light Infantry, 1887.

belonging to the Mahsuds were all driven off and by 21 January 1895 the tribes submitted and complied with the terms imposed upon them by the British. The losses to this very large Field Force was small, being just two men killed and only 22 wounded. The Brigades then returned to their bases and disbanded so that the units could return to their normal garrison. The troops taking part in the five-month campaign were awarded the Indian General Service Medal, 1854-1895, with the clasp 'Waziristan 1894-95' which was authorised by G.G.O. No 1082 of 1895.[19]

Whilst the campaign was being conducted against the Mahsud Waziris, the Indian Government was confronted by a further outbreak of unrest on the frontier, on this occasion at Chitral, which was to lead to the Chitral Expedition of 1895 and to the award of India Medal of 1895-1902. It was also required to provide troops for service in Central Africa and troops from Bengal were provided for this overseas campaign.

11th Bengal Native Infantry – by H. Bunnett.

Central Africa 1891-98

1   Cadell, Sir Patrick *History of the Bombay Army*, 1938, p246 and Journal of the Society for Army Historical Research, Vol LIII, No 215 Autumn 1975, article by Colonel (later General Sir John) J. L. Chapple, 'Disbanded Indian Army Regiments 1882'.

2   Cadell, op cit, p246.

3   Wilson, Lieutenant Colonel W. J. *The Madras Army*, Vol 4, Madras, 1888, p493.

4   Cardew, Lieutenant F. G. *A Sketch of the Services of the Bengal Native Army*, 1903, p394.

5   *History of the 5th Royal Gurkha Rifles (Frontier Force) 1858 to 1928*, c1928, p85.

6   *5th Royal Gurkha Rifles*, op cit, pp86 & 87.

7   *Beley, Captain Charles Harold Hepworth*, born 27 July 1855, commissioned 28 February 1874 in 1st Foot, transferred to Bengal Staff Corps 21 November 1876. Also Creagh, Sir O'Moore and Humphris, E. M., *The VC and DSO*, p23. *The London Gazette* dated 25 November 1887.

8   Abbott, P. E. and Tamplin, J. M. A. *British Gallantry Awards*, 1971, pp138-140.

9   Cardew, op cit, p397.

10 Cardew, op cit, p418.

11 *Berkeley, Lieutenant R. B.* Commissioned 7 February 1885 in Durham Light Infantry, transferred to Bengal Staff Corps (on probation) from 29 November 1886 and serving with 44th (Goorkha Light Infantry).

12 *Simpson, Lieutenant Walter Henry*, born 21 June 1860, comsioned Second Lieutenant, 39th Foot, 11 August 1880, promoted to Lieutenant from 1 July 1881, transferred to Bengal Staff Corps, 12 July 1883 and serving as Adjutant 43rd (Goorkha Light Infantry).

13 Cardew, op cit, p415.

14 Cardew, op cit, p416.

15 Ibid.

16 *Jihad* – Religious war of Mohammedans against unbelievers.

17 Gordon, Major Lawrence L. *British Battles and Medals*, 1962, pp244-245.

18 *Macaulay, Lieutenant Percy John Frederick*, commissioned Lieutenant 24 July 1886 in Royal Engineers. Prior to the operation, Lieutenant Macaulay was serving in the Quetta garrison.

19 Cardew, op cit, p422, and Gordon, op cit, p247.

CHAPTER TEN

Campaigns in East and Central Africa

During the period 1891-99 volunteers were granted permission to take temporary service with local authorities in British East and Central Africa. The first group of volunteers moved to Africa at the request of the British Central Africa Company. The party consisted of 60 soldiers, mostly Mazbi Sikhs with some men of the Hyderabad Contingent under the command of Captain C. M. Maguire of the 2nd Lancers, Hyderabad Contingent.[1] The small party was in support of the local police who were waging a campaign against the Arab slave hunters and traders. The expedition, under the command of Commissioner H. H. Johnston and Captain C. M. Maguire, first conducted an operation against Makanjira during October and the early part of November 1891. Later in November a second operation was mounted against Kawinga to free slaves who were being held by the Arab slave traders. Captain Maguire set out with a party of 30 sepoys but encountered a far superior force which caused his party to retire and during the action Captain Maguire was killed. The report on his death reads 'Captain Maguire met his death in the gallant manner that was to be expected of an officer of the Force to which he belonged [the Hyderabad Contingent]. Covering the retreat of his men to a boat, when attacked by a large hostile force, he remained on land until the last, and was then shot while swimming out to the boat which was waiting off shore for his party.'[2] Of the seven men who were from the Hyderabad Contingent, four were admitted to the 3rd Class of the Indian Order of Merit for 'conspicuous gallantry in the field'. Following this setback, a further contingent was sent to Africa early in 1892. Captain C. E. Johnson, 36th (Sikh) Regiment of Bengal Infantry, was sent as successor to the late Captain Maguire, together with ten Sikh volunteers who were to fill the vacancies created by the casualties sustained in the operations of 1891. There were minor operations during January and February 1892 against Zarifa, but in the following year Lieutenant C. A. Edwards, 35th (Sikh) Regiment of Bengal Infantry, together with 100 men, provided additional troops with which to mount two small operations. During November 1893 and January 1894 Commissioner Johnston organised a major attack against Makinjira's position using the contingent from the Indian Army, which was supported by two 'lake' gunboats. The outcome of this operation was to effect the release of many slaves who were awaiting transportation.

The officers and men who participated in the various expeditions that were conducted between 1891 and 1894, when ten small operations were conducted against the slave traders, were awarded the Central Africa Medal (1891-98), and for those who were engaged in later operations which were carried out between 1894 and 1898 the medal was awarded with the clasp 'Central Africa 1894-98'. The various operations covered by this clasp were:

January 1894	Operations around Fort Johnston.
March 1895	Expedition against Chief Kawinga of the Yaos.
September-Nov 1895	A series of expeditions against Yao chiefs which resulted in the pacification of the area at the southern end of Lake Nyassa.
December 1895	Expeditions mounted against slave traders around the Northern Region of Lake Nyassa.
January 1896	Expedition, led by Lieutenant C. A. Edwards, 35 Bengal Infantry (Sikhs), against Chief Tambola of the Angonis (who were of Zulu origin) who occupied an area to the west of Lake Nyassa.
October 1896	Expedition, led by Captain W. H. Manning, 1st Sikh Infantry, Punjab Frontier Force, against the Chewa Chief, Odeti, who was harbouring the fugitive Chief Tambola.
October 1896	A further expedition, led by Captain W. H. Manning,[3] against the Angoni Chief Chikusi.
August 1897	An expedition, again led by Captain W. H. Manning, to Chilwa to subdue the Anguru, led by Chief Serumba, in the area south of Lake Chilwa.
January-Feb 1898	Expedition led by Captain H. E. J. Brake, Royal Artillery, against the Angoni Chief Mpezeni and his son Singu, to the Luangwa Valley during which operation the Chief, his son and supporters were defeated.
April 1898	A further expedition to the south Angoniland to subdue Angoni raiders. The small force was led by Captain F. B. Pearce, The Prince of Wales's Own (West Yorkshire Regiment), and Lieutenant J. S. Brogden, Royal Marines.

Those taking part in these many minor operations were awarded the Central Africa Medal, 1891-98. The medal was issued on two occasions, the first time in 1895 for the ten small campaigns which were carried out between 1891 and 1894. The

35th Sikhs in the Soudan, 1896.

first issue was without a clasp, and with a swivel ring. The second issue, which covered the fourteen operations carried out between January 1894 and April 1898, was authorised in August 1899. The second issue was with a plain straight suspender and with the clasp 'Central Africa 1894-1898'. The medal is described as follows:

Obverse The diademed and veiled head of Queen Victoria with the legend 'VICTORIA REGINA'.
Reverse A scene of bush fighting around a tree between British soldiers and natives.
Size 36mm diameter.
Ribbon Three colours of equal width, reading from left to right (facing the wearer) black, white and terracotta. 32mm wide.[4]

The colours were selected as being symbolic of the troops who took part in the various campaigns, that is African, British and Indian. Although no regiment was sent to Central Africa as an entity, the force was made up of volunteers from a whole series of regiments within the Indian Army and the following breakdown of the volunteers shows the wide range of units that provided men for the first ten campaigns:

Parent unit	No of volunteers
Hyderabad Contingent	
1st Lancers	7
2nd Lancers	10
3rd Lancers	5
Bengal Infantry	
23rd (Pioneers)	26
32nd (Pioneers)	23
15th (The Ludhiana Sikhs)	14
22nd (Punjab)	6
26th (Punjab)	5
28th (Punjab)	19
30th (Punjab)	13
31st (Punjab)	14
35th (Sikhs)	15
36th (Sikhs)	26
45th (Rattray's Sikhs)	17
1st Sikh Infantry, Punjab Frontier Force	15
Indian Medical Service	2

The spread of units was wider for the operations from 1894-98 and the following breakdown shows the variety of units from which the volunteers were drawn:

No 2 Mountain Battery, Punjab Frontier Force	5
No 4 Mountain Battery, Punjab Frontier Force	5
1st Punjab Infantry	8
2nd Sikh Infantry	10
4th Sikh Infantry	10
Bengal Infantry	
14th (the Ferozepore Sikhs)	1
15th (the Ludhiana Sikhs)	11
19th (Punjab)	3
21st (Punjab)	1
22nd (Punjab)	1
24th (Punjab)	11
25th (Punjab)	9
26th (Punjab)	10
27th (Punjab)	10
28th (Punjab)	11
29th (Punjab)	10
30th (Punjab)	6
31st (Punjab)	12
35th (Sikhs)	50
36th (Sikhs)	10
45th (Rattray's Sikhs)	19
11th (Prince of Wales's Own) Bengal Lancers	1

The events of the campaign in what was originally the British Protectorate of Nyasaland, but was subsequently named the British Central African Protectorate in 1893 and Nyasaland in 1907, were partially chronicled by Captain F. T. Stewart of the 45th (Rattray's Sikhs) Bengal Infantry. In his account he wrote that the operations were 'to suppress the slave trade by every legitimate means' as the people of the Protectorate of Nyasaland were being raided, robbed and taken into captivity to satisfy the greed prevailing among a few of the chiefs of the Yao race who were being paid by Arab and Swahili slave traders for the people they sold into slavery. In July 1891 there were 71 Indian soldiers serving under Captain Cecil Maguire. The men were armed with Snider rifles and the force had been issued with two 9-pounder and one 7-pounder cannon from Woolwich Arsenal. Stewart reported that Captain Maguire was killed 'just north of Fort Maguire, on the S.E. coast of Lake Nyassa, on the 15th December 1891'.[5] In April 1893 Captain Edwards took 100 Jut Sikhs to Africa to relieve the time-expired Mazbi Sikhs, and the Indian Cavalrymen and this party was further reinforced by another 100 Sikhs who arrived under the command of Captain William H. Manning. The contingent of 200 Sikhs returned to India in June 1895 under the command of Captain Manning (later to become Colonel Sir William Manning, the Governor of the Protectorate). During the two years that the contingent were in Africa it is reported that the losses were one man accidentally drowned, three men killed or died of wounds, 13 men died of diseases, and of that number only three died of malaria. Six men were sent back to India, although for what reason the report does not indicate.

In 1895 a further contingent was formed which consisted of 202 Sikhs, 30 camp followers and three Hospital Assistants. The men were recruited from such diverse garrisons as Jhansi and Dera Ismail Khan and Bannu on the frontier. The contingent formed up at Bombay and was issued with warm clothing on 31 March, which consisted of a 'short black Souave jacket over a white "kurta", red "cummberbund", yellow knickerbockers and white spats'. (Black, yellow and white were the Protectorate colours.)[6] The movement through rocky country and dense bush under tropical conditions was far harder on the troops than the actual skirmishes when they encountered the enemy. The British Central Africa Gazette for 15 November 1895 makes the following report on the conduct of the Sikh soldiers. 'The ground was excessively difficult to fight over, as it consisted of very steep hill-sides strewn with gigantic boulders, but the British force took position after position in truly gallant style; the Sikhs especially distinguished themselves.'

A number of the Indians were admitted to the Indian Order of Merit for their gallantry during the numerous operations in the Nyasaland area; these included 'No 2162 Naik Atma Singh; No 3005 Sepoy Mahtab Singh . . . 1874 L. Havildar Bulaka Singh'[7] all of the 45th (Rattray's Sikhs), who were awarded the 3rd Class Indian Order of Merit, as were Jemadar Bhagwan Singh and three sepoys of the 14th (the Ferozapore Sikhs).[8]

Whilst volunteers from the Indian Army were on active service in Africa during 1895, far reaching changes were being made to the army structure in India. A reformation of the three Presidential armies had been recommended by the Army Organisation Commission as early as 1879 and had been placed before the Government in 1881, but at that time it was not considered expedient to press for the reorganisation and the proposals were shelved for the time being. The matter was again raised in 1885 and 1888 but it was not until 1892 that the proposals submitted by the Government of India, which at this time had been somewhat modified, were presented to Parliament. A Bill was passed by Parliament which resulted in the complete restructuring of the army in India. The Act brought the disbandment of the appointment and offices of Commander-in-Chief of the army in the Madras and Bombay Presidencies, and the Governors in Council ceased to have control of the army within their Presidencies. At the same time the Bengal Army was, for administrative purposes, divided into two commands, these being the Punjab and Bengal Commands. The changes were brought into effect from 1 April 1895[9] and saw the introduction of four commands within the Army of India. The four commands were the Punjab, Bengal, Madras and Bombay Commands, each having a Lieutenant-General who was given the title 'Lieutenant-General Commanding the Forces' and all were under the direct command of the Commander-in-Chief in India and thus under the control of the Government of India. A list of the regiments serving in the reformed commands is given at Appendix A.

During 1896 the 24th (Baluchistan, Duchess of Connaught's Own) Regiment of Bombay Infantry, less one company which was employed as a guard company for the Baluch-Afghan

Boundary Commission, was detailed to form part of the Mombasa Field Force, and embarked from Karachi on 5 March 1896. The regiment was brought up to full strength by the attachment of the Hazara Company of the 26th (Baluchistan) Regiment of Bombay Infantry. The force arrived at Mombasa Creek on 15 March and detachments were despatched to various locations by being transported in dhows. The Field Force had been sent to Mombasa to quell disturbances which had arisen due to a disagreement over the succession of chieftainship. The faction opposing the British-backed claimant gathered a large number of followers and attacked the British camp of the troops that had been sent to bring peace to the area. The British force attacked and secured Mweleh but the rebel leaders and their followers dispersed into the jungle. It was decided to wait for the Indian Field Force to arrive before pursuing the rebels, and in the meantime the rebels reformed and continued to attack villages. With the arrival of the Indian troops the operation commenced, and the enemy were dispersed and their villages destroyed together with food supplies and any ammunition that was found. The campaign was brought to a close when the column under command of Major J. W. G. Tulloch secured the stronghold of Mubarak, the rebel leader, and destroyed five outlying villages. Continuing the

35th Sikhs in the Soudan, 1896.

pursuit of Mubarak through the jungle under difficult conditions, the column found the main enemy magazine which was hidden in dense jungle and the contents were destroyed. Major Tulloch and his party continued to chase Mubarak, who was then heading almost due west. The column advanced ten miles in pursuit but then had to return to the captured stockade to await supplies. On 12 April news was received that Mubarak and his followers had crossed into German territory but about a week later the rebel chief and his men surrendered to the German authorities and were disarmed. This was virtually the end of the campaign and in June the Indian troops returned to India.[10]

The troops taking part in this operation were awarded the East and West Africa Medal (1887-1900), although no clasp was issued for the operations at 'M'wele' (Mweleh). The word 'Mwele' was impressed on the rim of the medal to the left of the claw and the date, either '1895' or '1895-6' to the right. The East and West African Medal 1887-1900 is described as follows:

Obverse   The diademed and veiled head of Queen Victoria with the legend 'VICTORIA REGINA'.
Reverse   A scene of bush fighting around a tree between British

Size   36mm diameter. It has been noted that the gauge is slightly thinner than that of the similar 1873 Ashantee Medal.
Ribbon   Yellow with black borders and two thin black stripes down the centre, 32mm wide.[11]

soldiers and natives (as used for the Central Africa Medal and the Ashantee Medal, 1873).

The Indian Army continued to have a presence in Africa during the remaining years of the 19th century. The operations were generally small and consisted of sections of the Indian Army giving support to British and locally (African) raised units in the suppression of rebels and tribes who continually raided settlements and peaceful native villages.

On 20 November 1897 a request for Indian troops was received by the Government of India for Uganda. The 27th Regiment (1st Baluch Battalion) of Bombay (Light) Infantry (referred to as the 27th Baluchis) were ordered to move to Uganda, and embarked on the troopship *Nowshera* on 3 December, arriving at Mombasa on 12 December. The battalion took into the field 14 British Officers and 743 Indian ranks under the command of Lieutenant-Colonel W. A. Broome, and on arrival in Africa the force moved to Ndi. On 9 January 1898 news was received that the Sudanese troops had mutinied and had killed Lieutenant N. A. Macdonald of the 14th (The Ferozepore Sikh) Regiment of Bengal Infantry, and a missionary. Sections of the Sudanese troops had previously mutinied and had killed some prisoners whom they had taken, which was why the 27th Baluchis had been sent from India to join the Expeditionary force. The terrain was extremely difficult and Colonel Broome wrote in his diary 'The country . . . is one mass of dense scrub jungle entirely uninhabited except on the mountains where the Wa-Teita live: there is but one road, the Mackinnon Road, which runs fairly parallel with the railway . . . The resources of the country are next to nothing, small quantities of mahendi [a cereal], goats, Indian corn, and fowls, but they [the local inhabitants] are not willing to sell.'[13]

The situation continued to deteriorate and it was necessary to send more troops to Uganda and a further contingent was sent from India, this being a contingent of 400 men of the 4th Regiment Bombay Infantry, who embarked at Bombay in the troopship *Dalhousie* on 25 February.

Mr Weaver, District Officer of Ndi, requested help from the troops as he had been threatened by a tribe numbering some 1,000 men armed with bows during his visit to the Mangangi tribal area, and on 21 March Colonel Broome set out with a small force to give assistance to Mr Weaver. The party, consisting of three British officers, two Indian Officers and 78 rank and file, reached the District Officer's camp in the Magangi valley on the morning of the following day. An attempt had been made to kill Mr Weaver, during which the local chief had been shot. Colonel Broome sent parties to apprehend the hostile natives and during the operations over the next three days about 40 or 50 of the enemy were killed, with only one casualty in Colonel Broome's force, this being one Indian officer slightly wounded. When the hostile tribe had been brought

under control the small Field Force returned to its base camp. Meanwhile severe fighting was going on in Uganda, where Chief Mwanga had assembled his men and the situation was being barely contained by the British Officers, with a very mixed force of Sudanese, Swahilis and other locally recruited troops. The rebels were attempting to meet up with a party of Sudanese mutineers who had assembled east of Mruli. After a number of encounters the enemy were dispersed, but not for long as the Sudanese mutineers reassembled and, moving near to Mruli, they constructed a small fort on the east bank of the Nile nearly opposite the settlement, and this move gave encouragement to the native followers of Mwanga. On 30 March Captain W. M. Southey, 27th Baluchis, with a force of 150 men arrived at Kampala and on 6 April set out for Mruli followed, after a few days, by Major C. G. Martyr DSO, DCLI with a force of 70 men. Arriving at Mruli on 24 April, Major Martyr decided to attack the enemy fort and, crossing to the east bank on 26 April, the enemy fort was taken by a small party mainly made up from the 27th Baluchis, supported by a detachment of the East African Rifles and a few Swahilis. The fort was taken and a number of the enemy escaped to the hills. The conflict was a fierce one and the Indian contingent lost Subadar Sher Din and five men, and Subadar-Major Yar Muhammad and nine men were wounded.

There were continued skirmishes throughout May and in June Captain W. H. Southey and a party of 44 men of his regiment, supported by 20 men of the Uganda Rifles and 75 Waganda, moved to reoccupy a post near the Murchison Falls which had previously been lost to the enemy. The post was reoccupied without opposition. The Sudanese mutineers, who had been driven from their fort near Mruli, reassembled near to the settlement and occupied a strong position from which they were a continued threat to the peace of the Protectorate. It was resolved to clear the mutineers from the area and on 3 August an offensive was mounted. The attacking force was organised into two columns:

No 1 Column – commanded by Major C. H. U. Price

| 27th Bombay Infantry (Baluchis) | – | 4 British officers and 237 rank and file |
| Uganda Rifles | – | 1 British officer and 24 natives |

No 2 Column – commanded by Major C. G. Martyr DSO

27th Bombay Infantry (Baluchis)	–	1 British Officer, 7 men
Uganda Rifles	–	2 British Officers, 159 Nubians
East Africa Rifles	–	1 British Officer, 53 natives
27th Bombay Infantry (Baluchis)	–	Lieutenant P. H. Dyke with three Maxim guns
One 7-pounder gun		

A detachment of No 1 Column secured a hill overlooking the enemy encampment and the force then advanced close to the enemy camp to await daybreak on 4 August. Meanwhile No 2 Column arrived within half-a-mile of No 1 Column at 5am, but owing to the jungle terrain, did not make contact with No 1 Column until 6am when a general advance was made. The troops charged the stockade and drove the enemy from that position and a small follow-up operation was carried out over the succeeding days.

Operations continued throughout September and October, all of them being carried out in difficult country. One incident which occurred on 10 October resulted in a number of casualties being sustained by the 27th Bombay Infantry (Baluchis) who fought a gallant defensive action. A patrol under command of Subadar Alahad Khan was attacked by a large party of rebels and, during the fierce action, Jemadar Muhammad Shah and 13 men were killed. The report on the action showed the gallantry of the Jemadar which reads: 'Jemadar Muhammad Shah exhorted his men to stand fast and die where they stood, setting the example on his side of the position and fighting to the last, and his men did the same. Naik Yusuf Khan, in charge of the rearguard in order to save the ammunition from falling into the hands of the enemy opened the boxes and distributed the cartridges to his men, under a heavy fire.'[14] The small party, much depleted in strength, eventually reached Kisalizi on the morning of 11 October and, apart from those killed in the action, one officer and eight men had been wounded.

During the following months small actions continued to be fought with major losses to the enemy and a lesser number of casualties being suffered by the British forces. During January 1899 the detachments of the 27th Bombay Infantry (Baluchis) returned to their headquarters at Kamapa as they were gradually relieved by detachments from the newly raised Indian contingent of the Uganda Rifles. The regiment then withdrew to the coast by detachments and on 11 May 1899 the regiment embarked on board the *Clive*, arriving at Karachi on 20 May. The casualty return for the Uganda operation was given as:

Killed	– Two Indian Officers, one lance Naik and 18 Privates.
Wounded	– One British Officer, one Indian Officer, one Naik, one Buglar and 17 Privates.
Died from disease	– One Indian Officer and 12 Privates.[15]

In addition to the Uganda operation, the Indian Government supplied a small force to take part in operations in Jubaland. A wing of the 4th Regiment Bombay Infantry and two companies of the 27th Regiment (1st Baluch Battalion) of Bombay (Light) Infantry were despatched to Jubaland to take part in the operations against the Oganda Somalis. The force was under the command of Major W. Quentin, 4th Bombay Infantry who set up his headquarters at Yonti. Believing it necessary to secure his position by building a stockade, he obtained permission to send a party into Italian Territory in order to fell palm trees for the building of his defences. On the evening of 21 May 1898 Lieutenant W. F. Stevenson, who was attached to the 4th Bombay Rifles, was returing from the Italian side of the river with an Indian Officer and 11 men, when the canoe in which they were travelling capsized. Lieutenant Stevenson and one Indian non-commissioned officer were drowned; the remainder managed to reach the bank safely. The small force lost a number of men who were killed on 22 June, when a party under the command of an Indian Officer was attacked by a force of about 400 Somalis, outnumbering the detachment by ten to one. The main body of the party were marching in single file, with advance and rear guards, and passing through thick bush country, when they were attacked from the right and the rear. The attack was so sudden that Jemadar Radha Singh, 4th Bombay Rifles, and several men were killed before they could even bring their weapons into use. A relief party set out from the nearby camp and recovered 27 bodies, and it was later discovered that one man from the ambushed party had disappeared and was later listed as 'missing'. During the skirmish the Somalis, who had afterwards retreated into the dense undergrowth, took with them 27 rifles and 1,640 rounds of ammunition. Despite this small victory, the enemy were continually harassed by the Field Force and eventually the Somalis' chiefs sued for peace which was granted, although two chiefs were held as hostage until the stolen arms had been returned. On 3 October, 22 Martini-Henry rifles and six Snider rifles were surrendered to the authorities. Peace having been achieved, the small expeditionary force was disbanded on 9 November, and the 4th Bombay Rifles returned to Bombay, embarking from Mombasa on 18 November. The detachment of the 27th Regiment (1st Baluch Battalion) was relieved by a further detachment of 150 men who were to serve in the Protectorate.[16]

Although hostilities commenced in South Africa in 1899 which developed into a major conflict, units of the Indian Army were not directly involved in the war. Nevertheless the conflict had an effect on the army within India. The Boer ultimatum was given on 9 October 1899 and the war commenced two days later. Prior to that date, the war had been anticipated and the Indian Government had been warned to hold in readiness a cavalry and infantry brigade for service in South Africa, particularly for the defence of Natal. On 7 September the troops were warned for active service and on the following day embarkation orders were issued. One advantage of despatching British troops from India was the travelling time. The average sailing time from Bombay to Durban was 15 days as compared with 20 days from Southampton.

All those concerned with the emergency reacted with great zeal and 22 vessels were chartered for the move of the troops and during the 16 days that the embarkation took place, 259 officers, 1,564 cavalry, 653 artillery and 3,427 infantrymen were taken on board. Additional troops were despatched from India between the period 11 October 1899 and the end of July 1900, amounting to a further 132 officers, 713 cavalry, 376 artillery and 670 infantry and mounted infantry.

Although during this time no actual Indian Army unit was despatched to the war in South Africa, it is recorded that, at different times, 469 Indian soldiers were sent as non-combatants, to serve in remount depots and to act as orderlies. In addition, 6,602 Indian civilian non-combatants were provided, which included a 'transport Corps' of 500 men as well as:

35th Sikhs in the Soudan, 1896.

Bheestie Corps (water carriers), 1,000 strong sent March 1900; Syce Corps (grooms), 1,000 strong in March and May 1900; Dhobie Corps (laundry Corps) in May 1900.[17]

In addition to the non-combatants sent to support the British war effort in South Africa, 6,761 remounts were sent during the period October 1899 to 15 June 1900. Many of these were withdrawn from Indian Cavalry units and others were 'given by native states with great loyalty and generosity'. In addition, 1,280 mules and ponies were despatched to the front.

1 *Maguire, Captain Cecil Montgomery,* commissioned in 8th Hussars 11 September 1876, transferred to 2nd Battalion, Hampshire Regiment, 15 August 1877, appointed to Indian Staff Corps 4 March 1878. Promoted to Captain 11 September 1887 and served with 2nd Lancers, Hyderabad Contingent.

2 Burton, Major R. G. *A History of the Hyderabad Contingent,* Calcutta, 1905, p289.

3 *Manning, Captain William Henry,* commissioned 25 August 1886, appointed to Indian Staff Corps, 14 July 1888, service with 1st Regiment of Sikh Infantry from 27 September 1891, promoted to Captain 25 August 1897.

4 Joslin, E. C.; Litherland, A.R.; Simpkin B. T.; *British Battles and Medals,* Spink, London, 1988, pp174-175.

5 McRae, Colonel H. StG. M. *Regimental History of the 45th Rattray's Sikhs,* Vol I, 1933, p468.

6 McRae, op cit, p469.

7 McRae, op cit, p475.

8 Talbot, Colonel F. E. G. *The 14th King George's Own Sikhs,* 1937, pp51-52.

9 G.G.O. 980 of 1894.

10 *Frontier and Overseas Expeditions from India,* Vol VI, Calcutta, 1911, p163.

11 Joslin, op cit, pp167-170.

12 *Frontier and Overseas Expeditions,* op cit, p172.

13 *Frontier and Overseas Expeditions,* op cit, p193.

14 *Frontier and Overseas Expeditions,* op cit, p203.

15 *Frontier and Overseas Expeditions,* op cit, p207.

16 *Frontier and Overseas Expeditions,* op cit, p173.

17 *Frontier and Overseas Expeditions,* op cit, pp212-213.

Left:
Garrison artillery with
40pr ML Gun drawn by oxen
and elephants.

Above:
5th (Bombay) Mountain Battery.

Right:
Mountain gun, Bombay Artillery.

Left top:
4th (Hazara) Mountain Battery.

Left below:
2nd Prince of Wales's
Own Gurkha Rifles, c1896.

Right:
Officer, NCO and Private,
5th Ghoorkha Rifles.

Below:
5th Gurkha Rifles – Piper, 1896.

CHAPTER ELEVEN

The North West Frontier Conflicts of 1895–1902

The North West Frontier of India, never a peaceful area, saw seven years of conflict which resulted in the award of the second of the India service medals and as the first 'general service' medal was issued 1854-95 with 23 bars, it was considered that it was time to institute a new award. The 'India Medal' was introduced which covered seven years and, during that time, seven bars were issued in conjunction with the medal; six with Queen Victoria's head on the medal and one with the head of King Edward VII. In the operations conducted in the North West Frontier area during the seven years, the Indian Army was fully committed throughout and there were many instances of gallantry by officers and men of the Indian units.

The first campaign covered by the 'India 1895 Medal' centred around Chitral. The background to the situation at that time is

summed up very clearly in a small publication printed at Allahabad immediately after the conclusion of the operation. The introduction reads: 'On New Year's Day of this year (1895) the ruling Mehtar of Chitral Nizam-ul-Mulk, was murdered by his half-brother Amir-ul-Mulk. From that time onward the active interference of Umra Khan in the State affairs of Chitral is to be detected . . . There seems no doubt, that Umra Khan received a letter from Amir-ul-Mulk, asking him for help directly he murdered Nizam-ul-Mulk; and Umra Khan, the redoubtable Chief of Jandoul, a man with apparently a natural genius for desperate measures, immediately concentrated 3,000 to 4,000 men, and crossed the Lowarai Pass . . . the result of a hundred skirmishes and the united testimony of the tribes of this frontier, gave Umra Khan the first place on the N.W. border as

Chitral, 1895. (Courtesy of Miss L. Fowler and the Royal Signals Museum.)

Chitral Fort, 1895. (Courtesy of Miss L. Fowler and the Royal Signals Museum.)

an expert and enterprising soldier.'[1]

The British sent Surgeon-Major George S. Robertson CSI, as Political Agent of the Gilgit area, but trouble soon developed when the Mehtar was murdered by his brother and, having killed his rival, Amir-ul-Mulk had the Newab, the Aksagal of Shogat, and his three sons killed. Lieutenant B. E. M. Gurdon was the Political Agent at Chitral with an escort of just eight Sikhs and, judging the situation to be extremely serious, he sent for the remainder of his escort of 100 men who were at Mastuj, some 65 miles north-east of Chitral. It was fortunate that this small party was able to reach the Political Agent at Chitral without attack and as the message concerning the murder of the Mehtar reached Surgeon-Major Robertson, the Political Agent at Gilgit, he was able to form a small party to proceed to Chitral. The complete story of the siege and defence of the garrison at Chitral is given in detail in two main works on the subject, these being *Chitral – The Story of a Minor Siege* by Sir George S. Robertson, and *The Relief of Chitral* by Captains G. J. and F. E. Younghusband, published in 1898 and 1896 respectively. The force actually involved in the defence of Chitral, is given as being '370 combatants'. These are shown as '90 rifles of the 14th

Sikhs, the remainder of the 4th Kashmir Rifles. The officers of the garrison were Captain Townsend, Central India Horse, in command after Captain Campbell was wounded; Captain Colin Campbell, who accompanied the British Agent inspecting; Lieutenant Gurdon, Assistant British Agent; Surgeon-Captain Whitchurch and Lieutenant Harley, 14th Sikhs.'[2] The events leading up to the siege record that on 3 March news was received that a large hostile force, led by Sher Afzul, was approaching Chitral. A party under Captain Colin Campbell was despatched to meet the oncoming hostile force and, after various attempts to remove the enemy from a village in which they had taken shelter, Captain Campbell was attempting to get more men up to a position whereby the village could be taken when he was shot through the knee. Captain Townsend then attempted to take the village when two Indian officers were shot on either side of him and his advance came to a halt. It was then necessary to withdraw and with the enemy now in the advantage, the Chitral defenders had no alternative but to retire to the fort. The cost had been high, with two Indian officers killed, Captain Campbell severely wounded and Captain Baird wounded and 22 men killed. Captain Baird had been reported missing with Surgeon-Captain Whitchurch, but Baird was rescued and 'carried in by Whitchurch, and a few Gurkhas, under the circumstance of the most extraordinary gallantry.' Robertson's

The bridge at Chitral, 1895. (Courtesy of Miss L. Fowler and the Royal Signals Museum.)

diary at this stage records that 'We are all now safe in the fort, with three months' provisions and a sufficient number of sepoys. Jemadar Rab Nawaz Khan was severely wounded by a rush of swordsmen. We must now wait for reinforcements, which will have to come by Drasan.' Captain Baird, who had been wounded three times, died on 4 March.[3] The small defending force had lost 54 casualties out of the 200 men engaged, and Robertson attributed the high casualty rate 'due to the excellent shooting of Sher Afzul's men . . . combined with their superior numbers'.

The fort at Chitral was besieged from 3 March until 19 April 1895, when it was relieved by a force led by Lieutenant-Colonel J. G. Kelly. Meanwhile in another part of the Gilgit Agency, Lieutenants Fowler and Edwardes,[4] together with a mixed party of Indian Sepoys and Kashmiri soldiers, set out to march to Chitral. The party reached the village of Reshun on 6 March and received information that there was a hostile party between them and Chitral. On the following day Lieutenants Fowler and Edwardes moved forward with a party of 30 men, leaving the Kashmiri Subadar, with the remainder of the small party, as a rearguard. They had not proceeded far when they were attacked by a strong enemy force and, with Lieutenant Fowler and three

men wounded, the party retreated and met up with the rear party where they made a stand for the remainder of the day. At night they withdrew to the deserted village of Reshun, and strengthened a corner of the village. The enemy attacked again the next morning and continued to do so for the next week. The defenders had to exist on three days' rations, and with only two earthen vessels of water the situation was quite perilous. One night a party made a sortie to get water from a stream about a mile away and was able to bring in a small supply. On the eighth day the enemy asked for talks and the leader of the hostile group proved to be Isa Khan, a younger brother of Sher Afzul. It was agreed that two letters would be written, one by the British Officers to Surgeon-Major Robertson at Chitral, and the other by Isa Khan to his brother. Over the next three days Isa Khan ensured that the small British party had food and water, and on the third day Isa Khan organised a game of polo and invited the two British officers to watch. The two officers, with Jemadar Lall Khan and two men, accepted the invitation and went unarmed to the ground where the match was to take place. They were given beds to sit on and suddenly a large force of some 700 or 800 men surrounded and secured them. The remainder of the village was attacked and many of the small British-Kashmir force were killed. Only the Mohamedans were spared, or those of other faiths who agreed to be converted. In all, the two British officers and 12 sepoys were captured and taken to Chitral where they arrived on 19 March. The two officers were permitted to write to Surgeon-Major Robertson who sent them eating utensils, clothes and blankets. The prisoners were kept in confinement at Chitral until 24 March, when they and the captured sepoys were marched to Drosh. After leaving Chitral the party was better treated and the two officers were given a horse each to ride. The party reached Drosh on the second day and were taken before Umra Khan. On the evening of the third day at Drosh, the two British officers were again taken to Umra Khan who gave them the option of returning to Chitral and joining the besieged garrison, staying on at Drosh, or accompanying Umra Khan to Bajour. The officers asked for the sepoys to be allowed to go with them to the fort at Chitral but as Umra Khan refused this request they elected to remain with Umra Khan with their men. The two officers were guarded by ten armed men, but generally Umra Khan treated them very well and both believed that he did not intend them any harm. Lieutenant Edwards was released on 12 April and before he was released he had a final meeting with Umra Khan. The event is recorded in the diary of Lieutenant John Fowler. A sword had been brought into the room where the two officers were being held and Lieutenant Edwardes thought that it was his own sword which he had lost when he had been captured. The entry in the diary reads 'Just before E started UK [Fowler refers to Umra Khan as 'UK' throughout his diary] said "Give me that sword" and handed it to us, saying, "I think this may belong to one of you. It was sent to me as a present from Chitral." E looked at the sword, and knew it as his at once, and handing it back told UK so. UK then said "I am very glad to give it back to you, and you can take it with you." E made UK a very nice little speech thanking him.'[5] Lieutenant Fowler remained a prisoner with Orderly Rashid Khan, Sapper Chandar Singh and two Kashmir sepoys. Edwardes reached the British relief column without trouble and gave the Commander of the relief force, Lieutenant-General Sir R. C. Low, the offer of submission from Umra Khan.

On 16 April, Lieutenant Fowler had a final meeting with Umra Khan and agreed to act as a mediator on his behalf. Fowler was then sent off towards the Relief Force with an escort of 30 cavalrymen and 30 infantry, accompanied by the other four prisoners. The diary gives a very graphic account of the meeting with the out picquet from the force. Lieutenant Fowler had been ordered to wear Pathan clothes over what little remained of his uniform and when the picquet lines were approached the cavalry escort bade him 'a cordial farewell'. When the infantry reached about 600 yards from the outposts they also turned back. The diary records the actual meeting 'I tied a white rag to the end of my stout bamboo, which was my only weapon, and kept it over my head. As we advanced I could see some of our Sepoys coming towards us, and soon I was

among a party of the 4th Sikhs. I was still wearing my Pathan clothes, and they told us to halt. I asked if there was an officer anywhere about, and they said in a casual way there was one up the hill. I proceeded to get off my pony, when they saw I was not the Pathan they had taken me for but a 'Sahib'. Then there was great excitement, and they showed the keenest joy and interest. The officer in charge of the picquet came down, and jolly glad I was to shake hands with him.'[6] The two British officers had been prisoners of Umra Khan for a month but had been treated quite well and their release permitted the British authorities to be generous to Umra Khan. It was generally conceded that Umra Khan 'had behaved like a gentleman'.[7]

To return to the siege of Chitral, as soon as the authorities became aware of the siege they mounted a relief expedition which was under the command of Lieutenant-General Sir Robert C. Low KCB, with the following troops under his control:

Captain of the 9th Bengal Lancers. AMOT

1st Infantry Brigade
1st Battalion, King's Royal Rifle Corps
1st Battalion Bedfordshire Regiment
15th (Sikh) Bengal Infantry
37th (Dogra) Bengal Infantry
No 1 British Field Hospital and No 14 Native Field Hospital

2nd Infantry Brigade
1st Battalion Gordon Highlanders
2nd Battalion King's Own Scottish Borderers
4th Sikh Infantry
Corps of Guides (Queen's Own) Infantry
No 2 British Field Hospital and No 35 Native Field Hospital

3rd Infantry Brigade
2nd Battalion Seaforth Highlanders
1st Battalion East Kent Regiment
25th (Punjab) Bengal Infantry
2nd Battalion 4th Gurkha Rifles
No 8 British Field Hospital and No 19 Native Field Hospital

Divisional Troops
Corps of Guides (Queen's Own) Cavalry

11th Bengal Lancers
13th Bengal Infantry
23rd Pioneers
No 15 Field Battery Royal Artillery
No 3 Mountain Battery Royal Artillery
No 8 Mountain Battery Royal Artillery
No 4 (Hazara) Mountain Battery
No 1 Company Bengal Sappers and Miners
No 4 Company Bengal Sappers and Miners
No 6 Company Bengal Sappers and Miners
Engineer Field Park, from Roorkee
No 4 British Field Hospital, A and B Sections
No 17 and 18 Native Field Hospital
Veterinary Field Hospital No 1, from Rawalpindi
Maxim gun and detachment of 8 men, 1st Battalion Devonshire
  Regiment

British officers of the 15th (The Ludhiana Sikhs) taken during the Chitral relief operation, 1895.

Lieutenant John Fowler (front left) on release from captivity by Umra Kahn. (Courtesy of the Royal Signals Museum.)

Lines of Communication Troops
1st Battalion East Lancashire Regiment
29th (Punjab) Bengal Infantry
30th (Punjab) Bengal Infantry
No 2 (Derajat) Mountain Battery (4 guns)
No 4 British Field Hospital, C and D Sections
No 24 Native Field Hospital
Nos 5 and 6 British Field Hospitals
Nos 28 and 29 Native Field Hospitals
Departmental Units
Veterinary Field Hospital No 2, from Rawalpindi
Field Medical Store, from Mian Mir
British General Hospital, Peshawar
Native General Hospital, Peshawar
(Half) General Veterinary Hospital, Umballa
(Half) Base Veterinary Store Depot, Umballa
Ordnance Field Park, Rawalpindi
Reserve Brigade
The reserve brigade was held in readiness at Rawalpindi
1st Battalion Rifle Brigade
26th (Punjab) Bengal Infantry

2nd Battalion 1st Gurkha Regiment
2nd Battalion 3rd Gurkha Rifles
(Half) British Field Hospital
(One and half) Native Field Hospital

In addition to the event at Chitral, and the capture of the Edwardes/Fowler party, Captain C. R. Ross and Lieutenant H. J. Jones together with 60 men of their regiment, the 14th (the Ferozepore Sikh) Bengal Infantry, moved from Buni on 8 March, intending to proceed to Reshun. The small party reached the Koragh Defile when they were attacked by tribesmen and, being heavily outnumbered, fell back to Koragh. Lieutenant Jones was instructed to secure the Koragh end of the defile with a party of ten men. In attempting to carry out this order, eight of his ten men were wounded and he then informed Captain Ross of the situation. The two groups reunited and secured a position in two caves by a river bank. Attempts to break out failed and they maintained their position in the caves during 9 March and resolved to break out and make for Koragh on the following day. At 2am, when it was thought that the tribesmen would be resting, the attempt was made but the party came under heavy fire and a large number of the sepoys were killed. Captain Ross was killed in front of one of the enemy sangars. Lieutenant Jones was able to withdraw from the defile and reach Koragh where they were again attacked. By this time the small party had been reduced to Lieutenant Jones and nine sepoys, all of whom had been wounded. Lieutenant Jones's report on the final stages of this ill-fated party reads 'We retired slowly on Buni, where we arrived about 6am. It was quite impossible to bring away any wounded men who were unable to walk with us. It was equally impossible to bring their rifles, and therefore a certain number of these, about forty, fell into enemy hands.'[8] Lieutenant H. J. Jones was later made a Companion of the Distinguished Service Order for his gallant conduct during the ill-fated attempt to reach Reshun.

The relief force was quickly mobilised and orders were given for the 1st Division to concentrate by 1 April at Hoti Mardan, Peshawar and Nowshera, ready for an advance to Chitral. The

'a burning sun and . . . in the face of galling fire.' However, the advance did continue. The report by General Low on the events of 3 April gives the basic details:

The action was begun at 8.30am and concluded at 2pm. The total numbers of the enemy are variously reported but the actual numbers on the pass were probably about 10,000 to 12,000 men, some 3,000 armed, and the rest using rocks and stones (a quite adequate weapon on troops attempting to scale steep hillsides). The enemy's loss was said by themselves to be about 500, and the road down the other side was covered with signs of numbers of wounded men having been carried away. Our loss was 11 men killed, and 8 officers and 39 men wounded. The 1st Brigade remained at the top of the pass holding it, while the mules of the brigade passed up; but the path was so bad that only a few mules reached the top that night.

30th Punjab Infantry, 1897.

advance was made on 1 April as planned, and a report on this part of the operation gives the movements of the brigades as follows: 'From Hoti Mardan the 2nd and 3rd Brigades marched to Jalala under Generals Waterfield and Gatacre, whilst General Kinloch took the 1st Brigade direct to Lundkhawar . . . The original intention was for General Waterfield to advance by the Malakand Pass and form a junction with General Kinloch at the Swat River, whilst the latter took the Shahkot Pass route . . . It was hoped that passages of Shahkot and Malakand would be facilitated, and a more rapid advance made to Chitral be secured.'[9] The enemy had collected at Shahkot and Morah Passes and their numbers were said to be about 10,000. The fighting was fierce and whilst the tribesmen had the advantage of defending the heights, the combined British and Indian Field Force had to advance over open ground, storm heights all under

On the following day, 4 April, the 1st Brigade, under Brigadier-General A. A. A. Kinloch CB, moved down at 2pm and found the enemy in strength and far from suppressed. After a short action which culminated with a charge by the Guides Infantry and the 37th Dogras, the enemy fled leaving about 30 dead. Over the whole operation it was estimated that about 500 were killed and wounded. The advance continued with the concentration of the Field Force at Camp Khar. General Kinloch's 1st Brigade moved to Aladand and covered the crossing of the 3rd Brigade and the remainder of the 2nd Brigade. On 12 April the Guides Infantry crossed the Panjkora by the bridge but unfortunately, on the following day, part of the bridge was washed away when some heavy logs were washed

Mundiah Fort, March 1896. (Courtesy of Miss L. Fowler and the Royal Signals Museum.)

down river. This left the Guides Infantry isolated on the opposite side of the flooded river and they were neither able to withdraw, nor could they be reinforced. The Guides Infantry were ordered to fall back to the Panjkora in order that they could be covered by the guns on the left bank of the river. The Guides, under command of Lieutenant-Colonel F. D. Battye, proceeded to clear the area of the enemy, but at about one o'clock, having been warned that two columns of the enemy were approaching, he ordered his men to fall back to the river. In doing so high ground was to be held so as to give cover for the withdrawal. The enemy force completely outnumbered the Guides but, despite this, the Guides withdrew gradually, repelling rush after rush from the tribesmen. On each occasion, when the order to retire was given, Colonel Battye was the last to move back but eventually he fell, killed instantly by a sharp-shooter's bullet. The Guides briefly broke ranks and surged forward to avenge their lost Colonel and it was with difficulty that Captain F. Campbell, who took command at that time, brought the Guides back into line and completed the orderly withdrawal, with the loss of three men killed and ten wounded.[10]

The Guides, who had advanced to clear the area were further forward than had been expected and, when confronted by two columns of about 2,000 men each, had no option but to retire to a point where they could be given covering fire from the opposite bank of the river. The allegation that the advance of the battalion had exceeded the orders given was later refuted and no criticism was made against the Commanding Officer, who lost his life bringing his men back to a position where they could, and did, repulse the enemy.

Whilst the main relief force was gradually advancing towards Chitral, a smaller relief force, under the command of Lieutenant Colonel J. G. Kelly, 32nd Bengal Infantry (Pioneers), left Gilgit on 23 and 24 March. The first party consisted of 200 men of the 32nd Pioneers; and the second party, which departed on 24 March was made up of 200 men of 32nd Pioneers, 2 Guns of the Kashmir Battery, together with 60 Kashmir sepoys, 40 Kashmir sappers and '100 Hunza Nagar Levies'. When the party reached Ghizr it snowed for five days, thus holding up any advance. The first attempt to get over the pass failed due to heavy snow which continued to delay the advance. There were casualties from snow blindness and

Chitral Fort, 1896. (Courtesy of Miss L. Fowler and the Royal Signals Museum.)

frostbite but the advance resumed on 5 April. On 7 April they met with opposition but after a determined attack on the enemy position at Nisa Gol, the force, under Colonel Kelly, were able to advance again. The diary giving details of the advance to Chitral records that on 18 April 'This morning the force had but 2½ days' provisions, so foraging parties were sent forward and about half a day's more was obtained.' On 19 April they reached Khozagi without opposition and learned that in fact the enemy had departed from Chitral.

The diary of Captain C. V. F. Townsend who had taken command of the force at Chitral, as Captain C. P. Campbell had been severely wounded, records the events of 19 April as follows:

About 3am this morning Lieutenant Gurdon, who was on middle watch, reported that a man outside was calling out under the fort wall that he had important news to tell. All precautions were taken; he was admitted to the main gate, and he told us of the flight of Sher Afzul and the Jandoul Chief (Umra Khan) about midnight, and of the near approach of Colonel Kelly's column from Mastuj. All the sangers were deserted. In the morning not a man was to be seen about Chitral. The siege, which had lasted 46 days, was at an end . . . The Gilgit column

accordingly arrived at 2pm on the 20th, the 32nd Pioneers looking in very good trim and good condition.[11]

The losses of the garrison at Chitral during the 46 days, including the fight on 3 March, were 104 killed and wounded out of 370 combatants which formed the British Agent's escort.

On 16 May, Major-General Low entered Chitral at 8am and was received by the troops drawn up on parade. He was met by Surgeon-Major Robertson and Captain Townsend and then inspected the troops drawn up in a square. He addressed them saying:

This is a remarkable parade, on which are assembled Colonel Kelly's troops and those of the 3rd Brigade of the force sent by the Government of India to relieve Chitral. All here have already received the congratulations of the *Queen-Empress* and I need not enlarge on the achievements of the troops or their consequences. The devoted gallantry and heroic courage of the garrison are the pride and admiration of their comrades, and will pass into history and form one of the highest achievements of the British-Indian and Kashmir armies.

Chitral had been defended and relieved and, apart from the award of the India Medal (1895-1902) with either the clasp

'Defence of Chitral 1895' for the period 3 March to 19 April 1895; or 'Relief of Chitral 1895' for the period 7 March to 15 August 1895, a number of honours were awarded to officers and men of the Indian Army who took part in either of the operations. These included:

Surgeon-Major G. S. Robertson became a Knight Commander of the Star of India; Lieutenant-Colonel J. G. Kelly, and Brevet-Major C. V. F. Townsend, Indian Staff Corps were appointed Companions of the Most Honourable Order of the Bath.

Eight officers were made Companions of the Distinguished Service Order, including six officers serving in the Indian Staff Corps, these being:

Captain Henry Benn Borradaile
Lieutenant Herbert John Jones
Lieutenant Stanley Malcolm Edwardes
Lieutenant Bertrand Evelyn Mellish Gurdon
Lieutenant William George Lawrence Beynon, and
Lieutenant Henry Kellet Harley

The other two officers, although shown as being British Army, were in fact serving with Indian based units, being Lieutenant Cosmo Gordon Stewart RA, serving with No 3 (Peshawar) Mountain Battery; and Lieutenant John Sharman Fowler RE, employed on special duty at Gilgit whilst on the strength of the Corps of Bengal Sappers and Miners.

Surgeon-Captain Harry Frederick Whitchurch, Indian Medical Service (Bengal) was awarded the Victoria Cross for 'conspicuous bravery and devotion to his country displayed by him in having, during the sortie from Chitral Fort on 3 March 1895, at the commencement of the siege, gone to the assistance of Captain Baird, 24th Bengal Infantry, who was mortally wounded and brought him back to the fort under heavy fire from the enemy.'

The Indian Officers and men also were awarded for numerous acts of bravery and gallant conduct which included Subadar Gurmukh Singh, 14th (The Ferozepore Sikhs) Bengal Infantry, who was awarded the order of British India, 2nd class, with the title 'Bahadur'. The 3rd Class of the Indian Order of Merit was awarded to two Havildars, a Lance Naik and 11 men of the same regiment; four sappers of the Bengal Sappers and Miners; three officers and three men of the 32nd Bengal Infantry (Pioneers); and, in addition, a further group of one officer and six men of the 14th (The Ferozepore Sikhs) Bengal Infantry, were given the award from 17 April 1895. The same award was given to three officers and 17 men of the 4th Kashmir Rifles for their gallant conduct during the operations.

The troops taking part in the defence and relief operation were awarded the India Medal (1895) which is described as follows:

Obverse – The crowned and veiled head of Queen Victoria with the legend 'VICTORIA REGINA ET IMPERATRIX'.
Reverse – A British and Indian soldier both supporting the

same standard and on the left is the word 'INDIA' and on the right '1895'.
Size – 36mm diameter.
Ribbon – 32mm wide. Crimson with two dark green stripes down the centre.

The medal, together with the clasps 'Defence of Chitral 1895' and 'Relief of Chitral 1895' were authorised by Army Order dated 1 April 1896.

Conflict continued in the North West Frontier area over the remaining years of the 19th century and the next major incident which was serious enough to warrant the issue of another clasp to the India Medal 1895 was for the defence and relief of Malakand during mid-1897, when the award of the clasp 'Malakand 1897' was issued for service during the period 26 July to 2 August. During July 1897 an estimated 20,000 Afridi tribesmen suddenly attacked the Malakand garrison. The posts of Chakdara and Malakand were commanded by Colonel W. H. Meiklejohn CB CMG, and consisted of troops of the 11th (Prince of Wales's Own) Regiment of Bengal Lancers; No 8 (Bengal) Mountain Battery; No 5 Company Madras Sappers and Miners; 24th (Punjab) Bengal Infantry; 31st (Punjab) Bengal Infantry and the 45th (Rattray's Sikhs) Bengal Infantry. The tribesmen first attacked Malakand but, after several days' fighting, were beaten off and then turned their attention to the Chakdara Post which held out although water and ammunition became scarce. The Malakand Field Force was formed under the command of Brigadier-General Sir Bindon Blood KCB, and consisted of a mixed British and Indian force made up of the following units:

The India Medal.

The 36th Sikh Regiment, 1896.

1st Brigade
1st Battalion Royal West Kent Regiment
45th (Rattray's Sikhs) Bengal Infantry
24th and 31st (Punjab) Bengal Infantry

2nd Brigade
11th (Prince of Wales's Own) Regiment of Bengal Lancers
No 5 Company Bengal Sappers and Miners
1st Battalion, The Buffs (East Kent Regiment)
Corps Guides (Queen's Own) Infantry
35th (Sikh) Bengal Infantry
38th (Dogra) Bengal Infantry

3rd Brigade
1st Battalion The Queen's (Royal West Surrey) Regiment
39th (The Garhwal Rifle) Regiment of Bengal Infantry
22nd (Punjab) Bengal Infantry

In addition, a squadron of cavalry from the 10th and 11th Bengal Lancers and Corps of Guides (Queen's Own) Cavalry was provided, and artillery support from 10 Field Battery (RFA) with Nos 1 and 7 Mountain Batteries RA, and No 8 (Bengal) Mountain Battery. Sappers and Miners supplied three companies, No 3 (Bombay), No 4 (Bengal) and No 5 (Madras), with 21 (Punjab) Bengal Infantry and 2nd Battalion Highland Light Infantry giving additional infantry support.

Malakand was reached first and, having relieved that position, Sir Bindon Blood despatched a column to relieve Chakdara which was successfully carried out but only after fierce fighting. An advance was made from Thana on 17 August and the enemy were encountered at Landaki where a large concentration of tribesmen held a flat-topped spur which dominated the valley. Colonel Mieklejohn moved his brigade and, ascending the hill, surprised the enemy on the left flank. The main force had kept the 5,000 tribesmen occupied on the front whilst this flanking movement was carried out, which succeeded in surprising the enemy and they fled from the area which then brought about an end to hostilities for the time being. The Malakand Field Force was then disbanded and the battalions returned to their normal stations. During the conflict two Victoria Crosses were awarded, one to Lieutenant Edmond William Costello, 22nd (Punjab) Bengal Infantry, who was awarded the VC for his gallantry on 26 July 1897;[12] and the second award was to Lieutenant Viscount A. E. Fincastle who was with the force as a war correspondent of *The Times*.

Within three weeks of the Malakand operation being concluded another disturbance occurred which resulted in the clasp 'Samana 1897' being awarded to troops who served in the garrisons beyond Kohat. Tribesmen attacked Fort Gulistan, which was at the gateway to the Afridi hills, and although a spirited resistance was put up by the small garrison of one Indian officer and 20 men of the 36th (Sikh) Bengal Infantry, a relief force under the command of Major-General A. G. Yeatman-Biggs set out to restore order. The troops included 180 men of the 2nd Battalion, Royal Scots Fusiliers, with detachments from the 2nd and 5th Punjab Infantry, 3rd Regiment of Sikh Infantry, the 15th (The Ludhiana Sikh) Bengal Infantry and 36th (Sikh) Bengal Infantry, 21st Regiment of Madras Infantry (Pioneers)

Local tribesmen of the Khyber Pass, c1896. (Courtesy of Miss L. Fowler and the Royal Signals Museum.)

as well as the 1st Battalion, 2nd (Prince of Wales's Own) Gurkha Rifles (The Sirmoor Rifles), 1st Battalion 3rd Gurkha (Rifle) Regiment and the 5th Gurkha (Rifle) Regiment, Punjab Frontier Force. The first engagement resulted in many of the men of the 2nd Battalion, Royal Scots Fusiliers, having to be brought back to Kohat by ambulance due to heat exhaustion, brought on by the extremely high temperature. The force gradually relieved the various forts that were under siege by the Ovakzais and Chamkannis tribesmen who, apart from having attacked the forts, had raided and destroyed posts and villages. The Field Force eventually drove the enemy back and peace was restored to the area.

There were other problems for the authorities along the frontier and, as was often the case, whilst one operation was being conducted in one area, tribesmen in another area decided that the time was right to attack villages and posts and generally cause unrest. Such was the case when, on the afternoon of 7 August 1897, about 4,000 to 5,000 followers of Hadda Mullah attacked the Shab Kadar Fort and then looted and burned the village of Shankargargh. The attack on the fort had been repulsed by the small garrison of one Indian officer and 46 'Border police'. The enemy withdrew but did not move far away. A column, under the command of Lieutenant-Colonel J. B. Woon, arrived with two companies of the Somerset Light Infantry as well as Indian Army troops and engaged the enemy on an undulating plateau at the foot of some hills. Owing to the difficult nature of the terrain the enemy were able to make a flanking attack on the British column so that Colonel Woon was obliged to withdraw to avoid being cut off from his base at Dakka Fort. Brigadier-General E. R. Elles CB arrived from Peshawar and assumed the command of the Field Force and, having reorganised them, he mounted a cavalry attack on the left rear of the enemy and was able to put the tribesmen to flight.

It was estimated that the enemy lost about 200 killed, with the Field Force loss of nine men killed, and four officers and 61 men wounded. Again in August 1897 an expedition was mounted against the Mohmands who had been causing problems in the Dir territory and were threatening the safety of the Chitral Road. The Mohmand Field Force, under the command of Brigadier-General E. R. Elles, consisting of two Brigades of British and Indian troops, set out and after a long march under trying conditions of intense heat, advanced unopposed and met up with the Malakand Field Force on 22 September, where the two Field Forces combined and secured the Bedmanai Pass. Two days later they moved into the Mitai and Suran Valleys and destroyed all the villages and towers. On the next day, 25 September, the work of subduing the tribes continued against the fortified villages in the Shindarra gorge. The whole operation was proving successful and the advance continued and operated against the villages occupied by the Koda Khel Baezai tribe. Again, the tribesmen were defeated and although the tracks were difficult, the advance continued until 4 October by which time all the offending tribes had submitted and paid their fines, and so with the mission accomplished, the combined force withdrew.

The situation on the frontier remained uneasy and within a few weeks of the close of the Malakand operation troops were again called upon to defend frontier posts against attacks from rebellious tribesmen. For the minor operations that were conducted during the period 22 August to 2 October 1897, those stationed in the garrisons beyond Kohat were awarded the clasp

26th Madras Native Infantry, 1896.   AMOT

The heliograph in use with the Tochi Field Force.   The Graphic

Officers of the 36th Sikhs besieged at Gulistan.

'Samana 1897' to the India Medal (1895-1902). The detachment of 36th (Sikh) Regiment of Bengal Infantry, who defended Fort Gulistan, put up a gallant defence of their post and another detachment from the same regiment, consisting of one Indian Officer and 20 soldiers, were all killed in the defence of their post at Saragarhi. In a rare tribute, a special memorial was erected at Amritsar (the Sikh Holy city). The troops who were under the command of Major-General A. G. Yeatman-Biggs were all included, from 2 October, in the Tirah Field Force. The troops which formed the frontier garrisons were from the following units:

12th Regiment of Bengal Cavalry
18th Regiment of Bengal Lancers
3rd Regiment of Punjab Cavalry
3, 9 and 11 Field Batteries RA
No 2 Mountain Battery RA
No 2 (Derajat) Mountain Battery
No 4 Company Bombay Sappers and Miners
2nd and 5th Regiments of Punjab Infantry (Punjab Frontier Force)
3rd Regiment of Sikh Infantry

15th (The Ludhiana Sikhs) Regiment of Bengal Infantry
36th (Sikh) Regiment of Bengal Infantry
21st Regiment of Madras Infantry (Pioneers)
1st Battalion, 2nd (Prince of Wales's Own) Gurkha (Rifle) Regiment (The Sirmoor Rifles)
1st Battalion 3rd Gurkha (Rifle) Regiment
5th Gurkha (Rifle) Regiment
Kurram Militia

In addition, the frontier defence was supplemented by three British battalions which were 2nd Battalion Royal Irish Rifles, 2nd Battalion Royal Scots Fusiliers and the 1st Battalion Duke of Cornwall's Light Infantry.

The Tirah Expeditionary Force, which included all the above mentioned units who had qualified for the 'Samana 1897' clasp, was formed under the command of Lieutenant-General Sir William Lockhart KCB, KCSI who had been recalled from leave in England to take command of the operation, with the intention of bringing both the Afridis and Orakzais under control and to punish them for the numerous 'offences' they had committed in the frontier area. The plan was to take the force into the heart of the Afridis' and Orakzais' territories and, with a great show of strength, prove to the tribes that the British Government could move into their territories at any time they wished and control the area.

The plan was for the force to cross the Samana range by the Chagru Kotal, west of Gulistan, and then cross the Khanki valley, pass through the Sampagha and Archanga passes, enter Maidan and dictate peace terms to the Afridis. The Tırah Expeditionary Force, concentrated for the main advance, was organised into two Divisions, each containing two brigades consisting of four battalions, with two squadrons of cavalry, four mountain batteries, three companies of sappers and miners and a pioneer battalion. Four other battalions were standing by to protect the lines of communication and two additional columns were organised, one at Peshawar and the second at Kurram. As a final back-up to the large field force a reserve brigade was established at Rawalpindi. There were 44,000 combatant troops in the Expeditionary Force and one of the greatest problems facing the planning staff was the provision of sufficient

Royal Artillery group c1896. AMOT

transport. To this end officers were despatched throughout the Punjab to requisition bullock carts, camels, mules and ponies. The operation effectively began on 2 October and by 18 October the 2nd Division, who had concentrated at Shinawari, moved out to clear the enemy tribesmen from the village of Dargai and the ridges in that area where the enemy had been firing on working parties from the combined British and Indian force. The village of Dargai was on a cliff which was approachable only by a single precarious footpath. The attack on the village was made by the 1st Battalion 3rd Gurkha (Rifle) Regiment, supported by the 2nd Battalion King's Own Scottish Borderers who took control of the village with comparative ease, which was partially due to the fact that the area was defended only by the Orakzais. The remainder of the brigade did not join up with the two units who had secured the village, due to rough terrain, which resulted in all the transport being sent back to base camp. By the time the two parts of the brigade had joined forces, the several thousand Afridis had advanced from the Khanki valley and were lining the heights, and it was considered advisable to withdraw from the village of Dargai. The reason for the withdrawal has been criticised but there was little option but to withdraw as the troops were isolated, the nearest water being

'Screw Guns' on the move.

some three miles away across a track that was unsuitable even for mules. The height of the position was 6,000 feet and as the troops were without firewood or warm clothing, and were threatened by imminent attack by Afridis, there was little option but to pull back to a more defendable position. On 20 October the whole of the 2nd Division returned to take the village and heights. The advance commenced at 4.30am and reached Chagru Kotal unopposed. As a deception, the political officer let it be known that the main advance was to follow the line of the outflanking advance made during the previous attack. To a degree the plot worked, as some of the enemy were moved from the main battle to keep a watch on the right flank. It was estimated that 12,000 Afridis were located on the Dargai heights ready to meet the main attack by the 2nd Division. The position was ideal for the defenders and, in addition, they strengthened their defence line by the construction of sangars. As soon as the 1st Battalion 2nd (PWO) Gurkha (Rifle) Regiment commenced its advance it was halted by the rapid and accurate fire from the Afridis' defenders. The artillery fire proved to be almost non-effective against the rocks and defence works put up by the enemy. For five hours the Gurkhas fought supported first by the 1st Battalion The

Dorsetshire Regiment and then by the 2nd Battalion the Sherwood Foresters (Derbyshire Regiment), but still the rapid fire kept the advance pinned down. The 1st Battalion Gordon Highlanders and the 3rd Regiment of Sikh Infantry were then brought forward and, after a rapid and concentrated artillery fire lasting about three minutes carried out by the whole of the supporting artillery, the five battalions, led by the Gordons, advanced with the pipers of the Gordon Highlanders playing *Cock o' the North*. The enemy, reluctant to face such a formidable force, withdrew before being overrun. As a result of the determined attack by the troops of the Expeditionary Force, four awards were made of the supreme gallantry award, the Victoria Cross. The awards were to Lieutenant H. S. Pennell, Sherwood Foresters; Private S. Vickery, Dorsetshire Regiment; and two were given to men of the Gordon Highlanders; Private E. Lawson and Piper G. Findlater, who continued to play the bagpipes, spurring on the Gordon Highlanders, after being shot through both ankles.[13] In this fierce encounter the Expeditionary Force lost 36 killed and 159 wounded. The troops spent a cold night on the ridge, bivouacking where they were, and the following day moved down to the Khanki valley without any further opposition. The advance guard reached Maidan on 1 November and, although fighting had occurred in both the Samapagha and Arhanga Passes, neither side suffered many casualties. Notices were then sent out to all the tribes inviting them to attend meetings to hear the terms on which the British were prepared to leave their country. The Orakzais generally had had enough and by the end of the month paid the imposed fines in rifles and cash. The Afridis, and the Zakha Khels who numbered about 4,500 men, remained hostile to the British. On 9 November, following an attack on a Zakha Khel village, the 1st Battalion Northamptonshire Regiment came under heavy fire from Afridis who used high ground to inflict casualties on the British battalion. At 4pm the 36th (Sikh) Regiment of Bengal Infantry was moved back to take over the rearguard duties from the British battalion. Unfortunately, the battalion took what seemed to be a short route back to base camp and entered a deep nala and lost contact with the troops now providing the rearguard. They were then attacked from the rim of the nala by the Afridis who, through accurate and rapid fire, brought more casualties to the battalion. The Northamptonshire Regiment's casualties for that day were two officers and 17 men killed, and two officers and 35 men wounded.

On 13 November a brigade of five battalions moved through a low pass into Aka Khal country with the intention of bringing some of the more hesitant tribes under control. There was very little trouble until the troops were moving back to base on 16 November, when they came under attack from the wooded slopes above the pass. Once again the 36th (Sikh) Regiment of Bengal Infantry, who were well versed in frontier fighting, were given the task of providing the rearguard with two 'weak' companies of the 1st Battalion Dorsetshire Regiment. A detachment of the battalion was placed in a position to command the road. Unfortunately, they mistook the enemy for a detachment of the 36th Sikhs and, moving out from a house which was their cover, they were immediately attacked with the loss of two officers and nine men killed and a number of others were wounded. The party was rallied by the senior Sergeant, withdrew from the conflict and moved back to base camp.

On 26 November a decision was made to evacuate the Tirah, and while the arrangements were made for the backloading of all the heavy baggage the opportunity came whereby the Chamkannis, a small tribe overlooking the Kurram valley, were punished for their offences. During 7 and 8 December one brigade moved back over the Arhanga Pass to meet up with the 1st Division which was to withdraw to Fort Bara via the Mastura. The 3rd and 4th Brigades of the 2nd Division concentrated at the river junction of the Dwa Toi. The march down to Dwa Toi was made in terrible conditions with rain and snow and bitter cold. The withdrawal proper commenced on 10 December and from then until Barkai was reached on 14 December the whole column came under attack, not only the rearguard but from the flanks as well. On the 13 December the 4th Brigade took over the duties of the rearguard. Long before

the transport of the 3rd Brigade was clear of the first defile, the Afridis, who were particularly daring at this stage due to their success in causing casualties on the previous days during the withdrawal, moved in close and attacked whilst the followers were still loading up the animals. Followers and animals were hit and it was only with difficulty that the camp was eventually cleared, and then under cover of artillery fire. At a point where the track moved up from a river bed, the enemy swarmed across the stream in a concentrated attack but were beaten back by a cross fire of artillery, machine guns and concentrated rifle fire. Even though the tribesmen had many casualties they soon recovered and continued to harass the rear guard as fiercely as ever. It was only by the steadfastness of the Expeditionary Force troops, and the determined direction by the Brigade Commander, Brigadier-General R. Westmacott, that the force was saved from further serious casualties. On the following day the troops continued the move back to base and when they met the picquets which had been sent out from the Peshawar Brigade from Fort Bara, the enemy withdrew and the two brigades marched into camp without further opposition.

The 1st Division in the Mastura valley took the opportunity on 9 December to punish some of the Aka Khel villages who

Lt-Col A.W. Pennington, 9th Bengal Lancers, 1895.   AMOT

were known to have given assistance to the hostile tribesmen. The first phase of the Tirah campaign was then completed but the cost had been heavy with 'thirteen hundred casualties' among the combat troops.[14]

On reaching Fort Bara the 2nd Division assumed the responsibility for watching the mouth of the Bara valley, whilst the 1st Division and the Peshawar Column concentrated at Fort Jamrud. On 23 December the Peshawar Column reoccupied Ali Masjid, where it remained for two days to cover the advance into the Bazaar valley by the 1st Division. Landi Kotal was reoccupied although the place had been looted and a lot of damage done. With the help of Shinwaris, who had submitted and paid their fines, the water supply was restored and the fort reoccupied. The operations in the Bazaar Valley lasted five days and, although the rearguards were harassed, there was no serious fighting as there had been in the Tirah.

forward to help recover the casualties from the previous attempt to take the hill, and in doing so a bayonet charge was ordered to give cover for the evacuation of the wounded. Lieutenant-Colonel J. Haughton was in the van and carrying the rifle of a man who had just been killed at his side; the Commanding Officer was himself shot through the head, and almost immediately his Adjutant, Lieutenant R. G. Munn, was also killed.

It took time to bring the Afridis to agree terms and only a few of the 1,097 rifles demanded had been handed in. The Zakha Khel were equally reluctant to come to terms, but by mid-February the blockade was beginning to have effect and when it became possible for the reopening of the Khaibar Pass to caravan traffic to Afghanistan on 7 March, the tribes realised that the British were determined to see the operation through to their satisfaction. At a final jirga on 13 March, General Sir

During the following month there was little activity, although the tribesmen continued to attack convoys and make other minor raids. The next major event occurred on 29 January 1898, during an operational sweep of the Kajuri plain. It was reported that a number of Afridis had brought their flocks down to graze but no trace could be found of the party. The 4th Brigade did, however, meet up with the enemy and, due to an error in the delivery of a message, a picquet was withdrawn prematurely and this allowed the tribesmen to occupy a vital high position. The 2nd Battalion King's Own Yorkshire Light Infantry, which was brought up to recapture the hill then occupied in force by the enemy, failed to regain the position. The 36th (Sikh) Regiment of Bengal Infantry, who had performed superbly when acting as rearguard troops during the main Tirah operation, were brought up to help retake the hill. The 36th Sikhs moved

William Lockhart fixed 17 March as the date on which he would resume the offensive unless all the fines were paid. On that date he returned to Fort Jamrud in person, while transport animals commenced moving out from Peshawar. On the same day a brigade moved a few miles into the Bara valley and this show of determination brought the tribes to sue for peace. Hostages were given and hostilities ceased on 3 April. It was officially over on 6 April and General Sir William Lockhart departed to continue his interrupted leave in England.

It was a tribute to his standing within the frontier community, both with the peaceful and sometimes hostile tribes, that at his departure 'some hundreds of Afridis, including large numbers of Zakha Khel, surrounded his house and begged to be allowed to draw his carriage to the railway station.'[16]

The troops who took part in the Tirah operation were

Fort Jamrud – at the entrance to the Khyber Pass.

Lt-Col Augustus Frederick Williams, c1897.

awarded the India Medal (1895-1902) with the clasp 'Tirah 1897-98' for service during the period 2 October 1897 to 6 April 1898. The award was also given to troops involved in the line of communication and in the Swat Valley.

The Indian Army units that took part in the campaign were, in addition to those already listed as being in the Samana operation:

20th (The Duke of Cambridge's Own Punjab) Regiment of Bengal Infantry
2nd Battalion, 1st Gurkha (Rifle) Regiment
34th Native Field Hospital
All parts of 1st Division, 1st Brigade

In the 2nd Brigade:
2nd Battalion 4th Gurkha (Rifle) Regiment

28th Regiment of Bombay Infantry (Pioneers)
51st Native Field Hospital

In the 1st Division troops were:
No 1 (Korat) Mountain Battery
No 3 Company Bombay Sappers and Miners
28th Regiment of Bombay Infantry (Pioneers)
63rd Native Field Hospital

Within the 2nd Division the following additional troops took to the field:
44th Native Field Hospital
48th Native Field Hospital
5 Bombay Mountain Battery, Rocket Battery
No 4 Company Madras Sappers and Miners
Sirmoor Sappers and Miners
42nd Native Field Hospital

In the Kurram Column, under command of Colonel W. Hill:
6th (The Prince of Wales's) Regiment of Bengal Cavalry
Central India Horse
12th (The Kelat-i-Ghilzai) Regiment of Bengal Infantry
Karpurthala Infantry
Nabha Infantry
62nd Native Field Hospital

The Peshawar Column, under Brigadier-General
A. G. Hammond, VC CB, DSO, consisted of:
9th Regiment of Bengal Lancers
No 5 Company Bengal Sappers and Miners
45th (Rattray's Sikh) Regiment of Bengal Infantry
9th Gurkha (Rifle) Regiment of Bengal Infantry
45th Native Field Hospital

The Rawalpindi Brigade, (the Reserve Brigade) under
command of Brigadier-General C. R. Macgregor DSO,
consisted of:
Jodhpur Imperial Service Lancers
27th Regiment (1st Baluch Battalion) of Bombay (Light)
Infantry
2nd Regiment of Infantry, Hyderabad Contingent
53rd Native Field Hospital

and, finally, the Indian army units in the Line of Communication troops, who were under the command of Lieutenant-General Sir A. P. Palmer KCB:
No 1 Kashmir Mountain Battery
No 1 Company Bengal Sappers and Miners
39th (The Garhwal Rifles) Regiment of Bengal Infantry
2nd Regiment of Punjab Infantry, Punjab Frontier Force
22nd (Punjab) Regiment of Bengal Infantry
2nd Battalion, 2nd (Prince of Wales's own) Gurkha (Rifle)
Regiment (The Sirmoor Rifles)
Jodhpore and Gwalior Transport Corps

Although minor incidents continued to occur in the frontier area, no major operations were mounted and it was only due to unrest in the Mahsud and Waziri districts during the latter part of 1901 and early in 1902 that another clasp was issued to the India Medal (1895-1902). The medal and clasp were awarded to the troops who took part in various mobile columns which were mounted to operate against the Mahsuds in the Kabul Khel country. During the period 23 November 1901 to 10 March 1902 Major-General C. C. Egerton, CB organised four mobile columns for the operations. The following troops from the Indian Army were involved in the final campaign on the North West Frontier prior to the reorganisation of the army by Lord Kitchener while serving as Commander-in-Chief, India:

1st and 2nd Regiment of Bengal Lancers
5th Regiment of Bengal Cavalry
No 2 (Derajat) Mountain Battery
No 7 (Gujerat) (Bengal) Mountain Battery
1st Regiment Punjab Infantry
2nd Regiment Punjab Infantry
9th Gurkha (Rifle) Regiment of Bengal Infantry
27th, 28th and 29th (Punjab) Regiment of Bengal Infantry
3rd and 4th Regiment of Sikh Infantry
35th (Sikh) Regiment of Bengal Infantry
45th (Rattray's Sikh) Regiment of Bengal Infantry
17th (The Loyal) Regiment of Bengal Infantry
9th and 23rd Regiment of Bombay Infantry
4th (Baluchistan; Duchess of Connaught's Own) Regiment of
   Bombay Infantry
38th (Dogra) Regiment of Bengal Infantry
32nd (Punjab) Regiment of Bengal Infantry (Pioneers)
13th (The Shekhawati) Rajput Regiment of Bengal Infantry
3rd Gurkha (Rifle) Regiment
North and South Waziri Militia
43rd Native Field Hospital

Whilst the various campaigns were being waged by the Indian Army, Queen Victoria, Empress of India, celebrated her Diamond Jubilee, known at the time as the 'Sixty Glorious Years'. Representatives from the Indian Army attended the celebration in England. After a long and eventful reign Queen Victoria died at Osborne House, on the Isle of Wight, on 22 January 1901. The accession of King Edward VII to the throne brought about a change to the India Medal (1895-1902), in that the obverse was altered to depict King Edward VII in field-marshal's uniform, wearing a coat. The reverse side had the date '1895' removed, and the thickness of the medal was reduced from that of the original issue.[17]

Lt-Col J.C.F. Gordon, 6th (Prince of Wales's) Bengal Cavalry, c1897.

26th Madras Native Infantry, 1896. AMOT

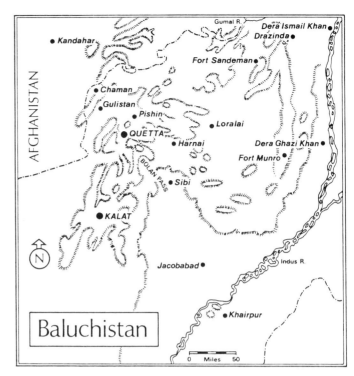

Baluchistan

1   *The Chitral Expedition 1895*, Pioneer Press, Allahabad, 1895, p1.
2   *The Chitral Expedition 1895*, op cit, pp15 & 16.
3   *Baird, Captain John McDonald,* born 12 March 1866, joined the 2nd Battalion, Royal Sussex Regiment on 6 February 1884 from the Royal Military College Sandhurst. After briefly serving with the Derbyshire Regiment's 1st Battalion, he joined the 2nd Battalion at Lucknow in December 1885. After service in Burma, he transferred to the Indian Army and served with 40th Bengal Infantry. He served with that unit during the Hazara campaign of 1888, and briefly returned to Burma. In September 1889 he transferred as Wing officer to the 24th Bengal Infantry at Sialkot. In the autumn of 1891 he was selected for special duty with the Kashmir Imperial Service Troops at Gilgit. After leave in Europe he returned at the end of 1893 to serve with the 4th Kashmir Rifles at Chitral. He was mortally wounded in an action near Chitral Fort on 3 March 1895 and died on the following day. He was buried at Chitral Fort.
    De Rhe-Philipe, G. W. *Inscriptions on Christian Tombs or Monuments in the Punjab, the North-West Frontier Province, Kashmir and Afghanistan* Part II, Lahore, 1912, p11.
4   *Fowler, Lieutenant John Sharman,* was commissioned into the Royal Engineers on 6 January 1886. He arrived in India on 14 March 1888 and then served with the Bengal Sappers and Miners. *Edwardes, Lieutenant Stanley,* was commissioned into the North Lancashire Regiment on 23 August 1884. He was appointed to the Bengal Staff Corps on 24 January 1886 and served with the 2nd Bombay Infantry from 29 April.
5   Fowler, J. S. *Extracts from the diary of John S. Fowler RE. Chitral 1895*, Dublin, 1895, pp92-93.
6   Fowler, op cit, p99.
7   Robertston, Sir George S. *Chitral, the Story of a Minor Siege*, 1898, p 361.
8   *The Chitral Expedition 1895*, op cit, p22.
9   *The Chitral Expedition 1895*, op cit, p27.
    The three Generals concerned with the operation were:
    Brigadier-General W. F. Gatacre DSO
    Brigadier-General A. A. A. Kinloch CB
    Colonel (Temporary Brigadier General) H. G. Waterfield
10 De Rhe-Philipe, G. W. *Inscriptions on Christian Tombs or Monuments in the Punjab, the North-West Frontier Province, Kashmir and Afghanistan* Part II, Lahore, 1912, p20.
    Lieutenant-Colonel Frederick Drummond Battye was the tenth and youngest son of George Wynyard Battye and was born at Chapra, Bihar on 27 May 1847 and entered military service through the Royal Military College Sandhurst and was commissioned into the 35th Foot. After service with the 35th and 62nd Foot Regiments, he became a Second Wing Subaltern in the 6th Punjab Infantry on 2 December 1869. In May 1870 he transferred to the Corps of Guides and remained with that Corps serving as Adjutant, and served in the Jowaki Campaign and the Second Afghan War. He was appointed to officiate as Commandant of the Corps and served in that capacity through the Hazara Campaign of 1891 and, following six months' leave, he was again appointed to command in March 1895 and in that post he took the Corps of Guides on the Chitral Relief Expedition. He was killed on 13 April 1895 and is buried at Mardan.
    Battye, E. D., *The Fighting Ten*, BACSA, 1984, p229.
11 *The Chitral Expedition 1895*, op cit, Appendix xvii.
12 *The London Gazette* dated 9 November 1897.
13 *The London Gazette* dated 20 May 1898.
14 Elliott Major-General J. G. *The Frontier 1839-1947*, 1968, p206.
15 *Haughton, Lieutenant-Colonel John,* born on 22 August 1852 and commissioned in the 24th Foot on 28 October 1871. He joined the Bengal Staff Corps on 2 September 1876 and after serving with the 18th, 10th and 35th Bengal Infantry regiments he joined the 36th (Sikh) Regiment of Bengal Infantry from 25 June 1894 and took command of the regiment from 1895. He was killed on 29 January 1898 and was buried at Peshawar.
    Lieutenant Reginald George Munn was commissioned into the Derbyshire Regiment on 23 March 1889. He was promoted to Lieutenant from 1 November 1890 and transferred to the Bengal Staff Corps from 28 September 1891. He was appointed Adjutant of the 36th (Sikh) Regiment of Bengal Infantry from 29 November 1896.
16 Elliott, op cit, p207.
17 Gordon, Major Lawrence L. *British Battles and Medals*, 1962, p274.

Subadar-Major Mukhlis Ali Khan, 14th Madras Infantry, 1897.

Above: 6th Bengal Infantry.

Below: 1st Regiment of Bombay Light Infantry (Grenadiers), 1897.

24th (Baluchistan) Regiment of Bombay Infantry, 1897.

Officers of the 26th (Baluchistan) Regiment of Bombay Infantry, 1897.

*39th Bombay Infantry
(The Garhwal Rifles).*

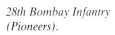

*28th Bombay Infantry
(Pioneers).*

CHAPTER TWELVE

The China Campaign and Reorganisation

The story of the campaigns of the Indian Army of the Empress commenced with a conflict in China, and in the closing years of the long reign of Queen Victoria the Indian Army was again called upon to serve in China. The movement known as 'Fists of Patriotic Union', whose members became known as 'Boxers' grew rapidly in strength in China. Such was their following that within China the members were seen to be invincible and as the movement received the unofficial approval of the Empress Dowager, there was no real attempt to curb the uprising by the Chinese forces. The target for the Boxers was the foreigners who were in China either for trading purposes or as missionaries.

The early attacks by the Boxers were against those Chinese who had converted to the Christian faith, resulting in the burning of property and, in some cases, the death of those converted. The assaults went unchecked by the local Chinese authorities and towards the end of 1899 attacks began on the Missionaries who were still attempting to gain converts in various parts of China. The position became critical, so far as the foreign ministers were concerned, when one of the Chinese commanders in the Chinese Army attempted to restrain a band of Boxers in one of the main streets of Peking and was dragged from his horse and killed. An appeal was made to the Chinese Government to stop the Boxers and although assurances were given to the effect that they would be kept under control, the Chinese authorities had no intention of acting and saw the uprising as an opportunity to rid China of all the foreign nationals who had taken up residence in the country. On 28 May 1900 the Boxers burnt Feng-tai railway station and destroyed part of the line. The situation was by now critical and the Ministers in Peking telegraphed for reinforcements from Tientsin and 337 men were despatched to reinforce the armed guards at the Missions at Peking. On the following day the Boxers again attacked the railway, this time at Po-ting Fu, and the European employees escaped by river for Tientsin but four were killed during the incident. The Chinese troops who had been brought back to Peking, supposedly to help in maintaining law and order, at once began fraternising with the Boxers.

All communications between the legations at Peking and the outside world were cut and on 9 June more Chinese troops entered the capital, but instead of keeping the Boxers under control they permitted them to enter the city in the 'uniform' of the Society and to parade there with their arms whilst declaring their intention to 'exterminate the foreigners'.[1] The situation continued to deteriorate and on 11 June the Japanese Chancellor, Mr Sugiyama, was murdered by the Chinese. Two days later the Boxers commenced their attack on the legations, as well as massacring a large number of Chinese Christians. In the meantime the situation at Tientsin had also become critical as the Boxers continued to stir up ill feeling towards the 'foreign devils'. Admiral Sir E. Seymour, the Naval Commander-in-Chief on the China station, received a telegram from the British Minister at Peking requesting assistance for the evacuation of Europeans. As a result of this message a mixed force of British, American, Austrian, French, German, Italian and Japanese, amounting to 2,066, was formed and departed from Tientsin on

10 June for Peking, but on 15 June the force lost all contact with Tientsin. Meanwhile, under the command of Rear-Admiral Bruce, the Allies had organised an operation to secure the Taku Forts in order that the line of communication with Tientsin could be kept open. The attack on the forts on 17 June was successful, but the position at Tientsin had deteriorated and when the Boxers attacked on 16 June all contact with the coast was lost. A mixed Allied force, which included the 1st Chinese Regiment from Wei-hai-wei (also known as the Wei-hai-wei Regiment), together with reinforcements from Singapore and Hong Kong, moved from the coast and relieved Tientsin on 23 June. Whilst this operation was underway the Peking Relief Column, under Admiral Seymour, had been blocked from reaching Peking; it was in fact holding a position at Hsi-Ku, only a few miles north of Tientsin and was unable to advance. A mixed force of British and Russian troops moved out from Tientsin and enabled Admiral Seymour to retreat back to Tientsin, which he successfully did on 26 June. After this the Allied troops were fully occupied in holding Taku and Tientsin but on 13 and 14 July the Chinese were defeated in the old native city of Tientsin. Following this setback the area around that city remained quiet. Reinforcements for the Allied force began to arrive from India on 18 July.

As a result of the conflict in China the Government of India

Interior of the Taku Forts.

was asked to provide troops for that theatre of operations. As a result of the request on 16 July, the Viceroy had placed the 7th Regiment of Bengal Infantry and the 1st Regiment of Sikh Infantry under orders to depart for China. On 18 June a further request was received and on this occasion an Expeditionary Force was placed under orders. It consisted of one battery of horse or field artillery, one regiment of Indian cavalry, three battalions of Indian infantry, and one company of sappers and miners, with land transport. In addition, two Indian infantry battalions were to be supplied for garrison duty at Singapore and Hong Kong.[2]

Brigadier-General Sir Alfred Gaselee KCB, ADC was appointed to command the Indian Expeditionary Force with Colonel E. G. Barrow, CB as 'second-in-command and infantry brigadier'. However on 22 June Lord Curzon received a further message requesting additional troops to be made available. As the force was to include a further cavalry regiment, and additional sappers and miners, in total amounting to 10,000 men, the local rank of Lieutenant General was given to Sir Alfred Gaselee and his second-in-command was given the local rank of Major-General. The force was organised into two brigades as follows:

Cavalry Brigade
B Battery Royal Horse Artillery
1st (The Duke of York's Own) Regiment of Bengal Lancers

14th Sikhs en route for China.

30th Bombay Infantry (Baluchistan Battalion) en route for China.

3rd (Queen's Own) Regiment of Bombay Cavalry
16th Regiment of Bengal Lancers
Section A No 22 British Field Hospital
Section C No 62 Native Field Hospital
Sections A and B No 57 Native Field Hospital
No 1 Brigade Supply Column

1st Infantry Brigade
7th (The Duke of Connaught's Own) Rajput Regiment of
    Bengal Infantry
26th (Baluchistan) Regiment of Bombay Infantry
1st Regiment of Sikh Infantry PFF
24th (Punjab) Regiment of Bengal Infantry
Nos 39 and 43 Native Field Hospital
No 2 Brigade Supply Column

2nd Infantry Brigade
2nd (The Queen's Own) Rajput Regiment of Bengal (Light)
    Infantry
14th (The Ferozepore Sikhs) Regiment of Bengal Infantry
1st Battalion, 4th Gurkha (Rifle) Regiment
30th Regiment of Bombay Infantry (3rd Baluch Battalion)
Nos 63 and 66 Native Field Hospital
No 3 Brigade Supply Column

3rd Infantry Brigade
6th (Jat) Regiment of Bengal Infantry
4th Regiment of Punjab Infantry PFF
20th (The Duke of Cambridge's Own Punjab) Regiment of
    Bengal Infantry
34th (Punjab) Regiment of Bengal Infantry (Pioneers)
Nos 51 and 61 Native Field Hospital

*Lt-Col Gartside Tipping and officers of the 1st (Duke of York's Own)
Bengal Lancers at Lucknow on the eve of the departure to China.*

No 5 Brigade Supply Column

4th Infantry Brigade
28th (Punjab) Regiment of Bengal Infantry
31st Regiment (6th Burma Battalion) of Madras (Light) Infantry
Alwar Infantry (Imperial Service Troops)
Bikaner Infantry (Imperial Service Troops)
Nos 53 and 58 Native Field Hospital
No 6 Brigade Supply Column[3]

In addition, the following 'Divisional' and 'Line of Communication troops' were included in the China Expeditionary Force:

12th Battery, Royal Field Artillery
1st Regiment of Sardar Ressala Jodhpur Lancers
1st Regiment of Madras Infantry (Pioneers)
Mounted Detachment of Bengal Sappers and Miners
No 4 Company Bengal Sappers and Miners
No 3 Company Madras Sappers and Miners
No 2 Company Bombay Sappers and Miners
The Maler Kotla Sappers (Imperial Service Troops)
A Photo-Litho Section each from the Bombay and Madras
    Sappers and Miners
1 Printing Section each from the Bombay and Madras Sappers
    and Miners
10 Special Signalling Units (British Infantry)
2 Special Signalling Units (Indian Army)
Section B No 22 British Field Hospital
Section D No 62 Native Field Hospital
No 42 Native Field Hospital
No 4 Brigade Supply Column

Line of Communication Troops
22nd Regiment of Bombay Infantry

British and Indian soldiers manning a heliograph station near the ruins of Feng-tai Junction Railway station, China.

Embarkation of Indian Troops for China – preparing food before embarkation.

3rd (Palamcottah) Regiment of Madras (Light) Infantry
5th Regiment of Infantry, Hyderabad Contingent
(*The above three units were earmarked as Garrison troops at Hong Kong*)
1 Telegraph Section each from Madras and Bengal Sappers and
  Miners
1 Railway Section
1 Ordnance Field Park
2 Engineer Field Parks
Sections A and B No 15 British Field Hospital
Sections A and B No 16 British Field Hospital
No 47 Native Field Hospital
Sections C and D No 69 Native Field Hospital
Section B No 5 Field Veterinary Hospital
Nos 3 and 4 Field Medical Store Depot

A number of minor store depots and hospital units were established for support of the large expeditionary force.

In addition to the official reinforcements for China, support was given from other sources in India, for example Khan Bahadur Dhanjibhoy of Rawalpindi provided nine ambulance tongas, with 20 horses and the necessary personnel, as well as twelve months' supply of 'repairing material'. The Maharaja Scindia of Gwalior offered to equip and maintain a hospital ship at the cost of 20 lakhs, and presented it to the British Government for use by the China Expeditionary Force. The gift was, of course, greatly appreciated by Queen Victoria. The vessel was refitted and renamed the *Gwalior* and sailed on its first voyage to China on 23 September.[4]

Whilst the China Expeditionary force was being organised the situation in China was worsening. The German Minister at Peking was murdered at Peking on 19 June, and in July the Roman Catholic Bishop Guillon was murdered at Mukden in Manchuria. On 9 July 54 missionaries were murdered in the province of Shansi. It was imperative that the Expeditionary Force be organised in India as, apart from India being the nearest major concentration of military units, the British Army was fully committed to the war in South Africa and was not able to spare troops from the home command.

With the unrest spreading, it became necessary for General Gaselee to detach the 2nd Brigade to Shanghai in order to support the defenders of the international settlement. There were, of course, problems with regard to the actual plans for the relief of Peking because of disagreement between the General

staff of the various nations taking part in the operation. General Gaselee had, on arrival, less than 4,000 of his troops available for the advance and the total strength of the allied force was 20,100 men with 70 guns, of which only 3,000 men and 12 guns were provided from the Indian Expeditionary Force. The Allied Force moved out to take Pei-t'sang on 5 August and four units of the Indian Army were included in the operation, namely:

1st Bengal Lancers	400 men
7th Bengal Infantry	500 men
24th Punjab Infantry	300 men
1st Sikhs	500 men

The Peking relief column followed the Pei Ho northwards in order that the river could be used as a supply route. The conditions under which the troops had to operate were appalling, with temperatures as high as 104°F and with little or no wind, the roads became a sea of dust. When the Allied force defeated the Chinese at Pei-t'sang the advance continued on the following day with the Chinese making another stand. Although many men collapsed under the weight of their packs and the continuous heat, the Chinese defences were gradually secured and by nightfall the Allies were in possession of Yang Tsun. The walled city of Tungchow was the next objective and this position was secured by the Japanese who found that both the Chinese Imperial troops and the Boxers had abandoned the city. On 12 August the Allied Generals decided that the cavalry should be sent ahead and move as close to Peking as possible. One of the problems facing General Gaselee was maintaining control of the various 'foreign' units who all wished to be the 'first to arrive' at Peking, the most difficult being the Japanese and the Russian.

The co-ordinated attack on Peking was to be made against the four gates in the city wall with the Russian, American, Japanese and British each taking a designated gate. It was intended that the assault would commence on the morning of 15 August. However, it was reported on 13 August that the Russian Cavalry had been able to advance within a few hundred yards of the Peking City wall. It was therefore agreed by the Allied General that the attack would be advanced by 24 hours and the troops moved into position on the night of 13 August. Unfortunately, the Russian troops were ordered to attack early and, in addition, their officers decided to attack the American objective instead of the gate allocated to them. By the morning of 14 August the Russians had failed to take the whole of the gateway. The Japanese not wishing to let the Russian troops

have the glory of capturing the city first, moved out ahead of time and General Gaselee, seeing that his overall plan was about to be ruined, gave the order to attack. The American force, who no longer had a gate to attack, attempted to scale the 30-foot high wall and succeeded in capturing that section of wall. The British advance began and, after a hole had been blasted in the wall by the artillery, the British force advanced towards the Legation. The troops entered the Legation compound via the sluice gate on the Imperial Drainage Canal. The relieving force reached the compound at about 2.30pm and those who had been besieged in Peking were delighted to welcome the first of the force 'led by their British officer, more and more sepoys [of the 1st Sikhs and 7th Rajput Bengal Infantry] poured through the Sluice Gate, up Canal Street and on to the tennis court.'[5]

The assault on the Forbidden City was then halted, and following further consultation it was decided that the Allies would hold a 'Victory Parade' on 28 August. The parade was held with each of the eight participating countries providing a contingent, with the local defenders and the foreign minister accompanying its own country's contingent.[6]

The main object having been achieved, the Allied forces turned their attention to the problem of subduing the remainder of the Boxer strongholds. To this end, a number of minor actions took place around Peking, Tientsin, Patachow and Pao Ting Fu. The Anglo-American force defeated the Boxers at

Patachow and sent the enemy fleeing into the hills in complete disorder. The German General, General von Waldersee, who had been given the over-all command of the campaign, eventually arrived at Taku on 21 September and, following a parade and review in his honour, it was agreed that he would lead the attack on the final Boxer position at Pao Ting Fu. When the Allied force approached the Boxers refused to surrender but the attack was made on 20 October and as the Boxers proved to be disorganised the town was taken. As a warning to others who might still consider pursuing the fight, General von Waldersee gave the order for the town to be completely destroyed.

In December 1900 it was decreed that all local Chinese officials were responsible for the safety of foreigners whilst in their area. On 1 February 1901 the Boxer Society was officially disbanded and Prince Tuan and his brother, Tsai Lan, who had supported the activities of the Boxers, were banished to the 'western regions of China for life'. An offer to pay £67.5 million

This page left: British and Indian Troops entering the city of Peking. Right: Captain Soady and his detachment of Sikhs scaling the wall at Pekin. (Sketches by John Schönberg.)   ILN

Left top:
German troops cheering a charge by the Bengal Lancers, 1900.

The Sikhs on the road to Peking.   ILN

indemnity to the Allies was made in May 1901 and on 7 January 1902 the Dowager Empress, Tzu Hsi, was permitted to return to the ruined city of Peking, although the Forbidden City and the Imperial Palace were intact. She spent the few remaining years of her reign (8 years) attempting to change the image of China.

An official summary of the operation, showing the award of a special medal, was published and reads:

An expeditionary force from India, under General Sir A Gaselee, operated in concert with the contingents of the other great Powers, was sent to relieve the Legations at Pekin, which had been besieged by the 'Boxers' since 13th June 1900. The relief was effected on 14th August. The British Force employed was 1,300 Imperial troops and 18,000 Indian native troops. The Imperial and Colonial forces employed were granted a special medal similar to that given for the China wars of 1842 and 1860 (A.O. 82 of 1902).[7]

The troops taking part in the China Expeditionary Force were awarded the Third China War Medal 1900, for service on operations during the period 10 June to 31 December 1900. The description of the medal is as follows:

Obverse   –   The crowned and veiled head of Queen Victoria with the legend 'VICTORIA REGINA ET IMPERATRIX'.

Reverse   –   A collection of war trophies with an oval shield, with the Royal Arms in the centre, all positioned under a palm tree. Above the legend 'ARMIS EXPOSCERE PACEM'. In the exergue is the word 'CHINA' with the date '1900' beneath.

Size   – 36mm diameter.
Ribbon   – 32mm wide. Crimson with yellow edges.

Three bars were issued, as appropriate, with the medal, these being 'Taku Forts', 'Defence of Legations' and 'Relief of Pekin'.[8]

Although the Indian Army was committed to providing a large expeditionary force for China it also had many other commitments to fulfil, which included keeping control of the North West Frontier, North East Frontier and many other internal duties. The most arduous task within the confines of India was, without doubt, the control of the North West Frontier area which was always a source of trouble. That area continued to pose problems for the military, for the British until 1947, and thereafter for Pakistan. The troubles with the numerous tribal areas resulted in many units being tied to the frontier area but, in addition, new calls were being made on the Indian Army, as from 1900 onwards it was to provide a garrison battalion for Hong Kong, and from 1903 another battalion for the Singapore Garrison. From time to time other calls were made upon the Indian Army, one such request came from West Africa. Lord Lugard recommended to the Secretary of State for

The Third China War Medal 1900, with clasp 'Relief of Pekin'.

Madras Sappers and Miners.

the Colonies that the Indian Army be invited to help the West African Frontier Force by seconding volunteers from the Sappers and Miners to assist the Force. A military despatch to the Viceroy, dated 3 February 1898, requested '20 Madras sappers for service in the Niger territories.' The request suggested that ideally the party should consist of 1 havildar (carpenter), 9 carpenters, 1 naik (smith), 2 smiths, a naik (mason), a mason, 2 surveyors, 1 sadler and 2 bricklayers. The terms of service in West Africa were to be for three years and such volunteers would be seconded from their corps and not be transferred. Also, special rates of pay would be granted. The party moved to the Niger Territories and in October 1898 a reference to the Indian Contingent in West African Frontier Force orders shows that 'No 1033 Lance-Naik Munisami' was promoted to Lance Havildar. The Madras Sapper and Miner party left Lokoja for the United Kingdom, having completed their work. The party was by then reduced to 17[9] although there appears to be no record as to the fate of the remaining three members of the original party.

Although the story of the Indian Army of the Empress should end at the time of the death of Queen Victoria in 1901, it is reasonable to extend the story two years and terminate it in

Bombay Sappers and Miners All Navy and Army Illustrated

19th Madras Infantry at Singapore on parade for the departure of Sir Harry Keppel, May 1903.

1903 when Lord Kitchener introduced sweeping changes in the Indian Army.

Lord Kitchener took over the post of Commander-in-Chief India in 1902, and completed the unification of the Indian Army which had been started in 1895. He abolished the system which held British officers on the strength of the Indian Staff Corps, whereas in actual fact they were not employed as staff but were serving as regimental officers. Officers were to be gazetted direct to the regiments of the Indian Army, a system that was in being prior to the 1861 reorganisation. Cavalry and Infantry regiments were renumbered in one sequence, and references to their former Presidential affiliation was discontinued.

Briefly, within the cavalry the former Bengal regiments retained their numbers, the Punjab regiments took numbers 21 to 25, Madras 26 to 28 and Bombay from 31 to 37. The Hyderabad Cavalry was reduced from four to three regiments and took the numbers 20, 29 and 30, whilst the Central India Horse were given the numbers 38 and 39. The infantry were reorganised in a similar manner with the Bengal regiments taking the numbers 1 to 48, Punjab regiments were given 51 to 59; Madras 61 to 93; Hyderabad 94 to 99 with Bombay taking 101 to 130. During the 1903 reorganisation three of the Madras regiments, the 5th, 8th and 11th were disbanded and a further 15 were converted to Punjabi regiments.

The role of the Indian Army was also changed and its main function was now stated to be the defence of the North West Frontier, a continuing task which gave those units stationed in the frontier area an 'active service' roll. Although there were years when there were no major campaigns warranting a campaign medal or bar, there were always minor incidents which ensured that those units serving in the frontier area were kept fully operational and the area was, without doubt, a hard training ground for what was supposed to be 'peacetime soldiering'.

The Indian Army of the Empress existed for 40 years and during that period the officers and men had time and time again proved their courage and had won many awards for gallantry, but even after a record of active service in many parts of the world Indian born officers and men were not eligible for the award of the Victoria Cross. It was not until 1911 that the Indian officers, non-commissioned officers and men became eligible for that most coveted gallantry award and it was three years later that the first Indian soldier was to be awarded a Victoria Cross. The soldier was Sepoy Khudadad Khan, of the 129th Duke of Connaught's Own Baluchis. On 31 October 1914, at Hollebeke, he was serving in the machine-gun section of his battalion and was working one of the two machine guns. The second gun had been put out of action by a German shell and the British officer had been wounded. The other five men of the detachment had all been killed but he continued to fire his machine gun until the position was overrun by German troops, who left him for dead. Later he was able to crawl away and rejoin his own unit. A month later his Victoria Cross was presented to him personally by King George V, during his first visit to the battle front. At this time Sepoy Khudadad Khan was still recovering from his wounds in the field hospital. The award was promulgated in *The London Gazette* dated 7 December 1914.[10]

The Indian Army had, at last, acquired its first award of a Victoria Cross, 16 years after the advent of the song *How India Kept Her Word*.

Dress helmet of the Scinde Horse.

1 *Frontier and Overseas Expeditions from India*, Vol VI, Calcutta, 1911, p452.
2 Ibid.
3 *Frontier and Overseas Expeditions from India*, op cit, pp459-60.
4 *Frontier and Overseas Expeditions from India*, op cit, pp456-57.
5 Fleming, P. *The Siege at Peking*, 1959, p206.
6 Bodin, Lynne E. *The Boxer Rebellion*, 1979, p19.
7 Chronology of Events Connected with Army Administration 1858-1907, *WO Publication 1/Gen No/890*, London, April 1908, p72.
8 Joslin E. C., Litherland, A. R; Simpkin, B. T. *British Battles and Medals*, 1988, p208.
9 Kirk-Greene, A. H. M. *Indian Troops with the West African Frontier Force, 1898-1900*, Journal of the Society for Army Historical Research, Vol XLII.
10 Smyth, Brigadier The Rt Hon Sir John *The Story of the Victoria Cross 1856-1963*, 1963, pp164-65.

Royal visit to Singapore 1901, 16th Madras Infantry on parade.

The Coronation of King Edward VII was to have taken place on 26 June 1902. However, on 24 June the Coronation was postponed due to the illness of the King. After an operation he made a swift recovery and the Coronation eventually took place on 9 August. Detachments from regiments of the Indian Army travelled to England and took part in the Coronation procession.

Left:
Cavalryman at Hampton Court, 1902.

Right:
1st Bombay Lancers at Hampton Court, 1902.

Below:
14th Bengal Cavalry at the Coronation of 1902.

APPENDIX A

The Indian Order of Merit

The definitive work on the Indian Order of Merit is the book *Deeds of Valour of the Indian Soldier which won The Indian Order of Merit* compiled by P. P. Hypher and published in 1925. The author commences his work with details of the regulations covering the award of the Order and the following extract from Hypher's publication records that detail:

The 'Order of Merit' is to the Indian Army, what the 'Victoria Cross' is to the British Army. The Order was instituted in 1837, and its object is to afford personal reward for personal bravery, irrespective of rank or grade, and without reference to any claim founded on mere length of service and general good conduct.

Prior to the institution of the Order, personal bravery was rewarded by the grant of money, or promotion, or the presentation of swords, turbans and shawls.

The Order of Merit consists of three classes, and is distinguished by a badge in the shape of a Military laurelled Star, bearing in its centre the inscription 'Reward of Valour'. The insignia are – for the first class, gold; for the second class, silver with a gold wreath; and for the third, silver only, to be worn on the left breast, pendent from a dark blue ribbon with red edges. A certificate detailing the grant of the Order and its concomitant advantages, is also given to each individual on his admission to, or advancement in, the Order.

The decoration is conferred by the Governor General of India in Council under the following conditions:–

(a) When the act of gallantry has been performed under the eye of a General Officer Commanding the Force.

(b) When the act of gallantry, having been certified to the satisfaction of the candidate's Commanding Officer, shall have been reported to the General Officer Commanding the Force, who shall have called for such description and assurance of the performance of the act (which assurance shall include a statement of the person who was an eye-witness of the act) and who shall have recommended the grant of the decoration.

The reward is only granted for conspicuous gallantry and not for an act of ordinary gallantry performed by a soldier in the simple exercise of his duty.

Admission to the 3rd Class is obtained by any conspicuous acts of individual gallantry performed by any Indian Officer (or officer of European or mixed parentage holding a similar position), or soldier in the field, or in the attack or defence of fortified places. Admission to the Second Class can be obtained only be members of the 3rd Class and for similar service; and in like manner the Order of the First Class is conferred only on members of the 3rd and 2nd Classes.

Admission into the Order confers on members an additional allowance, equal in the 3rd Class to one-third, in the Second, to two-

The Indian Order of Merit.

thirds, and in the First Class to the whole of the ordinary pay of his rank, over and above the pay or the pension he may be entitled to when invalided. The widow of a member is entitled to receive the pension conferred by the Order for three years after the date of his decease, and in the case of a plurality of wives the first married has the preference.

The Star of the Order is presented to the individual admitted, in the presence of the regiment assembled on parade, and is allowed to remain in the possession of the family of the deceased member. But on an individual being advanced from a lower to a higher class of the order, the inferior badge in his possession is returned to the Government of India.

The first awards of the Order of merit were made for acts of gallantry during the capture of Ghazni in 1839.

Changes were made to the Order in connection with the Royal Durbar which was held at Delhi in December 1911. The changes are set out in the second volume of the work which was also written by P. P. Hypher and published in 1927. The changes were:

(i) that from henceforth the loyal Indian Officers, men and reservists of His (Majesty's) Indian Army shall be eligible for the grant of the *Victoria Cross* for Valour, and

(ii) that the special allowances assigned for three years only, to the widows of deceased members of the Indian Order of Merit shall, with effect from the 12th December 1911, be continued to all such widows until death or re-marriage.

At the same time it was ruled that the Victoria Cross, with its monetary reward, should take the place of the First Class of the Indian Order of Merit. The Second and Third Classes were then changed to become First and Second Classes respectively. In addition, from that date His Majesty King George V authorised the use of the post-nominal letters 'I.O.M.' by all recipients of the Indian Order of Merit.

The following list gives the number of awards of the Indian Order of Merit made during the period 1860-1903.

AWARDS OF INDIAN ORDER OF MERIT

GGO Reference and Year	Campaigns/Operations	1st Class	2nd Class	3rd Class
734 of 1860	Mahsud Wazir operation, 1860			6
166 of 1865	Bhutan – Dalimkote, 1864		1	11
429 of 1865	Bhutan – Dewanigiri, 1865		1	4
572 of 1865	Bhutan – Dewanigiri, 1865			3
582 of 1865	Munnespooree Rebels, 1865			1
594 of 1865	Umbeyla, 1863			1
684 of 1865	Bhutan – Dewanigiri, 1865			7
78 of 1866	Bhutan – Dewanigiri		2	16
350 of 1866	Suliman Khefs, 1866			2
646 of 1866	Wagher Outlaws, 1865			1
8 of 1867	Munnipore Valley, 1866			2
424 of 1867	Manipur, 1866 and Marauders, 1867			7
1032 of 1867	Action against Murnees, Katerans & Booktees 1867, and Andamans 1867			6
76 of 1868	Katiwar, 1867, minor operations, 1868	1		5
657 of 1868	Bezotee Afridis, 1868			5
7 of 1869	Agrore, NWF, 1868			2
782 of 1869	Abyssinian Expedition, 1868			4
829 of 1872	Looshai Expedition, 1871		1	1
1277 of 1873	Andaman Islands, 1873			1
378 of 1878	Jowaki Expedition, 1877	1		5
516 of 1878	Utman Kheyls, 1878			2
33 of 1879	Afghan War, 1878-1880			1
106 of 1879	Afghan War, 1878-1880			1
164 of 1879	Afghan War, 1878-1880			7
230 of 1879	Afghan War, 1878-1880			8
271 of 1879	Afghan War, 1878-1880			1
299 of 1879	Afghan War, 1878-1880		1	
305 of 1879	Afghan War, 1878-1880			1
366 of 1879	Afghan War, 1878-1880			1
532 of 1879	Afghan War, 1878-1880	1		
533 of 1879	Afghan War, 1878-1880		1	5
583 of 1879	Afghan War, 1878-1880	1		4
605 of 1879	Afghan War, 1878-1880			5
736 of 1879	Afghan War, 1878-1880			4
797 of 1879	Afghan War, 1878-1880			1

GGO Reference and Year	Campaigns/Operations	1st Class	2nd Class	3rd Class
1260 of 1879	Afghan War, 1878-1880		1	11
10 of 1880	Afghan War, 1878-1880			1
117 of 1880	Afghan War, 1878-1880			1
131 of 1880	Afghan War, 1878-1880			2
132 of 1880	Afghan War, 1878-1880			1
133 of 1880	Afghan War, 1878-1880			1
190 of 1880	Afghan War, 1878-1880		1	
233 of 1880	Afghan War, 1878-1880			1
251 of 1880	Afghan War, 1878-1880	1	2	
252 of 1880	Afghan War, 1878-1880			40
294 of 1880	Afghan War, 1878-1880			1
336 of 1880	Afghan War, 1878-1880			2
425 of 1880	Afghan War, 1878-1880		2	4
426 of 1880	Afghan War, 1878-1880			1
432 of 1880	Afghan War, 1878-1880			1
(Note: Hypher's book gives year as 1887)				
443 of 1880	Afghan War, 1878-1880			1
471 of 1880	Afghan War, 1878-1880			1
533 of 1880	Afghan War, 1878-1880			6
563 of 1880	Afghan War, 1878-1880			15
638 of 1880	Afghan War, 1878-1880		1	
639 of 1880	Afghan War, 1878-1880			21
689 of 1880	Afghan War, 1878-1880			3
(Medals to widows)				
20 of 1881	Afghan War, 1878-1880			1
58 of 1881	Afghan War, 1878-1880			2
59 of 1881	Afghan War, 1878-18801	1	1	
60 of 1881	Afghan War, 1878-1880			20
136 of 1881	Afghan War, 1878-1880			2
222 of 1881	Afghan War, 1878-1880			2
351 of 1881	Afghan War, 1878-1880			3
438 of 1881	Afghan War, 1878-1880			1
59 of 1882	Afghan War, 1878-1880			1
356 of 1882	Afghan War, 1878-1880			8
493 of 1883	North East Frontier, 1882-1884			2
252 of 1884	North East Frontier, 1882-1884			4
298 of 1885	Suakin, 1885			10
421 of 1885	Suakin, 1885			1
278 of 1886	Burma, 1885-1886			1
556 of 1886	Burma, 1885-1886			1
561 of 1186	Burma, 1886			1
618 of 1886	Burma, 1885-1886			1
619 of 1886	Burma, 1885-1886			1
631 of 1886	Burma, 1885-1886			5
710 of 1886	Burma, 1886			1
787 of 1886 and 167 of 1890	Burma, 1886			4
30 of 1887	Burma, 1886			1
49 of 1887	Burma, 1886			1
124 of 1887	Burma, 1886			1
306 of 1887	Burma, 1886			5
395 of 1887	Burma, 1886			4
457 of 1887	Burma, 1886			1

GGO Reference and Year	Campaigns/Operations	1st Class	2nd Class	3rd Class
458 of 1887	Burma, 1886-1887			1
482 of 1887	Burma, 1886-1887			1
483 of 1887	Burma, 1886-1887			1
518 of 1887	Burma, 1886-1887			1
519 of 1887	Burma, 1886-1887			1
590 of 1887	Burma, 1886-1887			5
630 of 1887	Burma, 1886			1
675 of 1887	Burma, 1886-1887			1
755 of 1887	Burma, 1886-1887			1
911 of 1887	Burma, 1886-1887			2
954 of 1887	Burma, 1886-1887			4
371 of 1888	Burma, 1886-1887			2
391 of 1888	Burma, 1887			1
445 of 1888	Burma, 1886			1
542 of 1888	Burma, 1886-1887			6
654 of 1888	Burma, 1886			3
692 of 1888	North West Frontier, Black Mountain, 1888			2
733 of 1888	Burma, 1886			8
919 of 1888	Sikkim, 1888			1
1016 of 1888	North West Frontier, Black Mountain, 1888			1
1039 of 1888	North West Frontier, Black Mountain, 1888			1
123 of 1889	Black Mountain, Hazara, 1888			6
395 of 1889	Burma, 1889			3
637 of 1889	North West Frontier, Black Mountain, 1888			
(Gold bar to 1st Class Order)				
655 of 1889	Burma, 1889			1
515 of 1890	Burma (Lushai), 1890	1		
572 of 1890	Burma (Chin-Hills)			1
674 of 1890	Somaliland, 1890			1
769 of 1890	Burma, 1889			6
950 of 1890	Burma, 1889			8
354 of 1891	North West Frontier, Hazara, 1891			4
482 of 1891	South Lushai Hills, 1891			2
522 of 1891	North West Frontier, Hazara, 1891			2
558 of 1891	Burma, 1891			1
647 of 1891	Manipur, 1891			81
728 of 1891	Burma, 1891			1
862 of 1891	Manipur, 1891		1	4
951 of 1891	North West Frontier, Hazara, 1891			1
952 of 1891	North West Frontier, Hazara, 1891			1
1180 of 1891	Burma, 1891		1	1
129 of 1892	Burma, 1891			1
179 of 1892	North West Frontier, Hunza, 1891			6
614 of 1892	British Central Africa, 1891			16
659 of 1892	North West Frontier, Hunza-Nagar, 1891			6
683 of 1892	North West Frontier, Hunza-Nagar, 1891			1
(This does not include awards to the men of the Kashmir State Forces)				
709 of 1892	Defence of Sadon, Upper Burma, 1892			4
739 of 1892	Burma, Lushai Hills, 1892			2
740 of 1892	Burma, 1892			1
841 of 1892	Manipur, 1891			1
925 of 1892	Burma, Lushai Hills, 1892			2
255 of 1893	Capture of murderer at Benares, 1892			1

GGO Reference and Year	Campaigns/Operations	1st Class	2nd Class	3rd Class
613 of 1893	Burma, 1892			1
825 of 1893	Burma, 1892-1893			7
826 of 1893	Burma, 1892-1893			1
59 of 1894	Burma, 1892-1893			3
666 of 1894	Assam-Abor Expedition, 1894			3
728 of 1894	British Central Africa, 1894			1
793 of 1894	Burma, Kachin Hills, 1894			1
1022 of 1894	Burma, 1892-1893			6

(Three widows were admitted to 3rd Class pension)

GGO Reference and Year	Campaigns/Operations	1st Class	2nd Class	3rd Class
41 of 1895	Wazinstan Delimitation Escort, Wana, 1894			13
509 of 1895	North West Frontier, Chilas, 1893			5
657 of 1895	British Central Africa, 1895			2
742 of 1895	Defence and Relief of the Fort of Chitral, 1895			14
743 of 1895	Chitral, 1895			5

(This does not include men of the Kashmir Forces)

GGO Reference and Year	Campaigns/Operations	1st Class	2nd Class	3rd Class
744 of 1895	Chitral, 1895			8

(This does not include awards made to men of the Kashmir State Forces)

GGO Reference and Year	Campaigns/Operations	1st Class	2nd Class	3rd Class
745 of 1895	Chitral, 1895			6
970 of 1895	Chitral, 1895			1
1065 of 1895	Chitral, 1895			1
1228 of 1895	North West Frontier, Malakand, 1895			11
63 of 1896	North West Frontier, Tochi Valley, 1895			1
251 of 1896	Chitral, 1895			4
299 of 1896	Chitral, 1895			1
578 of 1896	Central African Slave Trade, 1895			6
1168 of 1896	Chitral, 1895			1
232 of 1897	Bajaur, 1897			25
785 of 1897	Attack on Political Officers' Escort at Manzai, 1897		1*	5

(*Widow granted pension of 2nd Class award)

GGO Reference and Year	Campaigns/Operations	1st Class	2nd Class	3rd Class
865 of 1897	Maizar, 1897		1	34
1211 of 1897	Maizar, 1897			2
1313 of 1897	Kurram Valley, 1897			2
1423 of 1897	Bara Valey, Tirah, 1897			1
49 of 1898	Malakand, 1897			73
101 of 1898	Malakand, 1897 and Tirah, 1897			2
133 of 1898	Samana, 1897			35
134 of 1898	Samana, 1897			21
231 of 1898	Bajaur, 1897		2	
394 of 1898	Shabkadr, 1897			6
429 of 1898	Shabkadr, 1897		1	
430 of 1898	Shabkadr, 1897			49
503 of 1898	Shabkadr, 1897			1
639 of 1898	Shabkadr, 1897			1
769 of 1898	Mekran, 1898			1
11 of 1899	Tirah, 1897		1	
12 of 1899	Tirah, 1897			4
99 of 1899	East Africa, 1897-1898			11
100 of 1899	East Africa, 1897-1898		1	
137 of 1899	East Africa, 1898			1
839 of 1899	East Africa (Uganda), 1898			1
45 of 1900	East Africa (Uganda), 1898			1
184 of 1900	British Central Africa, 1900			1
275 of 1900	Malakand, 1897			1

GGO Reference and Year	Campaigns/Operations	1st Class	2nd Class	3rd Class
276 of 1900	Malakand, 1897		1	
277 of 1900	Uganda, 1898			18
1054 of 1900	Burma, 1900			3
1239 of 1900	Burma, 1900			1
46 of 1901	China, 1900			1
115 of 1901	China, 1900			1
294 of 1901	Action against Dacoits, 1899			3
355 of 1901	China, 1900			3
419 of 1901	China, 1900			1
683 of 1901	China, 1900			2
875 of 1901	South Africa, 1900			1
259 of 1902	Tochi, 1896			1
264 of 1902	Mekran, 1901			3
403 of 1902	Mahsud-Waziri Blockade, 1901			14
547 of 1902	Kurram Valley, 1897			4
670 of 1902	Persia – Baluchistan, 1902		1	
1086 of 1902	Ashanti, 1902			1
382 of 1903	Gumatti, 1902		2	5

2nd Lancers Hyderabad Contingent.

Above:
20th Bombay Infantry.

Right:
26th (Baluchistan) Regiment
of Bombay Infantry, c1897.

Left:
10th Jat Infantry.

Left:
9th Bombay Infantry.

Below:
13th (The Shekhawati) Regiment of Bengal Infantry, 1897.

Right above:
8th Bengal Infantry, c1897.

Right below:
12th Infantry.

APPENDIX B

The Empress of India Medal, 1877

The medal was designed to be presented to senior English officials and to Indian native Princes and others on the occasion of the proclamation of Queen Victoria as Empress of India, at Delhi, on 1 January 1877. The Government of India, wishing to cease the 'oriental' custom of exchanging presents resolved that, on the occasion of the Grand Assemblage at Delhi, the presentation of a distinctive medal would be an ideal solution to the problem. The Government proposed that each Native Chief entitled to a salute should be presented with a gold medal and a large silken banner, with armorial bearings of the Chief on one side and, on the other, an inscription stating the banner to be the gift of the Empress of India.

The description of the medal is contained in *Medals and Decorations of the British Army and Navy* by John Horsley Mayo, which was published in 1897, and reads as follows:

Obv.   Bust of Queen Victoria, 1., wearing a small crown, and a veil which hangs down behind; ear-ring; necklace with portrait of the late Prince Consort; ermine tippet and Star of India. Beaded border. Leg. VICTORIA 1st JANUARY 1877

Rev.   The inscription EMPRESS OF INDIA in Persian, English and Hindi. Indented border.
      Circular 2.3 inches. Gold. Silver
      Artist. George G. Adams
      Struck by Mr G. G. Adams
      Ribbon, 1¾ inch wide. Dark red with yellow borders
      Worn round the neck.

The commemorative medals were distributed in two classes, that is gold and silver. The gold medals were awarded to senior Government Officials, Indian Native Princes, and to representatives of foreign governments who attended the Grand Assemblage at Delhi.

The military awards were in the silver medal class and the list of authorised recipients, by appointment, was given as:

1 Members of the Legislative Council.
2 Secretaries to the Government of India and Local Governments.
3 The Adjutant-General of the Army and Commanders of Divisions or Corps including the Volunteer Corps present at Delhi.
4 The Inspector-General and Deputy Inspector-General of the Police for the Punjab employed at Delhi.

5 The Deputy-Surgeon-General in sanitary charge.
6 The Deputy Commissioner of Delhi.
7 Mr Kirby, C. E. Executive Engineer, who constructed and in part designed the place of Assemblage.
8 Mr Kipling, who prepared the banners.
9 Each Native Noble and Gentleman who had been specially invited to Delhi by Local Governments and Administrations.
10 The Consuls of Foreign Governments present.
11 The members of the suites of the Khan of Khelat and of the Representatives of Foreign States.
12 The principal members of the suites of Feudatory Chiefs.
13 The Agents and Traffic Managers of the Sind, Punjab and Delhi, East Indian, and G.I.P. Railways, and the Deputy Consulting Engineer for Guaranteed Railways on special duty.

Obverse and Reverse of the Empress of India Medal, 1877.

14 The Political Officers in charge of Ambassadors, Native Chiefs, and Officers in charge of special camps.

15 The officials specially attached to the Foreign Office for duty in connection with the Imperial Assemblage.

16 The Members of the Viceroy's Personal Staff.

17 A selected private soldier or non-commissioned officer from each Regiment European or Native, serving in India.

There appears to be no record of which soldier in each Indian Army unit was presented with the medal. It would appear that the actual allocation was left to the discretion of the Commanding Officer and in the event there would be a great diversity of criteria for the allocation.

Later, in 1882, an order was issued forbidding the wearing of the medal when wearing uniform. The instruction reads:

No <u>0082</u>
   278

Horse Guards,
War Office,
12th June 1882

Sir,

By desire of The Field-Marshal Commanding-in-Chief, I have the honour to inform you that his Royal Highness has been pleased to decide that the 'Delhi Imperial Assemblage Commemorative Medal' awarded to certain officers and non-commissioned officers in 1877, is not to be worn by officers or soldiers of the Regular Army or Auxiliary Forces when in uniform, and I am to request that you will be pleased to issue the necessary orders accordingly.

I have, etc.,

R. B. HAWLEY, D.A.G.,

General Officers Commanding,
At Home and Abroad.

APPENDIX C

Composition of the Indian Army – 1895
(The regiments and Corps are in Indian Army List order)

Bengal
Governor-General's Body Guard
1st Regiment of Bengal Lancers
2nd Regiment of Bengal Lancers
3rd Regiment of Bengal Lancers
4th Regiment of Bengal Lancers
5th Regiment of Bengal Lancers
6th (Prince of Wales') Regiment of Bengal Cavalry
7th Regiment of Bengal Cavalry
8th Regiment of Bengal Cavalry
9th Regiment of Bengal Lancers
10th Regiment of Bengal (The Duke of Cambridge's Own) Lancers
11th (Prince of Wales' Own) Regiment of Bengal Lancers
12th Regiment of Bengal Cavalry
13th (The Duke of Connaught's) Regiment of Bengal Lancers
14th Regiment of Bengal Lancers
15th (Cureton's Multani) Regiment of Bengal Lancers
16th Regiment of Bengal Cavalry
17th Regiment of Bengal Cavalry
18th Regiment of Bengal Lancers
19th Regiment of Bengal Lancers
No 7 (Bengal) Mountain Battery
No 8 (Bengal) Mountain Battery
Corps of Bengal Sappers and Miners
1st Regiment of Bengal Infantry
2nd (The Queen's Own) Regiment of Bengal (Light) Infantry
3rd Regiment of Bengal Infantry
The 4th (Prince Albert Victor's) Regiment of Bengal Infantry
5th Regiment of Bengal (Light) Infantry
6th Regiment of Bengal (Light) Infantry
7th (The Duke of Connaught's Own) Regiment of Bengal Infantry
8th Regiment of Bengal Infantry
9th Gurkha (Rifle) Regiment of Bengal Infanty
10th Regiment of Bengal Infantry
11th Regiment of Bengal Infantry
12th (The Kelta-i-Ghilzai) Regiment of Bengal Infantry
13th (The Shekhawati) Regiment of Bengal Infantry
14th (The Ferozepore Sikh) Regiment of Bengal Infantry
15th (The Ludhiana Sikh) Regiment of Bengal Infantry
16th (The Lucknow) Regiment of Bengal Infantry
17th (The Loyal Purbiya) Regiment of Bengal Infantry

18th Regiment of Bengal Infantry
19th (Punjab) Regiment of Bengal Infantry
20th (The Duke of Cambridge's Own Punjab) Regiment of Bengal Infantry
21st (Punjab) Regiment of Bengal Infantry
22nd (Punjab) Regiment of Bengal Infantry
23rd (Punjab) Regiment of Bengal Infantry (Pioneers)
24th (Punjab) Regiment of Bengal Infantry
25th (Punjab) Regiment of Bengal Infantry
26th (Punjab) Regiment of Bengal Infantry
27th (Punjab) Regiment of Bengal Infantry
28th (Punjab) Regiment of Bengal Infantry
29th (Punjab) Regiment of Bengal Infantry
30th (Punjab) Regiment of Bengal Infantry
31st (Punjab) Regiment of Bengal Infantry
32nd (Punjab) Regiment of Bengal Infantry (Pioneers)
33rd (Punjabi Mohomedan) Regiment of Bengal Infantry
34th (Punjab) Regiment of Bengal Infantry (Pioneers)
35th (Sikh) Regiment of Bengal Infantry
36th (Sikh) Regiment of Bengal Infantry
37th (Dogra) Regiment of Bengal Infantry
38th (Dogra) Regiment of Bengal Infantry
39th (The Garhwal Rifle) Regiment of Bengal Infantry
40th (Pathan) Regiment of Bengal Infantry
42nd Gurkha (Rifle) Regiment of Bengal Infantry
43rd Gurkha (Rifle) Regiment of Bengal Infantry
44th Gurkha (Rifle) Regiment of Bengal Infantry
45th (Rattray's Sikh) Regiment of Bengal Infantry

Gurkha Regiments
1st Gurkha (Rifle) Regiment
2nd (Prince of Wales' Own) Gurkha (Rifle) Regiment (The Sirmoor Rifles)
3rd Gurkha (Rifle) Regiment
4th Gurkha (Rifle) Regiment

Punjab Frontier Force
1st (Prince Albert Victor's Own) Regiment of Punjab Cavalry
2nd Regiment of Punjab Cavalry
3rd Regiment of Punjab Cavalry
5th Regiment of Punjab Cavalry
(The Queen's Own) Corps of Guides (Cavalry and Infantry)
No 1 (Kohat) Mountain Battery

Central India Horse.

No 2 (Derajat) Mountain Battery
No 3 (Peshawar) Mountain Battery
No 4 (Hazara) Mountain Battery
The Punjab Garrison Battery
1st Regiment of Sikh Infantry
2nd (or Hill) Regiment of Sikh Infantry
3rd Regiment of Sikh Infantry
4th Regiment of Sikh Infantry
1st Regiment of Punjab Infantry
2nd Regiment of Punjab Infantry
4th Regiment of Punjab Infantry
5th Regiment of Punjab Infantry
6th Regiment of Punjab Infantry
5th Gurkha (Rifle) Regiment

Madras
Governor's Body-Guard
1st Regiment of Madras Lancers
2nd Regiment of Madras Lancers
3rd Regiment of Madras Lancers
Queen's Own Madras Sappers and Miners
1st Regiment of Madras Infantry (Pioneers)
2nd Regiment of Madras Infantry

3rd (or Palamcottah) Regiment of Madras (Light) Infantry
4th Regiment of Madras Infantry (Pioneers)
5th Regiment of Madras Infantry
6th Regiment of Madras Infantry
7th Regiment of Madras Infantry
8th Regiment of Madras Infantry
9th Regiment of Madras Infantry
10th Regiment (1st Burma-Gurkha Rifles) of Madras Infantry
11th Regiment of Madras Infantry
12th Regiment (2nd Burma Battalion) of Madras Infantry
13th Regiment of Madras Infantry
14th Regiment of Madras Infantry
15th Regiment of Madras Infantry
16th Regiment of Madras Infantry
17th Regiment of Madras Infantry
19th Regiment of Madras Infantry
20th Regiment of Madras Infantry
21st Regiment of Madras Infantry (Pioneers)
22nd Regiment of Madras Infantry
23rd (or Wallajahbad) Regiment of Madras (Light) Infantry
24th Regiment of Madras Infantry
25th Regiment of Madras Infantry
26th Regiment of Madras Infantry
27th Regiment of Madras Infantry
28th Regiment of Madras Infantry

29th Regiment (7th Burma Battalion) of Madras Infantry
30th Regiment (5th Burma Battalion) of Madras Infantry
31st Regiment (6th Burma Battalion) of Madras (Light) Infantry
32nd Regiment (4th Burma Battalion) of Madras Infantry
33rd Regiment (3rd Burma Battalion) of Madras Infantry

Bombay
Governor's Body-Guard
The 1st (The Duke of Connaught's Own) Regiment of Bombay Lancers
2nd Regiment of Bombay Lancers
3rd (Queen's Own) Regiment of Bombay Light Cavalry
The 4th (Prince Albert Victor's Own) Regiment of Bombay Cavalry (Poona Horse)
5th Regiment of Bombay Cavalry (Sindh Horse)
6th Regiment of Bombay Cavalry (Jacob's Horse)
7th Regiment of Bombay Lancers (Belooch Horse)
Aden Troop
No 5 (Bombay) Mountain Battery
No 6 (Bombay) Mountain Battery
Corps of Bombay Sappers and Miners
1st Regiment of Bombay Infantry (Grenadiers)
2nd (Prince of Wales' Own) Regiment of Bombay Infantry (Grenadiers)
3rd Regiment of Bombay (Light) Infantry
4th Regiment of Bombay Infantry
5th Regiment of Bombay (Light) Infantry
7th Regiment of Bombay Infantry
8th Regiment of Bombay Infantry
9th Regiment of Bombay Infantry
10th Regiment of Bombay (Light) Infantry
12th Regiment of Bombay Infantry
13th Regiment of Bombay Infantry
14th Regiment of Bombay Infantry
16th Regiment of Bombay Infantry
17th Regiment of Bombay Infantry
19th Regiment of Bombay Infantry
20th Regiment of Bombay Infantry
21st Regiment of Bombay Infantry (Marine Battalion)

22nd Regiment of Bombay Infantry
23rd Regiment of Bombay Infantry
24th (Baluchistan; Duchess of Connaught's Own) Regiment of Bombay Infantry
25th Regiment of Bombay Infantry
26th (Baluchistan) Regiment of Bombay Infantry
27th Regiment (1st Baluch Battalion) of Bombay (Light) Infantry
28th Regiment of Bombay Infantry (Pioneers)
29th (The Duke of Connaught's Own) Regiment of Bombay Infantry (2nd Baluch Battalion)
30th Regiment of Bombay Infantry (3rd Baluch Battalion)

Corps under the Orders of the Government of India
Hyderabad Contingent
1st Regiment of Lancers
2nd Regiment of Lancers
3rd Regiment of Lancers
4th Regiment of Lancers
No 1 Field Battery
No 2 Field Battery
No 3 Field Battery
No 4 Field Battery
1st Regiment of Infantry
2nd Regiment of Infantry
3rd Regiment of Infantry
4th Regiment of Infantry
5th Regiment of Infantry
6th Regiment of Infantry

Corps in Central India
Central India Horse (1st Regiment and 2nd Regiment)
Malwa Bhil Corps
Bhopal Battalion

Corps in Rajputana
Deoli Irregular Force (Cavalry and Infantry)
Erinpura Irregular Force (Cavalry and Infantry)
Meywar Bhil Corps
Merwara Battalion

BIBLIOGRAPHY

Allgood, Maj-Gen G, *China War 1860, Letters and Journal*, London 1901.

Atkinson, C. T, *A History of the 1st (PWO) Battalion, The Dogra Regiment, 1887-1947*, Southampton c1948.

Bamford, Lt-Col P. G, *1st King George V's Own Battalion, The Sikh Regiment*, Aldershot, 1948.

Barthorp, Michael, *The North West Frontier. A Pictorial History 1839-1947*, Poole 1982.

Barton, Sir William, *India's North West Frontier*, London 1939.

Battye, E. D, *The Fighting Ten*, London 1984.

Betham, Lt-Col Sir Geoffrey & Geary, Maj H. U. L, *The Golden Galley (2nd Punjab Regiment)*, Oxford 1956.

Beynon, Lt W. G. L, *With Kelly to Chitral*, London 1896.

Bodin, Lynne E, *The Boxer Rebellion*, London 1983.

Burton, Major R. G, *A History of the Hyderabad Contingent*, Calcutta 1905.

Burns, P. L. (Editor), *The Journals of J. W. W. Birch 1874-1875*, Kuala Lumpur 1976.

Cadell, Sir Patrick, *History of the Bombay Army*, London 1938.

Cardew, Lieut F. G, *A Sketch of the Services of the Bengal Army*, Calcutta 1903.

Cardew, Maj F. G, *Hodson's Horse 1857-1922*, London 1928.

Carman, W. Y, *Indian Army Uniforms – Cavalry*, Chatham 1968.

Carman, W. Y, *Indian Army Uniforms – Infantry*, London 1969.

Carter, Thomas & Long, W. H, *War Medals of the British Army*, London 1893.

Churchill, Winston L. S, *The story of the Malakand Field Force*, London 1898.

Condon, Brig W. E. H, *The Frontier Force Regiment*, Aldershot 1962.

Crawford, Lt-Col D. G, *Roll of the Indian Medical Service, 1615-1930*, London 1930.

De Rhe-Philipe, G. W, *A list of Inscriptions on Christian Tombs & Monuments*, (see also Irvine, M) *Part II Biographical Notices*, Lahore 1912.

Elliott, Maj-Gen J. G, *The Frontier 1839-1947*, London 1968.

Evatt, Brig-Gen J, *Historical Record of the 39th Royal Garhwal Rifles, Vol 1, 1887-1922*, Aldershot 1922.

Farrington, Anthony, *The Second Afghan War 1878-1880 Casualty Roll*, London 1986.

Farrington, S. M, *Peshawar Cemetery*, London 1988.

Featherstone, Donald, *Colonial Small Wars 1837-1901*, 1973.

Fleming P, *The Siege of Peking*, London 1959.

Fowler, J. S, *Extracts from the diary of John S Fowler, RE, Chitral 1895*, Dublin 1895.

Gordon, Maj Lawrence L, *British Battles and Medals*, Aldershot 1962.

Gorman, Maj J. T, *2nd Battalion, 4th Bombay Grenadiers (King Edward's Own)*, Weston-super-Mare 1933.

Hailes, Lt-Col W. L, *War Services of the 9th Jat Regiment*, Aldershot 1938.

Harfield, A, *British & Indian Armies on the China Coast 1785-1985*, Farnham 1990.

Heathcote, T. A, *The Indian Army (The Garrison of British Imperial India, 1822-1922*, London 1974.

Heathcote, T. A, *The Afghan Wars 1839-1919*, London 1980.

Hennell, Col Sir R, *A Famous Indian Regiment – The Kali Panchwin*, London 1927.

Hensman, Howard, *The Afghan War of 1879-1880*, London 1881.

HopeGrant, Gen Sir, *Incidents in the China War of 1860*, London 1875.

Hudson, Gen Sir H, *History of the 19th King George's Own Lancers 1858-1921*, Aldershot 1937.

Huxford, Lt-Col H. J, *History of the 8th Gurkha Rifles 1824-1949*, Aldershot 1952.

Hypher, P. P, *Deeds of Valour performed by Indian Officers and Soldiers during the period 1860 to 1925*, Simla 1927.

Irvine, Miles, *A List of inscriptions on Christian Tombs and Monuments in the Punjab, North West Frontier Province, Kashmir and Afghanistan*, Lahore 1910.

Jackson, Lt R. P, *Historical Records of the XIII Madras Infantry*, London 1898.

James, Lt-Col F. H, *History of the 1st Battalion, 6th Rajputana Rifles (Wellesley's)*, Aldershot 1938.

James, Lionel, *The Indian Frontier War (Mohmund & Tirah Expeditions of 1897)*, London 1898.

Joslin, E. C, Litherland, A. R. and Simpkin, B. T, *British Battles and Medals*, London 1988.

Lawford, Lt-Col J. P. and Catto, Maj W. E. (Editors), *Solah Punjab (16th Punjab Regiment)*, Aldershot 1967.

Leslie, N. B, *The Battle Honours of the British and Indian Armies 1695-1914*, London 1970.

MacDonnell, R. and Macaulay, M, *A History of the 4th (Prince of Wales's Own) Gurkha Rifles 1857-1957, Vol I*, London 1940.

Maunsell, Col E. B, *Prince of Wales's Own, The Scinde Horse*, Private 1926.

Maurice, Col J. F, *Military History of the Campaign of 1882 in Egypt*, London 1887.

Maxwell, W. E, *Capital Campaigners (3rd Battalion Queen Mary's Own) (The Baluch Regiment)*, Aldershot 1948.

McFall, Capt C, *With the Zhob Field Force*, 1895.

McNair, Maj The Hon T. F. A, *Perak and the Malays*, 1878.

McRae, Col H. StG. M, *Regimental History of the 45th Rattray's Sikhs, Vol 1*, Glasgow 1933.

Mollo, B, *The Indian Army*, Poole 1981.

Mullaby, Capt B. R, *History of the 10th Gurkha Rifles*, Aldershot 1924.

Myatt, Frederick, *The March to Magdala*, London 1970.

Neville, Capt H. L, *Campaigns on the North West Frontier*, London 1912.

North, R, *The Punjab Frontier Force, A Brief Record of their Services 1846-1922*, Dera Ismail Khan 1934.

Qureshi, Maj Mohammed Ibrahim, *History of the 1st Punjab Regiment 1759-1956*, Aldershot 1958.

Rawlinson, H. G, *8th King George V's Own Light Cavalry*, Aldershot 1948.

Rawlinson, H. G, *Outram's Rifles*, London 1933.

Rawlinson, H. G, *The History of the 3rd Battalion, 7th Rajput Regiment*, London 1941.

Rawlinson, H. G, *The History of the 2/6th Rajputana Rifles*, London 1936.

Rawlinson, H. G, *History of Napier's Rifles (5th Battalion 6th Rajputana Rifles*, Oxford 1929.

Robertson, Sir George S, *Chitral, The story of a Minor Siege*, London 1898.

Robson, Brian, *The Road to Kabul, 2nd Afghan War 1878-1881*, London 1986.

Roe, Lt-Col C. H, *Historical Record of the 2nd Queen's Own Sappers and Miners, 1790-1909*, 1909.

Sandhu, Maj-Gen Gurcham Singh, *The Indian Cavalry*, New Delhi 1982.

Shadbolt, S. H, *The Afghan Campaign of 1878-1880*, London 1882.

Shadwell, Capt L. J, *Lockhart's Advance Through Tirah*, London 1898.

Shakespear, Col L. W, *History of the 2nd King Edward's Own Gurkha Rifles (The Sirmoor Rifles)*, 1912.

Smyth, Brig The Rt Hon Sir John, *The story of the Victoria Cross 1856-1963*, London 1963.

Tamplin, J. M. A. and Abbott, P. E, *British Gallantry Awards*, London 1971.

Talbot, Col F. E. G, *The 14th King George's Own Sikhs*, London 1937.

Trousdale, Wm (Editor), *War in Afghanistan 1879-80*, Detroit 1985.

Vibart, Maj H. M, *The Military History of the Madras Engineers & Pioneers*, London 1883.

Waters, Maj R. S, *History of the 5th Battalion (Pathans) 14th Punjab Regiment*, London 1936.

Watson, Maj-Gen W. A, *King George's Own Central India Horse*, London 1930.

Wilson, Lt-Col W. J, *The Madras Army, Vol 4*, Madras 1888.

Woodyatt, Maj-Gen N. G. (Editor), *Regimental History of the 3rd Queen Alexandra's Own Gurkha Rifles*, London 1929.

Wylly, Col H. C, *From the Black Mountains to Waziristan*, London 1912.

Younghusband, Capt G. J. and Capt F. E, *The Relief of Chitral*, London 1896.

Younghusband, Col G. J, *The Story of the Guides*, London 1908.

Yule, Col H. and Burnell A. C, *Hobson-Jobson*, London 1903.

Regimentally published histories

15th Lancers (Cureton's Multanis) 1858-1908, Calcutta 1910.

History of The Guides 1846-1922, Aldershot 1938.

History of the 2nd Punjab Infantry, Privately Printed c1903.

Record of Services, 3rd Sikhs Punjab Frontier Force.

Historical Record of the 4th Battalion, 16th Punjab Regiment.

Regimental History of 4th Battalion, 13th Frontier Force Rifles (Wilde's).

Regimental History of the 6th Royal Battalion, 13th Frontier Force Rifles (Scinde) 1843-1923, Aldershot 1926.

A History of the 4th Battalion 19th Hyderabad Regiment, Aldershot 1933.

Historical Records of the 20th (Duke of Cambridge's Own) Infantry (Brownlow's Punjabis), Devonport 1909.

Records of the 1/XXI Punjabis, Aldershot 1919.

35th Sikhs Regimental Record 1887-1922, Peshawar 1923.

The 101st Grenadiers Historical Record 1778-1923, Aldershot 1928.

Government Publications

Chitral Expedition, 1895, Allahabad 1895.

Chronology of Events Connected with Army Administration, War Office publication, London 1908.

Frontier and Overseas Expeditions from India
Vol III, Calcutta 1910.
Vol IV, Simla 1907.
Vol V, Simla 1907.
Vol VI, Calcutta 1911.

Indian Army Regulations, Dress, 1899, Simla 1899.

Manual for Bengal Punjab Cavalry, Calcutta 1893.

Second Afghan War, 1878-80, London 1908.

Standing Orders for the Cavalry, Simla 1875.

The London Gazette (1860-1903).

Newspapers and Journals

The Graphic.

The Illustrated London News.

Journals of the Society for Army Historical Research, Vols XLII and LIII.

The Navy and Army Illustrated.

The Straits Times (Singapore), 1857.

Indian Army Lists, 1861-1903.

Right:
Madras Pioneers,
Field Service Order.

Below:
Bombay Sappers
and Miners, 1897.

INDEX

Index of medals, persons, places and ships.

Note – Officers' ranks are shown giving the senior rank of the last entry.